GRACE LIBRARY CARLOW UNIVERSITY
PITTSBURGH PA 15213

D0005095

The Next 25 Years

The New Supreme Court
and What It Means for Americans

Martin Garbus

KF
8742
.G375
2007

SEVEN STORIES PRESS

New York ♦ Toronto ♦ London ♦ Melbourne

CATALOGUED

Copyright © 2007 by Martin Garbus

A Seven Stories Press First Edition

All rights reserved. No part of this book may be reproduced, stored in a retrieval system, or transmitted in any form or by any means, including mechanical, electric, photocopying, recording, or otherwise, without the prior written permission of the publisher.

Seven Stories Press
140 Watts Street
New York, NY 10013
http://www.sevenstories.com

In Canada: Publishers Group Canada, 559 College Street, Suite 402, Toronto, ON M6G 1A9

In the UK: Turnaround Publisher Services Ltd., Unit 3, Olympia Trading Estate, Coburg Road, Wood Green, London N22 6TZ

In Australia: Palgrave Macmillan, 627 Chapel Street, South Yarra, VIC 3141

College professors may order examination copies of Seven Stories Press titles for a free six-month trial period. To order, visit www.sevenstories.com/textbook or send a fax on school letterhead to (212) 226-1411.

Book design by Jon Gilbert

Library of Congress Cataloging-in-Publication Data
Garbus, Martin, 1934-
   The next 25 years : the new Supreme Court and what it means for Americans / Martin Garbus.
     p. cm.
   Includes index.
   ISBN-13: 978-1-58322-732-9 (hardcover : alk. paper)
   ISBN-10: 1-58322-732-6 (hardcover : alk. paper)
   1. United States. Supreme Court. 2. Judicial review--United States. 3. Political questions and judicial power--United States. I. Title.

KF8742.G375 2007
347.73'26--dc22

                                        2006037456

Printed in the USA.

9 8 7 6 5 4 3 2 1

To Alessandra, Amelia, Julian, and Theodore

Contents

◆   ◆   ◆

Acknowledgments

◆   ◆   ◆

In preparing this book, I primarily relied on the decisions and transcripts of the Supreme Court, published information, the private decisions of the justices at conferences discussing the cases, the papers of the Supreme Court justices, and the interviews I conducted with participants in those cases. I am indebted to the scholarship and graciousness of Professors Sanford Levinson, Jack Balkin, Marci Hamilton, Jeffrey Rosen, Sheldon Goldman, Tinsley Yarborough, Larry Kramer, Anthony Amsterdam, and Bernard Schwartz and Norman Redlich, my former professors at New York University Law School.

Secondary sources on events I was not at included David Savage's *Turning Right: The Making of the Supreme Court* (John Wiley, 1993), Sheldon Goldman's writings in *Judicature and Picking Federal Judges* (Yale University Press, 1997), and the books of Bernard Schwartz, including those containing unpublished opinions of the Warren, Burger, and Rehnquist Courts. *The Supreme Court in Conference (1940–1985): The Private Discussions Behind Nearly 300 Supreme Court Decisions* (Oxford, 2001), edited by Del Dickson, supplements the justices' papers and the work of Bernard Schwartz.

I thank my new legal colleagues, Michael Ditzian, Ron Urbach, Howard Nielson, Brad Schwarting, Curt Myers, Gerald Schwartz, Lew Rubin and Gerry Uram.

I express my very great appreciation to Dan Simon and Theresa Noll, two caring editors; and Fredda Tourin, who helped transform my scrawls into this book. Comments that I appreciated came from conversations with Marci Hamilton, David Cole, Donna Lieberman, Leslie Neuman, Marc Stern, Peter Parcher, Leonard Weinglass, Art

Eisenberg, Jonathan Kandell, Dan Cogan, Raymond Steckel, Ellie Klein, George Kendall, Will Helerstein, Theodore Shaw, Leon and Synthia Polsky, and Joan Biskupic.

Most of all, to Cassandra and Elizabeth Garbus, and Philip and Christopher Enock. Last, but first, to my wife, Sarina Tang, without whose support and encouragement this book would not have been done.

Introduction

◆   ◆   ◆

The United States Supreme Court's primary role is to adjust the power balance between the three branches of government. The Supreme Court, contrary to what Chief Justice John Roberts says, is not a neutral umpire at all and never has been. It is as political as our other branches of government.

Our Justices are human, subjective, and political, with their own value systems. As future Supreme Court Justice Felix Frankfurter advised President Franklin Roosevelt, constitutional law has little to do with the Constitution and much to do with the views of the judges. They decide political issues.

Alexis de Tocqueville was durably accurate when he said, "There is hardly a political question in the United States which does not turn into a judicial one."[1] And there are very few judicial decisions that do not have political components.

There is a tendency to understate the potential significance of the appointment to the chief justice. He is not one among nine. He can be a divider or a conciliator. A chief justice has power both explicit and implied. The chief justice leads the closed-door conferences where justices discuss and vote on cases; assigns who writes the majority rulings; manages the docket; controls the open-court arguments; and supervises the three hundred or so court employees, including clerks, secretaries, police, and support staff. Many chief justices, including Earl Warren, use their role to exert great influence on the Court's path. Warren succeeded in unanimity in *Brown v. Board of Education* and in pushing his civil rights agenda over the learned and more conservative justices. William Rehnquist, in his own different way, succeeded in pushing the Reagan agenda. Chief Jus-

1

tice John Roberts, presiding over a committed conservative Court, has already, at argument, made it clear he sees himself as becoming the Court's conservative leader. In the first significant decision of the new Court, the chief justice in a privacy case chose to personally attack Justice David Souter. Initially more respected than Rehnquist, his honeymoon period ended very quickly. With Justices Samuel Alito, Antonin Scalia, Clarence Thomas, and Anthony Kennedy at his side, this Court will be a conservative steamroller—the likes of which has not been seen before in American history. The absurd illusion that Roberts' apparent collegiality and scholarly reasoning would lead to a more harmonious court is over.

Because of the Court's unusually partisan makeup and the instability created by a lack of consensus around the outcome of the last two presidential elections, our democracy has never been so polarized. The country is more deeply divided than at any time in living memory. There seem to be two irreconcilable blocks, with their legal, cultural, and political wars increasingly being fought out in the court. Conservatives are profoundly frustrated with the Court because the three Republican appointees, Souter, Sandra Day O'Connor, and Kennedy, have not given them the votes on the issues they want. Conservatives claim they are reacting to the New Deal and Warren Courts in what they see as a battle to correct the imbalance caused by fifty years of courts being too liberal, too "activist"—of legislating rather than deciding cases. Liberals, fearful of increasing conservative dominance, are trying to hang on to the victories achieved before the Reagan landslide.

Most people won't or can't follow the Court battles. Except when they concern a woman's right to choose, legal arguments often seem too abstract for most Americans to care about. The ways decisions will affect each of us are obscured—both by the law's arcane language and the Court's secrecy. It's often hard to see how directly U.S. Supreme Court decisions affect us.

The facts of nearly all cases fall far below the radar. Cases of sexual harassment, torture, custody disputes, regulations interpreting environmental regulations, church-state issues, and affirmative action suits get some attention when they hit the Supreme Court, but even then the way these cases will impact citizens is never discussed. Hot button issues, such as torture and warrantless wiretaps, tend to be decided on technical points, and the larger issues get swallowed up. With forty- and fifty-page 5–4 decisions, parsing and understanding the text and subtext to see what truly is at stake is very difficult.

The Court's legal opinions themselves contribute to the confusion—by making it appear as if the rape case, the gun case, the case of the disabled, were battles over "federalism," or "standing," purely legal battles that didn't involve politics.

Newspapers most often print single sentences or paragraphs summing up fifty-page decisions—an impossible task. Very few lawyers or legal academics even read the cases that so affect our lives. It is understandable, for they are written in a legalese that can confound legal training and common sense.

Recently, eight separate opinions were rendered in one one-hundred-page-decision, a result that discourages even the most dedicated of court followers. As if all this were not enough, Supreme Court opinions today tend to be more nuanced and complex than in the past. It is nearly impossible for the better Supreme Court reporters, under deadline, to see long-term patterns, especially during the last months of the term, called the June "crunch," when most of the court's most important decisions come down. Although these decisions are available to anyone, they are not read, and a precious few public citizens and journalists watch oral arguments in the Supreme Court. Television coverage is nearly nonexistent.

The U.S. Supreme Court hears half the number of cases that it heard ten years ago. The cases it does decide often seem to announce few new dramatic changes in society, and the language of the decisions is increasingly technical. The Court's opinions often appear to be concerned with debates over legal matters that seem purely procedural. The Court operates nearly invisibly. At best, three or four cases a year catch the public eye.

The majority of Americans believe they live in a country in which the important political and legal cases of the twentieth century's liberal cycle—*Brown v. Board of Education*,[2] *Roe v. Wade*,[3] and *Griswold v. Connecticut*[4]—are, because of process and precedent, protected from reversal. Again and again, at the nomination hearings of liberals Stephen Breyer and Ruth Bader Ginsburg and conservatives Roberts and Alito, the justices tell us of their great respect for "correct" precedent. But the answers, from both sides, were disingenuous. Most justices, liberal or conservative, believe in precedent when it gets the result they want.

Robert Bork's much criticized statement that the value of precedent is overstated is correct. Despite the reverence they're given in history books and Supreme Court nomination proceedings, landmark decisions on abortion rights, one man/one vote, the Civil Rights laws, and racial equality no longer command very much respect on the contemporary Supreme Court. The landmarks need not be directly overruled to be rendered ineffective. They are avoided. They are strangled by limitation. They are defanged. The laws may remain in force but without much effect or meaning.

We are supposed to be a country with a rule of law. Often we are a country that honors rule by law—a profound difference. A proudly proclaimed and honored myth supposes that we are a government of laws, not men. That is not true. Nor are we a government of men, not laws. We are a government of laws and men.

A judge's outlook is shaped by his or her affiliations, interests, and identity; previous professional experiences; experience during the confirmation process; adherence to a particular judicial approach, if any, and the existing composition of the court.

Listen to Justice O'Connor describing Justice Thurgood Marshall, the great liberal Supreme Court justice:

> His was the eye of a lawyer who saw the deepest wounds in the social fabric and used law to help heal them. His was the ear of a counselor who understood the vulnerabilities

of the accused and established safeguards for their protection. His was the mouth of a man who knew the anguish of the silenced and gave them a voice.

The absence of a towering presence, a Marshall, a Brennan, or a Warren, can change the direction of a court as much as the presence of one can. Being a fundamentalist Christian, a Southerner, or someone with many friends who are corporate CEOs all exert influence over a justice's outlook.

Textualism—a mode of statutory interpretation guided by the text rather than by intentions or ideals external to it, and by the original meaning of the text rather than by its evolving meaning over time— provides jurists a seemingly neutral touchstone and protocol and can shield them from having to deal with some of a case's difficult human consequences. At a panel discussion at Harvard Law School, Justice Scalia lamented the "politicization" of the court and stated that "it will become unpoliticized, as it relatively used to be, as soon as we go back to saying the Constitution means what it says, and it means what it meant when it was adopted." His allegiance to rule-based textualism combined with his conception of his role as a judge helps him to distance himself from the particular parties and the societal implications of the case before him in each case. It provides him with a means of legitimizing troubling outcomes. Justice, for many of the conservative judges, is an irrelevance. "We don't really take a case in order to, quote-unquote, do justice" or "to make sure that the good guy won and the bad guy lost," Scalia has said.

Breyer, on the other hand, has said that "judges do judge; and were these things to decide themselves in some automatic way, what reason would there be for a court?" It is easier to apply a moral law or a social need when applying complex, context-specific standards that presume an evolving Constitution than it is when applying relatively simple and broad rules to interpret a Constitution that is presumed to have a fixed meaning.

Justices tend to surround themselves with like-minded law clerks, which can lead to further ideological anchoring. Alito's first action after nomination was to appoint Adam Ciongoli, a thirty-four-year-old former Justice Department lawyer who worked for John Ashcroft when the Patriot Act and torture memos came from Ashcroft's office. Ciongoli had also been Rehnquist's clerk and had clerked for Alito when the justice sat on the Third Circuit.

Considered one of Ashcroft's most influential advisors, Ciongoli, according to his colleagues, was Ashcroft's main sounding board. As Ashcroft put it, "He has participated in a wide variety of matters, from helping formulate, construct, and shape the Patriot act to counseling me on items related to security."

When Ashcroft's Senate opponent, Missouri Democratic Governor Mel Carnahan, died in a plane crash on October 16, 2000 and was replaced on the ballot by his widow, it was Ciongoli who stayed up nights preparing a challenge to the outcome of the election, though Ashcroft decided against filing suit and eventually lost his Senate seat at the polls.

When Ashcroft got the call from Austin, Texas, that President George W. Bush wanted to interview him for the attorney general's post, it was Alito's new law clerk who got on a plane to Springfield, Missouri, that very night to brief Ashcroft. Ciongoli had also written memos in support of the Bush unitary president theory—those are all issues that will come before the court.

Prior to Ciongoli's appointment, the time-honored practice was that a justice's clerk either came fresh from law school, or had worked for one Circuit Court judge before. The justices hire researchers and aides, not policy- or decision-makers. Thus Alito's choice was, to say the least, a highly unusual appointment.

Justice Thomas has been the only justice to select all of his clerks from judges appointed by presidents of one political party. Revealing the extent of his us-versus-them mentality, Thomas likens choosing clerks to "selecting mates in a foxhole." Professor Jeffrey Rosen of Georgetown Law School has observed that "justices who lack confidence and have a simplistic view of the law tend to be more susceptible to their clerks' influence and therefore rarely diverge from the party line."

Judges can of course be powerfully affected by the individual personalities and demeanor of their peers on the court. Justice Scalia's slashing style and acerbic comments on Kennedy's and O'Connor's work helps explain O'Connor's and Kennedy's reluctance to join him. Justice Brennan's charm and tact probably helped keep the 1990s court on a liberal course.

The mechanisms designed to keep the judiciary independent of the other branches of government are incomplete, and good evidence suggests that judges frequently interpret laws in ways that align with the particular policy desires of sitting members of Congress and the current president. This is not surprising given the forces that Congress and the president can bring to bear on the judiciary—including limiting or even stripping jurisdiction in certain areas, altering the size of federal courts, and instituting impeachment hearings. Just as important is the fact that the court cannot implement its orders without the aid of other branches of government.

Justice Kennedy was influenced by the international outcry over the Abu Ghraib and Guantanamo prisons and the use of torture when he decided to apply the Geneva Conventions to detainees' trials. He has already broken with Scalia, Rehnquist, and Thomas by agreeing to look at foreign law to help influence his opinions. Looking at foreign law, whether it be in the area of the Geneva Convention, juvenile justice, or social welfare legislation, means listening to a view more liberal than ours. It also means seeing the United States in relation to the rest of the world. Whether this will influence any one case other that the Guantanamo cases remains to be seen. Kennedy's rejection of the president's legal scheme for detainee trials does not mean he will, in other areas such as surveillance, be a swing vote on the side of the "liberals."

Justice Kennedy may also be influenced by the opportunity to make this new Court "his court" in the same way that Justice O'Connor did during her last few years. Clearly Scalia and Thomas helped push Kennedy away in the areas of gay rights and capital punishment. He has shown extraordinary constitutional pride, and seems to have a different feeling of responsibility than before. Like O'Connor, who became responsible for many of the Court's ultimate positions, he may emerge more from The Nine.

Or he may be persuaded by the intellectual might that justices Roberts and Alito bring to the bench to reach the same conclusions as Scalia and Thomas, but through a different legal path. The few areas where he has been liberal do not go to the heart of Kennedy's already enunciated jurisprudence in the areas of states rights, race relations, affirmative action, criminal defendants, and environmental issues.

Senate Majority Leader Bill Frist was correct when he said Alito was the Democrats' worst nightmare. He would have been equally correct had he said it about Roberts.

Roberts and Alito have been consistent throughout their professional lives. In 1985, Alito wrote on an application for a job in the Reagan Justice Department, "I am particularly proud of my contributions in recent cases in which the government has argued in the Supreme Court that . . . the Constitution does not protect a right to an abortion." And, further, that "in college I developed a deep interest in constitutional law, motivated in large part by disagreement with Warren Court decisions, particularly in the areas of criminal procedure, the Establishment Clause, and reapportionment."

Justices, as we know, occasionally change or modify their views while on the Court. Justice Powell, Justice Blackmun, and Justice Brennan are the best-known examples. Unlike these justices, Roberts and Alito are committed warriors on the battlefield. They are ideologues, celebrated and banqueted by their dominant Federalist constituency encased in a supporting Washington world. Now, having secured the position they wanted all their professional lives, they are free to go as far as they want.

Rarely would I say a Supreme Court Justice is legally wrong, or right. By the time a case gets to the Supreme Court, for example, in the abortion area or the affirmative action or gerrymandering cases, hundreds of judges (federal and state, appellate and trial) have spoken out on the issues—we find 100 lower court judges on one side and 100 on the other. Then we get 5–4 Supreme Court decisions, often changing as the justices change. Most all the judges are very bright—it cannot be said that 105 are right on the law and 104 are wrong. No, it is their values that clash. Most "precedents" can be read every which way. Justice William Brennan put it best. When asked what the law was, he spread the five fingers of his hand. "Five." The law, says Justice Brennan, is whatever the five justices say it is.

Historically, most justices who modify their views shift to the left. But Roberts and Alito will not. Powell, Brennan, and Blackmun came from outside Washington and were influenced by finding themselves in more liberal circles than they had been before. But Roberts and Alito are both Washington players, part of an arch conservative world—Roberts for his entire professional life and Alito during his long formative Reagan years. Roberts and Alito most certainly cannot be expected to change their long-held, deeply felt conservative views. They have already staked out positions on the great issues that will face this and future courts.

Roberts and Alito were more than brilliantly evasive during the hearings—they lied. They wanted the job. Whether discounting their past views, forgetting them, or answering questions with skilled sophistry that befuddled most of the senators, Alito and Roberts provided unforgettable commentaries about the face of justice today, about their own willingness to sacrifice personal dignity in the service of their political causes, and on the paltry role of honesty in their performances. The extent of Roberts' and Alito's deceit will be revealed when we receive their decisions. Only then will most Americans fully appreciate the brilliance of their performances at their hearings.

The conservatives, as we saw at the hearings, claim high moral ground. Yet Justice Thomas, according to the *Los Angeles Times* in 2004 and the *New York Times* in 2006, has accepted tens of thousands of dollars in gifts since joining the bench, including an $800 leather jacket, a $1,200 set of tires, and an extravagant vacation from a conservative activist. Justice Scalia, unbothered by the criticism of his duck hunting with Vice President Dick Cheney while Cheney had legal issues before the Court, skipped the swearing-in of Chief Justice Roberts for a paid trip to the Ritz Carlton at the Beaver Creek ski resort. And O'Connor, when asked by Ken Starr, then an assistant attorney general, who vetted her, whether she had supported a 1970 bill to decriminalize abortion in Arizona, told him she could not remember. Starr did not check it out—she had voted for the bill and Reagan, misled, vouched for her anti-*Roe* credentials. And O'Connor, before the *Bush v. Gore* case, and Scalia, before the Guantanamo cases, both expressed their political biases and then refused to recuse themselves.

Justice Roberts relentlessly articulated his commitment to the right of privacy at his hearing. But in the first substantial case, *Georgia v. Randolph*, decided March 22, 2006, his minority opinion said that a police invasion of a defendant's house over the defendant's objection was proper because the wife, involved in a marital dispute with the husband, permitted it. Justice Souter—"a home is a man's castle"—and four other justices, including Kennedy, found the privacy violation that Roberts was ignoring to be a well-settled law protecting privacy.

Justice Souter said, "In the dissent's view, the centuries of special protection for the privacy of the home are over." He called Roberts' statement that this decision would interfere with the policy's ability to protect victims of domestic violence a "red herring"; of course, the police have the right to protect a crime victim. Justice Roberts said Souter's position was "overwrought." Justice Stevens and Justice Scalia argued over the method of constitutional interpretation: should we, could we, decide how James Madison and Alexander Hamilton would have decided this case?

Whereas the Warren Court was willing to void state law in the name of protecting and advancing the interests of "discrete and insular minorities," the Rehnquist Court did not, Kennedy will not, and the Roberts Court will not. The present and future Court brooks no coequal interpreter of the Constitution. It sees itself as the supreme arbiter of state and national conflict. It enforces this vision against encroachments by governments at *all* levels—local, state, and national. *Bush v. Gore*, with Kennedy and O'Connor in the majority, led the Court toward a new understanding of the equality principle and the very role of the Supreme Court as *the* final arbiter in American politics.

Conservatives routinely strike down environmental laws and uphold laws protecting property rights. Their expansive view of presidential power goes along with their commitment to limit the Congress' power to make laws that protect campaign finance reform or restrict gun control. This is not surprising, but it is disturbing. Their view of the law exactly matches the conservative political platform, while at the same time, they claim that the Court is not political.

The new Court is on a crusade to end decades of regulation. Their justification is a conservative ideology that credits liberals with having pulled the court too far left.

Lino Graglia, a right-wing professor at the law school of the University of Texas, says that the

> Court's constitutional decisions of the last four decades have . . . overwhelmingly served to substitute the policy preferences of persons on the far left of the American political spectrum for the policy preferences that prevailed in the ordinary political processes.

Robert Bork adds,

> Liberals for half a century have been using their control of the Supreme Court to erode our most basic freedom—the free-

dom, unless the Constitution actually says otherwise, to make our own moral and prudential choices democratically.

Roberts argues that sixty years of federal regulating agencies, first put into place during the Roosevelt years, are "constitutional anomalies." His views, if taken up by the court, would roll back the past seventy years of American law. He was the most conservative member of the second most important federal appeals court in the country. Alito's forty-one dissents in the two hundred forty opinions he rendered show him to be the most conservative member of his twenty-two judge court. Ninety-one percent of his dissents (thirty-eight of forty-one), according to University of Chicago law professor Cass Sunstein, are more conservative than those of his colleagues—including judges appointed by presidents George H. W. Bush, Reagan, and George W. Bush. Roberts' and Alito's opinions are framed differently than Bork's, Scalia's, or Thomas's, but they wind up in the same place.

As the political deputy in the Solicitor General's office under Reagan and George H. W. Bush, Roberts, selected primarily for his ideology to supervise the political positions taken in the briefs, argued in the Supreme Court to overrule *Roe*, to permit prayer in schools, and to punish dissidents. The briefs express his personal views. He wouldn't have had the presidential appointment if they did not. It insults him to claim otherwise. During his two years as a judge, he consistently voted in support of authority—for governments, corporations, the military, and the police. Roberts' brief in *Rust v. Sullivan*[5] called for *Roe v. Wade* to be overturned, even though the constitutionality of *Roe* was not at issue.

In *Bray v. Alexandria Women's Health Clinic*,[6] Roberts coauthored an amicus brief on behalf of various radical antichoice groups that argued that blocking access to abortion clinics was not an act of discrimination against women. Amicus briefs are often more reflective of a lawyer's view than briefs authored on behalf of a litigant. The author is freer to say what he thinks.

Roberts, referring to his major influences, Judge Henry Friendly and Justice Frankfurter, talks about his and their respect for precedent and *stare decisis*. But he coauthored a government brief urging the Court to disregard long-established law and to find it constitutional for a public school to sponsor a prayer at graduation ceremonies. That issue will soon again be before the Court. Roberts, the swing vote, will disregard *Lee v. Weissman*,[7] the 1992 precedent that found public prayer unconstitutional. He agrees with Justice Frankfurter's dissent in *Baker v. Carr*,[8] perhaps the most important case of the twentieth century, that established the most fundamental tenet of a democracy to be the principle of one man-one vote. Precedent notwithstanding, he and Alito reject the majority view.

Roberts, Rehnquist's clerk during the 1980 term, talks reverently about Rehnquist, the man and his legal decisions. Alito's clerk also clerked for Rehnquist. We should look more closely at who Rehnquist is.

David Savage, in his fine book *Turning Right*, reported that in 1964 Rehnquist opposed a citywide "public accommodations" law that the Phoenix City Council was considering that would forbid discrimination against customers based on race, color, or religion. "I oppose the ordinance because I believe that the values it sacrifices are greater than the values which it gives," he declared. The issue as he saw it was "freedom" of an individual against heavy-handed government interference. Later he wrote, "The Founders of this nation thought of it as the 'land of the free' just as surely as they thought of it as the 'land of the equal.' . . . The ordinance summarily does away with the historic right of the owner of a drug store, lunch counter, or theater to choose his own customers."

Rehnquist argued that no law, in fact, could remedy the racial problem, because it "stems from the state of mind of the proprietor . . . unable to correct the source of the indignity to the Negro, it redresses the situation by placing a separate indignity on the proprietor. It is as barren of accomplishment in what it gives to the Negro as in what it takes from the proprietor. The unwanted customer and the disliked proprietor are left glowering at one another across the lunch counter." Despite Rehnquist's rhetoric, the measure passed by an overwhelming vote. Later, as the top legal theorist of the Nixon administration, Rehnquist defended the government crackdown on Vietnam War and civil rights protesters along with initiatives such as wire-tapping, "no-knock" searches, and the FBI's surveillance of private citizens. When a later case came before the Court challenging the very surveillance practices in which Rehnquist was involved, he refused to recuse himself.

Memoranda he wrote to Justice Jackson that surfaced during his confirmation hearing make clear that the then law clerk was no friend of minorities, first railing at "the liberals" who were breaking down segregation in the South, then expressing his belief that the Court was wrong in deciding *Brown*. Rehnquist first laid out his philosophy on this point in a 1952 memo to Justice Jackson, advising the justice to "reaffirm" the separate but equal doctrine of *Plessy v. Ferguson* because it "was right." Rehnquist wrote:

> To those who would argue that the "personal" rights are more sacrosanct than "property" rights, the short answer is that the Constitution makes no such distinction. To the argument made by [plaintiff Brown's attorney] Thurgood, not John, Marshall that a majority may not deprive a minority of its constitutional right, the answer must be made that while this is sound in theory, in the long run it is the majority who will determine what the constitutional rights of the minority are. . . . I realize that it is an unpopular and unhumanitarian position, for which I have been excoriated by "liberal" colleagues but I think *Plessy v. Ferguson* was right and should be re-affirmed.

When the *Plessy v. Ferguson* memo initialed "WHR" surfaced during the 1986 hearing on Rehnquist's nomination to be chief justice, Senators Metzenbaum and Biden hammered at the use of the "I" in the memorandum, trying to get Rehnquist to concede he was expressing his own views and not Jackson's, as he was steadfastly maintaining. Senator Carl Levin of Michigan told the Senate:

> We now have had a better opportunity to examine the evidence relating to this memo than the Senate had in 1971. . . . [I]t is very difficult to conclude anything other than that the memo does not contain Justice Jackson's views, and must therefore have been either an expression of law clerk Rehnquist's views or an attempt on the part of law clerk Rehnquist to provide Jackson with the pro-*Plessy* point of view. In either case, the evidence casts serious doubt on Justice Rehnquist's account of the nature of his memorandum.

Senator Robert Dole, arguing in Rehnquist's favor, said that "the people voted for Ronald Reagan by landslide proportions in 1980 and 1984" and "they expect the President to carry their mandate all the way to the Supreme Court." After the hearings ended, the Republican-controlled Congress and the president's extensive lobbying led to a 65–33 victory. It was the most votes ever cast against a chief justice nominee.

In 1988, Professor Bernard Schwartz found further evidence bearing on Rehnquist's candor and view on *Plessy*. He was given access to Justice Jackson's concurring draft opinion in the *Brown* case, which was never issued. The draft showed that Jackson clearly believed that school segregation was unconstitutional. Schwartz concluded logically, "It is hard to believe that the man who wrote the sentences holding segregation invalid in his draft held the view only a few months earlier attributed to him by Chief Justice Rehnquist—'that *Plessy v. Ferguson* was right and should be reaffirmed.'"

Roberts and Alito probably share those views. The majority's theme in the school segregation, discrimination, and affirmative action cases is that the injury to minorities has been sufficiently rectified and, if not, the Court should no longer try to redress the injury. As Justice Scalia proudly said in justifying the conservative view, "We are all Americans." From the Right's viewpoint, we have already passed too many laws to protect individuals from racial discrimination, unfair legal systems, and indifferent educators.

Their legal view is based on a fundamental misreading of the Fourteenth Amendment. Clause 5 reads, "nor shall any State deprive any person of life, liberty, or property, without due process of law; nor deny to any person within its jurisdiction the equal protection of the laws." The operative questions are: How does one define liberty in the first part of the sentence? Does liberty in other parts of the document's first section mean something broader, narrower, or the same, as liberty in the Due Process Clause? These words have been fought over since the amendment was enacted, for their implications shape our understanding of how far the Due Process Clause of the Fourteenth Amendment may go in limiting state power. Today's majority thus finds the Court's minority interpretation of the Fourteenth Amendment extravagant: they claim that the liberals' definition of the words *liberty* and *due process* have gone too far in expanding individual rights and narrowing economic rights.

Roberts coauthored the government's brief in *United States v. Eichman*,[9] defending the constitutionality of the federal law criminalizing flag burning, even though the Supreme Court, one year earlier, in *Texas v. Johnson*,[10] had ruled a similar state statute unconstitutional. The Supreme Court rejected his argument. Roberts, who claims a commitment to *stare decisis* and precedent, was willing to urge a virtually instantaneous overruling of *Texas v. Johnson*.

Roberts knows that Republicans need not face the political fallout from a direct *Roe* reversal. *Brown v. Board of Education* and other landmark cases decided since the late 1930s have been eviscerated without being reversed through other rulings that limit the applications. *Plessy v. Ferguson*,[11] *Brown*'s predecessor that found segregation legal, was not reversed by *Brown*—it was, by legal legerdemain, pushed aside as not controlling.

Roberts' Circuit Court decisions are against federal regulation—

whether it be in the environmental, administrative, or economic areas. He is fully in agreement with The Federalist Society, which recently had a conference titled "Rolling Back the New Deal: A Review of Economic Regulation." "Let's Do Away with the SEC" was the headline of a Federalist newsletter. His District of Columbia Circuit decisions adhere to the line of cases, interpreting the Commerce Clause that lead to the dismantling of the administrative state. More economically sophisticated than either Scalia or Thomas, he can emerge as the conservatives' point man on economic matters, leading the already-started rejection of the New Deal Court's Commerce Clause decisions. He is the only justice whose knowledge of business and economics directly challenges Stephen Breyer.

The Framers meant for the legislative branch to be the most important branch in the federal government: Congress was to make the laws, the president was empowered to execute them, and the Court was required to interpret them. The very essence of a republic was that it would be governed through a deliberative legislature, composed carefully to reflect both popular will and elite limits on that will. The Framers were hostile to pure authoritarianism, including monarchies, and did not want the nation to be governed by an elected authoritarian any more than a nonelected one.

The argument has been made that O'Connor's departure does not fundamentally change the Court because Kennedy then becomes the swing vote. But Kennedy is very different from O'Connor in the three main areas in which the Court will deliberate in the next decades. He will vote to uphold Roe, but will continue to support severely limiting it; he will vote for the expansion of presidential powers, not giving Bush a blank check because of the war, but giving him far more than he is entitled to; he will support the expansion of state police powers and terrorism laws at the expense of privacy, due process, and freedom of speech. Describing Kennedy, a deep conservative, as a centrist, helps obscure this Court's sharp swing to the right.

Justice Kennedy agrees with Alito, Roberts, Scalia, and Thomas on most issues. But he voted for the majority in *Casey v. Planned Par-*

enthood, the most important abortion case since *Roe*, to uphold *Roe* solely on the basis of precedent. He does not agree with *Roe*'s broad sweep and will leave the liberals on most of the abortion cases that come up. On the important issue of one man-one vote, he is consistently with the conservative bloc—he rarely finds partisan gerrymandering that disenfranchises blacks, urban voters, or Democrats unconstitutional.

For example, let's take a look at the Supreme Court's 1987–1988 term, a more liberal court than today's. Justice Kennedy gave the conservatives the majority in seven of the eight 5–4 decisions in which the court's other eight members split along liberal-conservative lines. He voted for the rich and powerful and against the poor. He voted against giving women the same rights as men and against the rights of men charged with crimes.

Kennedy's votes in these split decisions were these:

♦ He supplied the fifth vote for the conservatives in the court's highly controversial decision overruling a major 1976 civil rights decision that transformed an 1866 law into a potent weapon against private racial discrimination, such as selling houses to "whites only."

♦ He joined the majority in the 5–4 decision upholding federal grants to church-affiliated groups to counsel teenage girls to be chaste and avoid abortion, a vote that tells us he may vote to uphold Bush's faith-based initiative, which is pouring hundreds of millions of dollars into churches.

♦ He joined the conservatives in a 5–4 decision favoring military contractors by giving a special defense against liability for injuries inflicted by defective products.

♦ He joined conservatives in a civil 5–4 decision evocative of a pre-Warren Court, upholding a rural county's denial of free school bus service to a family that could not afford the usual fee.

◆ He joined in two 5–4 decisions and one 6–3 decision upholding death sentences. In one of the death sentence cases he wrote a decision giving trial judges broad discretion to deny criminal defendants the attorneys of their choice. He cast two votes rejecting challenges to police interrogation techniques.

Justice Kennedy also sided with the conservatives in a 5–4 decision that pension funds that paid different benefits to men and women based on mortality tables showing that women generally live longer are not retroactively liable to pay higher benefits to those who retired. He did so by ignoring the precedent of the Court's earlier rulings, that the use of such tables was sex discrimination.

In that 1987–1988 term, Justice Kennedy voted in twenty-nine cases in which the Court's leading liberal, Justice Brennan, and the generally conservative Chief Justice Rehnquist, were on opposite sides. He agreed with the chief justice in eighteen cases, the most important ones, and with Justice Brennan in eleven. His pattern has been the same every year since. The only major change in his position since then was deciding in 2003 that consensual homosexual acts were not a crime. Previously he was the deciding vote in a 1986 case that held to the contrary.

While ostensibly testifying to explain the Court's budget requests each year, Kennedy has often been taken to task over controversies surrounding the Court. In March 2001, Congressman Jose E. Serrano of New York confronted and chastised Justice Kennedy over the Court's ruling in *Bush v. Gore*.[12] Serrano complained on behalf of his minority constituents that their voices had been muted in the 2000 election—he claimed the voting process was similar to corrupt electoral processes in other countries.

Justice Kennedy, before the Subcommittee, defended the U.S. Supreme Court's entry into the disputed 2000 presidential election. Explaining why the Court overcame "vital limits on judicial authority," the Bush Court notes that "when contending parties invoke the process of the courts . . . it becomes our *unsought* responsibility to resolve the federal and constitutional issues the judicial system has been forced to confront."

Kennedy attempted to distinguish the Court from the other two branches by virtue of its language, ethic, discipline, dynamic, grammar, tradition, and logic of the law that are all "different from the political branches." Hence, he concluded that this Court was indeed "first among equals."

Former *New York Times* writer David Margolick, writing in the October 2004 issue of *Vanity Fair* after interviewing lawyers who were clerks during *Bush v. Gore*, highlights those Kennedy characteristics that have not yet been fully recognized: his sensitivity to "real" politics and his very conservative instincts. Based on interviews with some of the law clerks of the Supreme Court justices, Margolick shows how Kennedy's basic feelings are nearly identical with those of other conservatives. Of course, Kennedy's vote, along with O'Connor's, denied Gore the presidency.

Kennedy decided to take *Bush v. Gore* despite his states' rights position and despite his aversion to political issues, as shown by the voting cases. Another conservative justice might not have taken the case—it was obviously hypocritical for them to interfere with the Florida state courts. While we might expect it from Rehnquist, Scalia and Thomas, it seemed surprising coming from Kennedy. And O'Connor might have also been embarrassed to vote to take the case without four justices on her side. Kennedy was the perfect justice. He was the justice who took all emergency motions from Florida, Georgia, and Alabama. Under court rules, Kennedy needed three other voters to grant Bush's application to get the Supreme Court to consider his case. He got four—Rehnquist, O'Connor, Thomas and Scalia—all states' righters, all who wrote and believed that the states should handle their own matters and the federal government should not intervene.

O'Connor's stated distress over Gore's victory was widely

reported and not denied. Recusing herself would have been appropriate, but it was not the course she took.

Kennedy, even as he took the case, let his clerks know he felt Bush's chances to have the Supreme Court reverse the Florida High Court's decision were not strong. But Justice John Paul Stevens, a Gerald Ford appointee, the oldest member of the bench, knew what Kennedy refused to say clearly.[13]

Stevens started writing a dissent the minute he heard that the Court had taken the case. Kennedy, pilloried by Robert Bork and the conservatives as a traitor and worse, whose pro-abortion votes were given reluctantly and sparingly, was the justice most taken up with the idea of the court as the preeminent branch of government. He spoke from the mount; his gaudy, red-rugged office was more appropriate for a self-important head of state than for a Supreme Court justice. His clerks were then, and are today, among the most conservative from the Federalist Society. Gore's lawyers failed to take on O'Connor, failing to see that her moderate legal stance had been overwhelmed by her politics. And they did not know that Kennedy had shifted positions and that a new argument was the only hope of reaching him.

The first Court decision showed its deep divide. Everyone other than Kennedy had committed themselves. Because they knew a decision on the merits of the case would have lead to open warfare on the Court, they successfully papered over their differences by punting. Their first decision, 9–0, asked the Florida Court to clarify its decision. But when the Florida Court instead ordered a recount, the Court again stepped in.

Gore's counsel pitched his argument to Kennedy, not knowing that Kennedy, according to his law clerk and memos he then wrote, had already made up his mind. At the argument, Kennedy asked questions intended to lead one to believe that he was against the Bush position. But given the speciousness of the Bush winning argument, he started to equivocate after he left the bench. Scalia saw this. He and Kennedy met within the hour after the argument and Kennedy, politically and legally corrected, joined the conservative majority.

Kennedy, in the internal memos circulated among the justices, asked the dissenting justices to tone down their criticism of the court to leave out the claim of partisan politics. He appealed to their sense that the Court would be impaired by their deeply felt criticism. He charged that the dissenters were "trashing the Court." In a draft of his opinion, he seriously misstated the Stevens dissent. Met with Stevens' outrage, Kennedy refused to step back.

Stevens put it well in his elegant, concise, sad dissent. "Although we may never know with complete certainty the identity of the winner of this year's Presidential election, the identity of the loser is perfectly clear. It is the Nation's confidence in the judge as an impartial guardian of the rule of law."

Make no mistake about it—Kennedy is the reason *Bush v. Gore* came out the way it did. Kennedy wrote most of the final short majority opinion. His statement of what the court had done was transparently false. *Bush v. Gore* applies only to Bush and is not of precedential value, he said. No Supreme Court justice has ever said that about a case the court decided.[14]

◆　　　◆　　　◆

America's democracy is at a watershed. In a country always at war, we pass and interpret laws that forever place our democratic values at risk, as competing values assert pride of place. Because this new century poses problems that the writers of our two-hundred-year-old Constitution could not have imagined, we are increasingly writing on a *tabula rasa*—where no one can truly argue that the Constitution and eighteenth, nineteenth, and twentieth century cases provide the anwers we need. The concept of three equal branches has little meaning. Now the president has accrued power already contrary to the wishes of the Founding Fathers, who feared a too strong executive. That our government now has echoes of a theocracy would horrify James Madison, Alexander Hamilton, and Thomas Jefferson. The Constitutional stricture that only Congress can declare war no longer has any meaning—it is the president who gets us into wars while Congress watches from the sidelines. The president has accrued power, and Congress' power, often through its own acquiescence, has diminished in ways contrary to the wishes of our Founding Fathers.

There has long been a desire in America for restrictions on democratic rights and for an authoritarian government, propelled by a combination of religious and nationalistic fervor. The helplessness caused by the events of September 11 and the domestic and international war against Muslim "terrorists" deepened this need. History shows that a government powered by God and "unilateral executive power" can easily give rise to tyranny.

◆　　　◆　　　◆

De Tocqueville, in *Democracy in America*, feared that in America power would come to reside with a single person and then the country's citizens would be "reduced to nothing better than a flock of timid and industrious animals, of which the government is the shepherd." De Tocqueville also wrote that he knew of no country with "less independence of mind and true freedom of discussion" than America. De Tocqueville foresaw a time when an American strongman would cow Congress and the justice system.

De Tocqueville saw, as did the writers of the Constitution, that the American majority would trample the minority. A firm supporter of our unique and cherished system of checks and balances, he believed in the possibility of America's rule of law to limit the excesses of the ruler—the exact issue in today's debate over the mangled jurisprudence of detainee detention, the refusal to provide the citizenry with information, and warrantless wiretapping of American citizens. He had known that the Court, without money or armies to enforce its decisions, was of limited power against a tyrannical strongman. "The courts correct the aberrations of democracy," he wrote, and "though they can never stop the movements of the majority, they do succeed in checking and directing them."

Tocqueville would believe all the false, empty justifications. He feared, and foresaw, that the newest incarnation of a dictatorship was likely to be created by the "avowed lover of liberty" who is a "hidden servant of tyranny." Or, as Senator Barry Goldwater justified it, extremism in the defense of liberty is no vice.

◆　　　◆　　　◆

How will the courts of America attend to the confrontations—legal, political, and cultural—that face us? For at least the next twenty-five years, a conservative Supreme Court is determined to eradicate much of twentieth-century law and establish an imperial presidency, while dramatically disenfranchising the voters by cutting down the power of Congress.

Below the Supreme Court are the twelve federal circuit courts. Today nine of those courts are firmly in the hands of conservatives. Three-quarters of those 165 appellate judges have views very similar to Alito, Roberts, Scalia, Thomas, and Kennedy.

The two-hundred-year struggle for racial, gender, and economic fairness, for educational equality, for federal laws protecting minimum wages, and for defense against corporate plunder and environmental destruction, all fall within the Supreme Court's decision-making power. All are at risk.

The Supreme Court and our lower federal court judges are restructuring our government, reallocating power in ways that the people have not shown they want.

Money is power. The enormous amount of money flowing into churches and religious schools is barely noticed. Bush's faith-based initiative, the voucher programs in twenty-two states, and the support of religious schools, while at the same time withholding monies from public schools, serve as compensation to the Religious Right for their support. A powerful radical conservative bloc is becoming a permanent part of our landscape.

The Rehnquist era started the shift of power to the states and away from the federal government—away from Congress, away from the federal agencies, and away from the regulatory system created to protect employees, consumers, small investors. The Roberts-Scalia-Alito-Thomas-Kennedy Court will continue the work of the Rehnquist Court and make the rightward swing more dramatic. It will preside over the expansion of presidential powers in ways never before imagined. And as it expands those powers, it will insulate the president from accountability. The chief executive, under the new regime, will be responsible to no one.

Our Founding Fathers created a republican form of government in which the supreme power rests in the people through their elected representatives, a government based on our Constitutionally created structure of checks and balances.

The story goes that, as Benjamin Franklin (whose 300th birthday we celebrate this year), left the Constitutional Convention in 1787, he was approached by a Mrs. Powel, who asked him, "What have you given us, Dr. Franklin?"

"A republic," he replied, "if you can keep it."

In the next twenty-five years, the Roberts court will not be able to effectively check or balance the president. We can see where this Court is going by looking at some of the writings and statements of Robert Bork, the intellectual father of the Conservative movement that was seeded in the Reagan years. The majority of the present Court are members of The Federalist Society, a group formed and fostered by Edwin Meese, Boyden Gray, Ken Starr, Charles Fried, and Bork. Much of what Starr (a former sitting judge), Roberts, Alito, Scalia and Thomas say has been said before by Bork. Alito, in 1985, said what most conservatives believe: Bork is America's greatest living jurist. Even though Bork was famously blocked from ascending to the court, I would argue that not enough attention has been paid to what he believes—for his beliefs are the essence of the new court. His profile was low during the Roberts and Alito hearings—his name was never mentioned by the nominees. But no amount of evasive answers at nomination hearings can hide the fact that the man who called the Rehnquist court "too liberal" is the new Court architect.

When Bork attacked a book I'd written for saying he was the power behind the throne of the new regime, he said I had to be "counting on the gullibility of the public where the constitutional function of courts is concerned, for the picture [Garbus] draws of an imminent conservative takeover of the Court is a stranger to reality." He wrote further, "The 2000 presidential election, according to Garbus, gave the 'partisans of the political and religious right' the chance to add to their Supreme Court majority. What majority? He claims that the Rehnquist Court 'has already substantially eviscerated the work of the Warren and early Burger Courts in areas of abortion, school prayer, affirmative action, and school integration. Would that it were so, but it is not."

But when Alito was nominated, Bork said, "the Conservatives have the Court we want."

♦   ♦   ♦

The conservatives have spent the past thirty-six years changing the law. All that Edwin Meese, Robert Bork, Charles Freed, Boyden Gray, Samuel Alito, and John Roberts wanted when they formed the Federalists in 1982 has come to pass.

Today's conservatives rely on the laws of a previous conservative cycle—cases that recall and revive a culture that existed one hundred thirty-five years ago. During the Reconstruction, a conservative Supreme Court took control for seventy years, ending in 1937 when a more liberal court was created. After the assassinations of Martin Luther King, Jr. and John F. Kennedy, and after the 1972 *Roe v. Wade* decision, the country and the Court were in transition from 1972 to the Reagan-landslide Rehnquist Court in 1980. The Rehnquist Court's decisions cite law and value from the 1870s, the Reconstruction era, and 1910, the *Lochner*[15] period. By looking at the basis for past and present Conservative decisions we can predict what the future holds.

The 1937 Roosevelt expanded economic rights, and after 1952, the Warren Court attempted to create racial equality and protect the economic and voting rights of minorities. It attempted to give full force to the Constitution's mandate—to stop the tyranny of the majority over the minority. The Rehnquist-Roberts Court seeks to encourage the power of the majority over the minority.

Because justices are appointed for life, cycles of control of the Supreme Court extend for decades. This has happened before. There have been other long-sitting courts. But never like this. The Roosevelt and Warren Courts marked a liberal period of thirty-five years from 1937 to 1972. The Rehnquist Court had a thirty-six-year lifespan, and the present court will most probably be controlled by "conservatives" for the next twenty-five years. The three youngest justices are conservatives. Thomas is fifty-eight, Roberts is fifty, Alito is fifty-one. It will probably get even more conservative in the future. The two oldest justices most likely to next leave, Ruth Bader Ginsburg, seventy-three, and John Paul Stevens, eighty-six, are the two liberal members of the Court. Scalia, at age sixty-nine, is a few years older than the moderates, Breyer and Souter, both sixty-seven. Kennedy is seventy.

Lifelong appointment to our nation's judiciary has tended to mean just that. Hugo Black, appointed in 1937, stayed thirty-four years; Felix Frankfurter, appointed in 1939, stayed twenty-three; William O. Douglas, appointed in 1939, stayed thirty-six. In more recent times, Harry Blackmun and Thurgood Marshall stayed twenty-four years. Justice Rehnquist has been there for thirty-four years, Justice Stevens for twenty-nine years, Justice O'Connor for twenty-five. Scalia, only forty-seven years old at the time of his appointment, has already served nineteen. These appointees long outlasted those who appointed them. The circuit courts of appeals and many of the federal trial courts have judges with comparable lengths of service. Lifespans are lengthening. Absent unforeseen events, Roberts, Alito, and Thomas will be on the bench twenty-five years from now. Assuming Scalia and Kennedy stay until they are eighty-five, there will be a solid conservative bloc of five conservatives and two moderates on the bench for the next two decades. Assuming future justices are appointed equally by the two parties, there will be a solid conservative bloc for the next twenty-five years.

There is an old adage. "He who tries to predict the future through a crystal ball winds up eating broken glass." There are, of course, many unforseen events that will occur over the next quarter of a century. Nonetheless, the courts' past, present and probable future fortells a long conservative cycle. The November 7, 2006 elections, which saw moderate republications replaced by conservative democrats, will not change that cycle. The white evangelicals and born-again Christians who constituted 24 percent of those who voted in the November 2006 election will continue to intimidate the Senate and mobilize on their red button issues. Even a more liberal Senate Judiciary Committee will not stop the conservative cycle.

The American dream seemed possible in 1865 after the Civil War. Reconstruction promised to give the country a breath of equality and freedom. But that promise was short-lived. The Reconstruction Court, immediately after the Civil War, attempted to fully undercut the Civil War Amendments, the Thirteenth banning slavery, the Fourteenth Amendment which stopped any state from depriving "any person of life, liberty or the pursuit of happiness, without due process of law; nor denying to any person within its jurisdiction the equal protection of the laws"; and the Fifteenth giving all male citizens the right to vote. Poll taxes restricting voting rights were upheld, the federal government's power to move toward equality ended, and segregated schools were upheld.

Starting with *Dred Scott* and finishing with *Plessy v. Ferguson,* which found segregation constitutional, the Conservative Court continued into the twentieth Century, called the Lochner Era. This court denying the rights of individuals and gave corporate interests enormous powers over its employees by banning minimum wage and maximum hour laws, banning any attempts to enforce safety regulations, issuing injunctions to stop unions in labor disputes, and imprisoning labor leaders. We are reliving, as if for the first time, that kind of retrenchment.

We are better than military commissions, Abu Ghraib, Guantanamo, the Patriot Act, the Military Commissions Act of 2006, and "rendition," the sending of prisoners overseas to be tortured at CIA-controlled prisons, paying journalists to write propaganda in the form of news—practices justified by the attorney general, the vice president, the CIA, and others in the administration. No previous administration ever sought to justify such practices. No American government has been so criticized and seen as so radical and dangerous to the rest of the world. Skepticism or disbelief is appropriate when a potential police state committed to misinformation starts talking about spreading its democracy.

Chapter One

The President against the People

The accumulation of all powers, legislative, execu-
tive, and judiciary, in the same hands, whether of
one, a few, or many, and whether hereditary, self-
appointed, or elective, may justly be pronounced the
very definition of tyranny.
—James Madison, *The Federalist*, ed. Benjamin F.
Wright, No. 47, p. 336 (1961)

◆   ◆   ◆

Surprisingly few cases have dealt with the powers of the president. How much power this President gets depends in large part on the people, on Congress, and on the new Supreme Court. Attorney General Alberto Gonzales has claimed that the President is the "sole organ of foreign policy in the nation." It is safe to say the new Court is prepared to give a President and his Attorney General permission to violate the Constitution not only in the war on terror but also on domestic issues. Astonishingly, on November 15, 2005, Carl Levin, the liberal Democratic senator from Michigan and an outspoken present opponent of the war, joined his Republican counterpart from South Carolina, Lindsey Graham, in passing legislation validating the President's broad claim of domestic and foreign powers. The *habeas corpus* right was stripped from anyone the government decided to brand as an enemy—Congress did what even the Court would have hesitated to do. The Senate vote was 79–16 in favor of the legislation. Passed by the House, in an overwhelming majority, it gave the President what he wanted. And then the McCain anti-torture bill was in fact the first law in the United States that legitimized torture.

The Pentagon has already expanded its domestic surveillance

activity beyond that of any time in history. In 2004, President Bush's State of the Union speech assured Americans that there are no warrantless searches. We now know that since 2001, National Security Agency (NSA) and Pentagon operatives break into homes; wiretap and eavesdrop at will; monitor protests of every kind, from environmental to antiwar; and build secret dossiers on citizens while arguing that there can be no judicial review of their activities. The President claims that there were less than twenty-five hundred intercepts; James Branson, a former NSA official, claims that the figure is closer to three hundred thousand. We later learned that at least two million Americans had their financial records looked at. The President also argues that there can be no judicial review of any decision he makes of whether an alien or an American citizen is an enemy combatant. Congress supports this. So, too, I fear, will this and future courts.

Created in 1952, the NSA is the biggest American intelligence agency, with more than thirty thousand employees at Ft. Meade, Maryland, and listening posts around the world. Part of the Defense Department, it is the successor to the State Department's "Black Chamber" and American military eavesdropping and code-breaking operations that date to the early days of telegraph and telephone communications.

The NSA runs the eavesdropping hardware of the American intelligence system, operating a huge network of satellites and listening devices around the world. Its mission has been to gather intelligence on foreign enemies by breaking codes and tapping into telephone and computer communications.

The disclosure in the 1970s of widespread surveillance on political dissenters and other civil rights abuses led to restrictions at the NSA and elsewhere on the use of domestic wiretaps. The NSA monitors United Nations delegations and some foreign embassy lines on American soil, but it is generally prohibited from listening in on the conversations of anyone inside the country without a special court order.

Since the reforms of the late 1970s, the NSA has generally been permitted to target the communications of people on American soil only if they are believed to be "agents of a foreign power"—a foreign nation or international terrorist group—and a warrant is obtained from the Foreign Intelligence Surveillance Court.

Months after the terror attacks of September 11, 2001, President Bush signed a secret executive order that relaxed restrictions on domestic spying by the NSA. The order allows the agency to monitor without warrants the international phone calls and e-mails of some Americans and others inside the United States.

Not until recently did the public became significantly aware that the government had, prior to the 2001 NSA oversight, passed the 1978 Foreign Intelligence Services Act (FISA) and the courts it created. It is not surprising that very few people know of its existence. The courtroom is in a windowless room on the top floor of the Department of Justice. There are eleven rotating judges. The Court meets in secret, with no published opinions or public records. Nearly all those spied upon will never know they were under surveillance. No one, except the FISA judge involved and the Department of Justice, knows what is done. No one, except the government and FISA judge, knows who the warrants are aimed at. There is no review by anyone, neither the regular federal Appellate Court nor the Congress, of its decisions. More than fifteen thousand search warrants, permitting eavesdropping, surveillance, and break-ins, have been sought by the government. From 1979 to 2001, twelve thousand warrants were sought. Not one was denied. From 2001 to the present, fifty-two hundred were sought and four were sent back to the government for more evidence. Of the four, two were modified and granted. Thus, although the FISA court is required to determine if enough facts are present to justify a warrant, only twice has it ever denied a warrant. Even though the FISA law gave the government the right to tap, and then either wait seventy-two hours to tell the FISA court or discontinue the tap, that was not sufficient for the President. Not one single case has been successfully prosecuted based on evidence obtained through one of these wiretaps.

If there is another terrorist attack, and it is very likely there will be one, the government will seek more powers, claiming that the new attack proves the present laws are inadequate. We will certainly see, as we recently saw in Britain, the head of government ask for ninety-day detentions without access to court. Blair said more time was needed to get information from the terrorists. He compromised with a twenty-seven-day detention period. The attempt to end habeas corpus and permit unlimited surveillance starts in wartime at Guantanamo and then spreads in peacetime to the rest of America. We are outraged, as we should be, that China, fearing dissent, uses the massive machinery of the state and thirty thousand men to spy on and jail Internet users. And yet we cannot weaken our claim that the United States provides a strong alternative in defense of democratic principles.

In 2006, the New Patriot Act was passed. Two out of three branches of the federal government are left out of the loop in that act.

Through the Patriot Act—a brilliant public relations acronym for "Uniting and Strengthening America by Providing Appropriate Tools Required to Intercept and Obstruct Terrorism"—and the September 18, 2001, use of military force authorization, Congress has consistently driven power to the President while lessening its own role, as well as the role of the judiciary, in decisions about foreign and our domestic war. The enormity of the preemptive war claim that the delegation of war powers authorizing the President to "use all necessary and appropriate force against those nations, organizations, or persons he determines planned, authorized, committed, or aided the terrorist attacks that occurred on September 11, 2001, or harbored such organizations or persons" is apparently not fully appreciated by Congress. This gives him the right to start a preemptive war against anyone anywhere in the world.

The Patriot Act is only the tip of an iceberg of amended legislation. Few in the public and few in Congress understand that its endless deletions and amendments of previous legislation, impossible to follow unless you know the previous law by heart, dramatically change the law in many areas.

The Patriot Act surveillance provisions, like the NSA surveillance, provide federal agencies with more surveillance options and less judicial supervision. The principal statute governing electronic surveillance in criminal investigations passed in 1968, Title III of the Crime Control and Safe Streets Act, tried to answer Supreme Court doubts about the constitutionality of electronic surveillance under the Fourth Amendment by seemingly providing a judicial check that, in effect, is no check at all. Except in emergencies, the Bush Administration must persuade a judicial officer that they have probable cause that the interception they seek may provide evidence of one of a number of listed offenses. The court order permitting surveillance requires investigators to submit to limitations and judicial supervision. Evidence intercepted in violation of Title III's central provisions is made inadmissible in Court.

The Patriot Act rejects the Safe Streets Act. It allows surveillance of U.S. citizens beyond FISA standards and beyond the criminal law even where there is no probable cause and, in effect, no judicial involvement. FISA warrants freely obtained may now be used even if intelligence is not the primary purpose of an investigation. In "Roving Wiretaps" Bush gives us new language and new concepts. If you wiretap an individual's phone, the government says you can tap any phone, cell phone, or street call that the person uses, as well as the phones of anyone he calls. One wiretap provision, unchecked by a judge, can lead to hundreds or thousands of other calls. The Patriot Act authorizations, not based on probable cause, are nationwide.

Probable cause, an extraordinarily important Constitutional protection, is gone. It is not an exaggeration to say that it is the linchpin of the Constitution—the linchpin of protection against a police state. Prior to the Patriot Act, the government could and did order telephone companies to turn over lists of the numbers being dialed to and from a particular telephone. If the government certified that the information sought was "relevant to an ongoing criminal investigation," a judge "must" grant the order, regardless of whether the judge agrees with the government's conclusion. The government, on the same unexamined certification, traps and traces orders providing access to "dialing, routing, and signaling information" in connection with computers. The government has access to lists of e-mails sent and received, as well as a list of Web sites visited on a particular computer. In the telephone context, getting a "pen register," with its list of telephone numbers dialed to a particular phone, offered no opportunity to hear the individual's conversations. However, the information about e-mail addresses and Web sites evidently travels with the content of the e-mail. The Department of Justice promises to separate the two and not pry into content. There is no way of supervising whether this promise is kept. In addition, it seems that if a target uses a computer in a cybercafé or the public library to check e-mail or visit a Web site, surveillance of that computer will continue, giving the government access to the e-mail and Internet activities of thousands.

The Patriot Act and the Military Commissions Act gives our attorney general the power to detain and deport noncitizens with only the pretense of judicial review. The attorney general certifies only that he has "reasonable grounds to believe" that a noncitizen endangers national security. The attorney general and secretary of state are designating domestic groups as terrorist organizations, and deporting any noncitizen who belongs to them.

The new Supreme Court will not resist many of the president's attempts to keep the judiciary from reviewing legislation aimed at terror. The justices are likely to throw themselves on this year's security train, since neither Congress nor "We the People" are expressing sufficient dissatisfaction.

In 2001 the attorney general announced that he intends to eavesdrop on inmates' attorney-client conversations. He also announced plans to have state and local law enforcement officials question five thousand people who appear to have been selected according to their ethnicity or religion. He acted to expand his power to detain immigrants, and to make information from the Freedom of Information Act less available. At the same time, NSA admits that the increased surveillance has not made us safer.

We are selling our birthright for a vague language that means anything the president says it means. The president's position is essentially that "Congress is not doing the right thing, so I'm going to act on my own."

Richard Epstein, a University of Chicago law professor who is among the most conservative scholars in America, said he believes "the President's argument that he can override FISA is wrong. I find every bit of his legal argument disingenuous."

The Supreme Court and Congress have the power to affect what happens at the detention and torture centers, but they barely exercise it. Five years after we opened the Guantanamo prison, not one person has been found guilty of anything. Not one person has been convicted after trial in an American court of terrorism. Even though there have been many federal court orders, not one detainee, either in the United States or Guantanamo or the CIA overseas bases, has been better off because of them: the detainees continue to be showpieces in the war on terror.

The Bush legal system of warrantless searches, enemy combatants with so few rights as to turn their trials into "Kangaroo courts," and insufficient judicial oversight shall continue for as long as the war on terror continues. No one has ever before even suggested an abridged legal system that could affect the rights of so many Americans. Bush, referring to Roosevelt and Lincoln, uses history as a defense and refers to World War II and the Civil War—far different situations. Roosevelt's concededly awful internment policy was directed at declared enemies, the Germans and Japanese, when we were at war, saw sabotage, and feared invasion. We now recognize that it was wrong. Lincoln's suspension of habeas corpus came during the Civil War, when six hundred thousand Americans were killed. But even that Congress never gave Lincoln the other powers that George W. Bush seeks.

Youngstown Sheet & Tube Co., et al. v. Sawyer,[16] the framework for any discussion of the limitations of presidential powers, which is more than fifty years old, is iconic. It took center stage minutes into the Supreme Court confirmation hearings of Judge Samuel A. Alito, Jr. when Senator Arlen Specter, the Republican chairman of the Judiciary Committee, named it as one of three decisions he addressed in his opening statement. The June 1952 case arose when President Harry S. Truman tried to stop the unions from interfering with the nation's steel mills during the Korean War. In a 6–3 decision, the Supreme Court said he did not have the power to do so merely because we were at war.

Chief Justice John G. Roberts, Jr., at his confirmation hearings in September 2005, endorsed *Youngstown.* He "set the framework for consideration of questions of executive power in times of war and with respect to foreign affairs since it was decided." But limiting the precedent to the facts and the time when *Youngstown* was written permitted him to pay fealty to the decision while he was on the circuit court while reaching totally contrary results.

Writing the majority opinion in *Youngstown,* Justice Hugo Black said the president's power was extensive but not unlimited: "Even though 'theater of war' be an expanding concept," Justice Black wrote, "we cannot with faithfulness to our constitutional system hold that the commander in chief of the armed forces has the ultimate power as such to take possession of private property in order to keep labor disputes from stopping production. This is a job for the nation's lawmakers, not for its military authorities." Justice Robert Jackson's concurrence seemed to be aimed at the rebuilt and newly packaged conservative argument that there is a "unitary president," one with nearly unchecked powers. "That comprehensive and undefined presidential powers hold both practical advantages and grave dangers for the country," Justice Jackson wrote in the concurrence, "will impress anyone who has served as legal adviser to a president in time of transition and public anxiety." He proposed three categories to decide the constitutionality of broad grants of executive power. The president's authority is at its maximum, Justice Jackson wrote, when he "acts pursuant to an express or implied authorization of Congress."

This administration has said that congressional authorizing of the use of military force after the September 11 attacks gave him the right to use his maximum powers. The president says that any laws Congress passes, such as the 1978 Foreign Intelligence Security Act, that wrongfully limit the president's powers are unconstitutional.

Justice Jackson's second category was a middle ground in which Congress has not passed any laws dealing with the legal issue before the Court. In that case, he said, "any actual test of power is likely to depend on the imperatives of events and contemporary imponderables rather than on abstract theories of law." In other words, it is pretty much up for grabs.

The third category is when the president takes action at odds with the will of Congress, exactly the case here. In this tarea, Justice Jackson said, the president's power is "at its lowest ebb," and claims of presidential authority "must be scrutinized with caution." President Bush's opponents say that FISA is at odds with the president's interpretation of the broad power to get warrantless tapes. FISA, says the president, gives him the power to wiretap without warrants for fifteen days after a war starts. Attorney General Gonzales says this proves that if the president were given fifteen days, Congress recognized the need for warrantless searches and gave it to him for as long as the president felt he needed it. The attorney general also says that if FISA is interpreted to limit the president's present wartime power, it is unconstitutional.

Our Framers could not have foreseen the present age of nuclear missiles and cataclysmic terrorism. But they understood political accountability, and—as their deliberations in Philadelphia attest—they knew that sending Americans into battle demanded careful reflection and vigorous debate. So they created a simple means of ensuring that debate: in Article I, Section 8, of the Constitution they gave Congress the power to declare war. At that time no one had the temerity to conceive of preemptive war.

What would have happened if there had been a full congressional debate on Iraq? Congress could then have tried to learn about the existence of weapons of mass destruction and whether, as the government claimed, oil revenues would pay for the quick war and short reconstruction. There might even have been a discussion.

A congressional declaration of war can stop a preemptive war. It forces public debate—not just congressional debate. And it can give the courts a chance to step in as they did in *Youngstown*. A report issued in 2006 by the Constitution Project, a group of eminent academics and policymakers assembled by Georgetown University's Public Policy Institute, argues that Congress and the courts must take responsibility and be able to stop a president.

Congress' practice of failing to insist on its congressional rights began early in our country's history, when President James Madison demanded a declaration of war against Algiers to stop the Barbary pirates. Congress did not give the declaration but authorized him to use "such of the armed vessels of the United States as may be judged requisite." Authorizations of this type continued over the centuries and have become fast tracks to war. Congress, fearful of being attacked as not warlike enough, votes on the president's misleading military proposals without accepting responsibility for judging the objectives of the war or the plans for waging it.

This president and this Congress are not the first to collaborate in acts that lead to tragedy. The Gulf of Tonkin Resolution, based on falsehoods unexamined by Congress, led to Vietnam. After the Vietnam War, Congress passed the 1973 War Powers Act, saying that troops sent into combat by the president must be withdrawn within sixty days unless Congress specifically approves an extension of combat. But after passing the law, Congress permitted it to fall into disuse. Richard Nixon vetoed the Act. When Congress overrode the veto, he reaffirmed his right to go ahead with war regardless of what Congress said.

The War Powers Act recognized a formal congressional process and declaration constitutionally impossible for the president to ignore.

Leslie Gelb, a former Pentagon analyst, proposed a new set of procedures for sending troops into what may become a drawn-out war. The president would be required to present to Congress an analysis of the threat, specific war aims, the rationale for those aims, the feasibility of achieving them, a general sense of war strategy, plans for action, and potential costs. Congress would hold hearings of officials and nongovernmental experts, examine evidence of the threat, assess the objectives, and explore the drawbacks. A full floor debate and vote would follow.

In the case of a preemptive strike on the United States, the president, under Gelb's proposal, retains his power to fight the attackers without a congressional declaration. But any sustained operation would require congressional involvement. The president could send troops to Iraq if they attacked us. But if he planned to keep troops there he would need a congressional declaration. Without one, funding for troops in the field would be automatically cut off.

Gelb's concept is a good one if Congress presses its constitutional and institutional rights. And if a future court backs it up. This process would put considerable pressure on the president to develop his case with far greater care than has been the norm over the past fifty years. Mandating that Congress must act before troops are in the field would make it more difficult for Congress to run away.

The time for such legislation is better now than at any time in history. The majority of the country is ready for it. The cost of the war, the certainty of result, and the killings demand that such legislation be passed. Yet Congress remains silent.

Today an Alaskan bridge to nowhere bill gets more deliberation than a decision to send American troops to war. That is not what Thomas Jefferson, James Madison, and John Adams intended.

"When the president does it, that means it's not illegal," Richard

Nixon infamously said. Alito, when working for Reagan, defended Nixon's statement and the actions he took under that plan. Nixon was proved wrong. The wiretapping plan ended when J. Edgar Hoover, of all people, objected to it. Nixon's approval of it was listed in the articles of impeachment. The rejection by the courts of Richard Nixon's expansive claims did not stop the steady increase of that power. Nor did the congressional rebuke to Reagan's support of the Contras.

"When the commander in chief does it, that means it's not illegal," is Bush's claim too. That claim, as Bush seems to understand it, goes beyond Nixon, beyond Johnson, beyond any previously-sought power over citizens in wartime or peace.[17] The new Supreme Court will unfortunately further expand the president's powers and curtail the powers of Congress. And the administrative agencies created by Congress in a wide range of areas, from disaster relief to drug approval to imposing clean-air standards, will be all but destroyed.

Will the new Supreme Court effectively ban torture, as the Israeli and British high courts recently did? Probably not. Administration lawyers claim that the president as commander in chief is not bound by laws that ban torture because he is empowered by the Constitution to fight the nation's wars however he sees fit. A memo from the Department of Justice to the White House counsel dated August 1, 2002, argued that any attempt to apply Congress' antitorture law "in a manner that interferes with the president's direction of such core war matters as detention and interrogation of enemy combatants thus would be unconstitutional." It says, "Any effort by Congress to regulate the interrogation of battlefield combatants would violate the Constitution's sole vesting of the Commander-in-Chief authority of the President." Scalia has already said he agrees with this.

Had Reagan or Nixon been president at this time, they surely would have sought the same laws. But it is more of a threat because Bush and subsequent president will have a more conservative Court behind them. The public believes torture has been outlawed because the president says so, while at the same time he claims the power to decide when to do it. Furthermore, the much-applauded Bush-McCain agreement allegedly banning torture does not do anything of the kind. McCain and Congress, while claiming victory, actually capitulated. Torture has not been banned or in any way impeded. In fact, it is encouraged. Under the compromise, anyone charged with torture can defend himself if a "reasonable" person could have concluded he was following a lawful order. That defense "loophole" totally corrodes the ban. It is the CIA, or the torturing agency, that will decide what a "reasonable" person could have concluded. What is not "reasonable" if the interrogator (wrongfully or rightfully) believes he has a ticking bomb? Will a CIA or military officer issue a narrow order if he knows his interrogator believes, in this case, torture will work? The Military Commissions Act of 2006, in fact, encourages torture. It states that confessions obtained during torture may be used against the victim in their legal proceedings, an argument rejected by the Israeli and British courts. An interrogator can't lose by torturing. It also permits enemy combatants to be executed on necessary and classified evidence that the defendants cannot effecively challenge.

And, in any event, Bush said when signing the amendment barring "cruel, inhuman and degrading treatment" of terrorism suspects that he would interpret it in a manner consistent with the constitutional authority of the president to supervise the unitary executive branch as commander in chief. He said "alternative procedures" used by the CIA were acceptable. That means, of course, the President does whatever he wants. Vice President Dick Cheney does not rule out subjecting prisoners to a "dunk in the water" if it saves lives. Waterboarding and sleep deprivation sound "permissible".

The Bush-McCain torture compromise found in the Military Commissions Act legitimizes torture for the first time in this country. Not in the two World Wars, Korea, the Cold War, or Vietnam did the president ever seek or get the power this bill gives them.

And the new Court will confirm this procedure. The worse the victim is, the more information he supposedly has, the more he will be "permissibly" tortured.

The Roberts Court will uphold the McCain bill and the Military Commissions Act against constitutional power on the grounds Congress has laid out. It will also permit the president to violate international treaties if necessary to fight the war on terror. By these lights, the United Nations Convention Against Torture, the leading antitorture treaty, could constitutionally be violated even though the United States signed and ratified it, and even though the Constitution declares treaties to be "the supreme law of the land." The conservative Court majority, over a vigorous liberal dissent, will most likely uphold Attorney General Gonzales's view that the antitorture treaty does not as a matter of law apply to its actions outside the United States.

Legally, Guantanamo is being treated as a no-man's-land. The Cubans have no jurisdiction. It is not in United States territory, even though it is leased from Cuba by the American government, and the American government argued that neither the Constitution nor any other U.S. law applies there. Habeas corpus suits filed on behalf of those detained failed on the basis that American federal courts had no jurisdiction. An appeal to the circuit court upheld that decision, but in May 2004, the Supreme Court acknowledged that the court did have the jurisdiction to judicially review each individual detention since they were under the control of the secretary of defense, Donald Rumsfeld.

The administration argued to the Supreme Court on March 28, 2006, that the Geneva Convention does not apply because this is not a conventional war and the detainees are not entitled to the status and protections afforded to prisoners of war. The men in the camp were held in solitary confinement in cells which are six by eight feet; they were allowed to exercise only twice a week for fifteen minutes; letters from home are stockpiled for months and handed over in a bundle, undermining their potential to sustain emotional well-being. None of this fulfils human rights standards. Detainees were "rendered" throughout the world—to Pakistan and Afghanistan's security force—in the knowledge that they would be tortured.

Many children under sixteen have also been detained in the camp, contrary to the Convention on the Rights of the Child, never mind the Geneva Convention. The United States' response is that these are not children and they present a lethal danger that justified their detention. Every country in the world has signed the international Convention on the Rights of the Child except the United States and Somalia.

For five years, hundreds of men have been detained in conditions that are an affront to human rights. Links with Al-Qaeda have been made in very few cases. The majority are men who were in the wrong place at the wrong time or low-level members of the Taliban. Releases are slowly taking place, but without apology. The Red Cross has described the camps as principally centers of interrogation rather than detention. Officials have been reported as saying that the techniques of interrogation are "not quite torture but as close as you can get." Some of the prisoners have attempted suicide, and psychiatrists have expressed concerns about the damaging effects of indefinite incarceration. The prisoners have been essentially incommunicado from family and lawyers, with no sense of what the future holds. The uncertainty, psychiatrics say, is a recipe for mental instability.

As of this writing, detainees are being tried before military commissions. The judges are members of the armed forces, appointed army commanders committed to justifying a position. The defense lawyers come from a vetted military panel. Statements made by tortured prisoners are admitted. Delivering the F. A. Mann lecture in Lincoln's Inn in November 2003, Lord Steyn, one of the most senior judges in Britain's highest court, described these American military commissions as "a mockery of justice." The British court then stated unequivocally that torture cannot be condoned and that any evidence arising from that torture is inadmissible.

An exhaustive study published in the *National Journal* in 2006 examined one hundred thirty-two prisoners who filed habeas corpus petitions and three hundred fourteen other prisoners who appeared before the Combatant Status Review Tribunals. Connie Hegland, the author of the study, said that most of the incarcerated were not picked up on battlefields but came from Pakistan. Seventy-five percent of the men who filed habeas corpus petitions are not charged with taking part in hostilities against the United States; 80 percent of the total are not charged as being involved with Al-Qaeda.

Most of the prisoners were handed over by warlords and are charged with associating with either Al-Qaeda or the Taliban, or supporting them, often in the most tenuous way.

Fliers distributed to the bounty hunters said "Get Wealth and Power beyond your dreams . . . You can receive millions of dollars helping the Anti-Taliban forces catch Al-Qaeda and Taliban murderers."

Torture, as we know, is very effective in getting information. Hegland reported that a prisoner, following repeated torture, identified sixty fellow inmates (more than 10 percent of the Guantanamo's population) as suspects.

Seton Hall professor Mark Denbeaux subsequently published a study whose statistics and analysis came very close to Hegland's. Eighty-six percent of prisoners, he found, were captured by the Pakistanis at a time when the U.S. government was awarding large bounties for suspected enemies.

Michael Scheur, who headed the CIA's Osama bin Laden unit from 1999 until he resigned in 2004, previously concluded that no more than 10 percent of prisoners could be found guilty of anything. The *National Journal* study and the Denbeaux study say it cannot be higher than 10 percent.

A third report, issued by the UN Commission on Human Rights, concludes an eighteen-month investigation by five investigators. The document discusses detainment conditions, which they found inhuman. One hundred eighty men have been released—some for "extraordinary rendition"—to countries that practice torture. Others have been freed.

No court yet has all the statistics before it in any one case. Presumably the Supreme Court will in the next few years.

The Supreme Court's 2003 decision in *Rasul v. Bush*[18] gave enemy combatants the right to challenge conditions of their detention in American courtrooms. It was proclaimed as a liberal victory for it confirmed the two-hundred-year-old right to challenge a government detention. But three years later, no detainee has benefited from it.

In the Guantanamo case *Hamdan v. United States,* issued on the last day of Roberts' first term, the president's claim that he had a nearly blank check was firmly rejected after Kennedy joined the four-member liberal bloc in a 5–3 decision. Roberts did not vote because he had sat on the case at the appeals court level, voting in favor of the administration. Bush's military commissions could not be used to try Guantanamo detainees because they were not authorized under any law or by the Geneva Convention, the Court said. The Court required minimum procedural safeguards if Congress tried to pass laws peculiar to the Guantanamo detainees. The majority opinion was written by Justice Stevens, a World War II veteran and the only justice who served in the military.

But *Hamdam* is not, as many liberals claim, "a dramatic refutation of the Administration's entire approach on the 'War on Terror.'"[19] Conservatives' apocalyptic forecasts have also been wrong. John Yoo, the former Justice Department lawyer, who wrote the torture memo sounding the same note, criticized the Court, saying "what the Court is doing is attempting to suppress creative thinking. . . . It could affect every aspect of the war on terror." But it is not so.

While the Court powerfully rejected the president's broad claim of "inherent authority to convene military commissions to try and capture enemy combatants in wartime," it left the door open for Congress to pass a military tribunal scheme that violates many aspects of the Code of Military Justice. Congress did just that in

2006. Congress is now behind legislation that makes a mockery of the legal system and cuts back on *Hamdan*.

With one additional conservative, the vote would have gone the other way. Scalia's vote was foretold. But his bias was shown when the case was before the Court and he publicly spoke of enemy soldiers "shooting at my son" in Iraq.

Often when the Supreme Court hears a case in which the president claims enhanced powers, the situation becomes worse for the people as well as for Congress. The Court may find in favor of the president. And even if the Court does not, as they did not in the *Hamdi*[20] case, both the majority and dissenters can give the president language he can use as justification for the next power grab; and then we wait another five years for a decision. It is sad that the Supreme Court cannot see that the detentions, torture, surveillance, and expanse of presidential powers to declare war by himself is an emergency equal to Truman's steel mill seizure.

Detention of detainees without giving them constitutional rights is permitted, say many in Congress and the president's men, because the *Hamdi* and *Hamdan* Court did not say it wasn't. Domestic warrantless tapping is also permissible because the *Hamdi* Court did not say it wasn't. The fact that the *Hamdi* Court did not have the detention, or surveillance issue before them, claims the President, only means that their authorization was implicit rather than explicit. There are very few statements from any justice that cannot be fitted into arguments on both sides. Scalia's dissent in the *Hamdi* case says that an American citizen in his home country is always entitled to a judicial hearing justifying detention—unless Congress suspends the writ of habeas corpus. If Congress is prepared to suspend that writ, and Scalia does not say they cannot, then American citizens can be endlessly detained.

Justice Thomas' frightening words are less ambiguous. "It is crucial to recognize that judicial interference in these domains destroys the purpose of vesting primary responsibility in a unitary executive. Judges lack the information and expertise to second-guess determinations made by the President."

Congress has even failed to get the president to turn over documents concerning prewar intelligence about weapons of mass destruction in Iraq, documents relating to Hurricane Katrina, to Supreme Court nominees, to energy policies, and to surveillance.

Congress can, when the president wrongfully exerts his "executive privilege," exert its own power and go to court, as they did in the Nixon era. They can also stop cooperating with the presidential agenda and stop funding the president's choice programs. Hearings accomplish very little alone, but thus far it is the option of choice. The ultimate sanction, impeachment proceedings, mobilized twice in recent times, against Nixon and Clinton, may be the only option.

Congress' abdication of responsibility can be seen in some of their most recent acts. Representative Nancy Pelosi, the Democratic leader in the House, and Senator Jay Rockefeller, the Democratic senator from West Virginia, both known for sensitivity to civil liberties infringements, together with a substantial number of congressmen, were "briefed" by the president on the new NSA program. Pelosi, Rockefeller, and several other congressmen "confidentially" expressed concern but did nothing else. They claim they could do nothing. Of course, that's wrong—as members of Congress, they have immunity and could have, on the floors of Congress, demanded more information.

Congress deludes itself, and Congress is afraid that the extent to which they have abdicated their responsibilities will become widely known. But the point is that a Roberts Court will not permit Congress to reassert itself. The imbalance will become much more extreme. The president's usurpation of congressional oversight will be actively endorsed by the Supreme Court.

It is certainly arguable, if not totally obvious, (1) that the FISA statute specifically prohibits NSA surveillance authorization, and (2) that the congressional permission to use force to fight overseas does not permit illegal surveillance.

You need not be a lawyer to know that the surveillance law is illegal—anyone who can read or understand English can see the plain language of the statute and the military force authorization. Why didn't Pelosi, Rockefeller, and the others take a closer look at the illegal surveillance? Even people in Ashcroft's Justice Department far senior to John Yoo[21] recognized it was illegal—they refused to sign off. Many of these career attorneys were effectively demoted as punishment for their stand.

On January 7, 2006, the Congressional Research Services, a nonpartisan arm of Congress, said that the "legal rationale . . . does not seem to be as well-grounded. As the Bush team now argues, it is inconsistent with the law." Why then didn't Pelosi, Rockefeller, and others, immediately after learning of the programs, at least get a legal analysis of the program's constitutionality? Instead, they ignored the democratic process and let go unchallenged a program that authorized unconstitutional physical break-ins and the surveillance of millions of Americans. The only time the politicians reacted was when they saw the public rage.

The members of Congress seem to react slowest when it is not their ox being gored. They know most Americans do not believe in or support the Bill of Rights. The benefits of liberty, freedom, and privacy rights are too ephemeral—especially so when people are faced with what appears to be the real threat of terrorism. Most politicians believe that those ephemeral rights fall in the face of Bush's claims of national security damage.

Pelosi, Rockefeller, and other members of Congress can be said to have "collaborated" with Bush for years to keep this information from the American public. But now that the entire Congress as well as the American public knows what is being done, they can no longer claim that we did not know. No one is doing anything on behalf of the millions of Americans who were being spied upon. No one tried to stop it or even examine it. Allegedly, Congress is looking into it. If Congress does do something, it will not be out of constitutional commitment but for the political benefit of the members. That says a great deal about our politicians' commitment to democracy and the Constitution.

The Supreme Court would seem to be the natural place to look for a restoration of the constitutional balance of powers. But the Court, faced with the most significant issue since the beginning of the Republic, the contentious problem of presidential rule, has thus far, in *Hamdan*, given the president pretty much what he wants.

The future Supreme Court will decide the surveillance issue in the president's favor and will find that he has most of the inherent power he seeks. It will rule that the Constitution gives him the power to authorize domestic warrantless wiretaps.

♦   ♦   ♦

President Bush directed the NSA to eavesdrop (and use data-mining technology) on private communications between the United States and foreign countries, without seeking warrants, to increase security. Those knowledgeable in security within the Bush administration point out that examining tens of thousands of conversations actually damages security. It is like looking for needles in a gigantic haystack you created. The bigger the haystack, the less chance you'll find anything. And that is so even if it weakens security and weakens legal prosecutions. Prosecutors are wrongfully using secret evidence in regular criminal trials and terror trials in which defendants, invoking their Fourth Amendment rights against unlawful search and seizure, ask courts to force the government to disclose whether there was illegal surveillance. The government then claims a national security defense, and then the defendants move to dismiss. Released detainees have already filed civil suits against the government charging torture, detentions, and renditions to foreign countries by United States personnel. Those suits now include claims for unlawful surveillance. Civil liberties challenges to the surveillance practices will filter through the Supreme Court for years.

When a new administration is elected, criminal prosecutions

could be brought against the intelligence officials who illegally authorized the wiretaps. But that is, of course, highly unlikely.

This country needs to revise its laws to respond effectively to terrorist threats—but that is Congress' job in open debate.

◆   ◆   ◆

Another significant presidential power issue the Court will decide in the next decades is the effect of "signing statements."

Presidential signing statements are old news, but Bush has used them as no other American president ever has. Bush's claim that he, rather than Congress, defines the intent behind a law. Phillip Cooper's 2002 book, *By Order of the President: The Use and Abuse of Executive Direct Action*, assessed the uses and abuses of signing statements by President Bush. Bush, according to Cooper, issued twenty-three signing statements in 2001; thirty-four statements in 2002, raising one hundred sixty-eight constitutional objections; twenty-seven statements in 2003, raising one hundred forty-two constitutional challenges; and twenty-three statements in 2004, raising one hundred seventy-five constitutional criticisms. During his first term Bush raised five hundred five constitutional challenges to legislation that became law.

What does this mean? It means that if Bush decides a law, or a part of the law, is unconstitutional, he does not enforce it. For example, if he decides that one part of an appropriations bill is unconstitutional, he does not permit the money to go where the bill says it should go. Bush effectively thwarts Congress' will without any legal challenge and, in most cases, without the public, or even members of Congress, being aware of it. He uses the signing statements as a line-item veto. But, unlike the public—and often fought-over—line item vetoes, the signing statements and their implications fly under the radar.

John Dean, Nixon's former counsel and later a convicted Watergate criminal, who is now an author and a lecturer, has written extensively on the subject. Bush is reserving the right to treat the laws as unconstitutional if they impede his grab for power at Congress' expense. He can do so with bills aimed at fair trials for detainees. The military then has a cover for improper acts—their defense is that the president said the law being applied to them is unconstitutional.

I, like most Americans, learned of the use of signing statements in January 2006, when President Bush used a signing statement to attempt to nullify the recent controversial McCain amendment regarding torture.

Bush's signing statement says that he will interpret the law "in a manner consistent with the President's constitutional authority to withhold information the disclosure of which could impair foreign relations, the national security, the deliberative processes of the Executive, or the performance of the Executive's constitutional duties." It is *Alice in Wonderland* talk—the law is what I say it is.

The expansive use of a signing statement violates Congress' power to make the laws by giving the president power to say what that law is. The Constitution provides that a veto is the president's only and exclusive avenue to prevent a bill from becoming law. Signing statements are, of course, not mentioned, and their use cannot rewrite the Constitution. Congress, not the president, interprets intent in passing laws.

The potential impeachment of Nixon was based on his abuse of power. Bush is pushing the powers of the presidency far beyond Nixon's limits. But this country does not have the energy to impeach Bush, let alone censure him.

The Roberts Court was to hear in 2006 another prominent case concerning the abuse of executive power—that of Jose Padilla, an American citizen arrested at O'Hare Airport in 2002 and then detained in the United States without trial. But Bush succeeded in avoiding an anticipated defeat.

What had already happened in that case prior to the Supreme Court's nondecision was remarkable. Even his friends on the very conservative Fourth Circuit Court of Appeals said that Bush had gone too far in trying to manipulate the law.

On September 9, 2005, circuit court judge Michael Luttig, who had been seriously considered for both the Roberts and Alito seats, stated that the president had the authority to hold enemy combatants who had taken up arms against the United States overseas and entered the country to blow up buildings in American cities on Al-Qaeda's behalf. At the time Luttig issued that opinion, Padilla had been imprisoned for three and a half years. He upheld the three-and-a-half-year imprisonment without any trial or hearing because the government claimed that Bush was acting under his war powers and in the interest of national security. Padilla appealed.

Bush reversed his position several weeks after Luttig's decision. The government indicted Padilla in a Florida court and no longer claimed that Padilla had entered the country to commit a terrorist act. Bush took this action a few days before the Supreme Court was to decide whether it would take Padilla's appeal. Bush told Luttig that Padilla no longer has to be held by the military—he could now go to the criminal courts, the Florida court, and Bush asked that Padilla be transferred to a federal jail.

Luttig was outraged. He saw that Bush was trying to avoid the Supreme Court's dealing with Bush's claim, now apparently false, that Padilla was an enemy combatant. Luttig saw that the Bush administration did not want to tell anyone what facts justified Padilla's three and a half years of imprisonment. Luttig denied Bush's attempt to transfer Padilla until the Supreme Court heard the case. Luttig's decision was totally unforeseen. Bush, in a remarkable request, also asked Luttig to withdraw the September 9, 2005, decision that had been in Bush's favor. Luttig refused to do so.

Luttig asked Bush to justify his change of heart. Bush refused to do so.

At first the Supreme Court decided both to hear the appeal and to permit the transfer of Padilla to civilian authorities. At the March 28, 2006, argument, the Court gave short shrift to the Bush administration claim that the new legislation had stripped the defendant of his right to habeas corpus, the right to have the Supreme Court hear his case. In April 2006 the Court decided not to hear the case on the grounds that Bush's transfer of Padilla to the civilian courts deprived it of jurisdiction. The Court gave Bush the victory he wanted.

The successful manipulation of the Court in this way by a president has not been seen before. And the Court's refusal to decide the case countenances that conduct. Padilla's trial is not likely to occur (if it ever occurs) until he has spent five years in jail.

The administration's constant legal misbehaviors are far below the radar. Only when a case gets to the Court does the public get any idea of the legal and moral issues. Ahmad Omar, an American citizen working in Iraq for an American construction company who was arrested in Baghdad at the end of 2004 is a case in point. For one and a half years, he was held in an American jail in Iraq, was not charged with anything, and was not allowed to see a lawyer. The Bush administration then tried to transfer him to an Iraqi jail. Omar filed an action in the Federal Court in Washington opposing the transfer. Judge Ricardo M. Urbina refused to allow the transfer and rejected the administration's argument that the jail, previously described in their legal papers as an American jail, was a Coalition jail.

In the case of the "twelfth" hijacker, Zacarias Moussaoui, the federal district justice was outraged by the government's witness tampering. Unfortunately, what the United States attorney did in that case, telling the witnesses how to testify, is often done by prosecutors, only they don't put it in writing.

The Bush administration keeps repeating, each time they are asked to justify constitutional invasions, that history is "authority" for Bush's actions. Nixon's era is their authority. But FISA was not enacted when Nixon committed his illegal acts. Through the FBI, Nixon had wiretapped five members of his own national security staff, two newsmen, a staffer at the Department of Defense, and Daniel Ellsberg. These people were targeted because Nixon's plans for dealing with Vietnam—we were at war at the time—were ending up on the front page of the *New York Times*.

Nixon had a plausible national security justification for the wire-taps: He claimed he had to stop the leaks because America's ene-mies were privy to its war plans. His illegal surveillance was never struck down, although many members of Congress believed that the wiretapping, combined with the misuse of the information it had gathered, was an impeachable offense.

Scholars at the conservative think tank, the Hoover Institute,[22] argue that the president must have the exclusive power to decide when warrantless taps are necessary. They argue that the president should have total control over all the security agencies and executive branch departments—the Department of State, Defense, Justice, Treasury, and Homeland Security, as well as all agencies within the U.S. intelligence community and enforcement wings such as the FBI. Attorney General Gonzales says the President is "the sole organ of foreign policy in the nation." The Hoover scholars point out, per-haps correctly, that the agencies spend more time in competition and negotiation rather than direction and management and that there is no central authority figure. No one is in command, and that is why, they say, September 11 occurred, why the WMD intelligence failed, why the space program has failed, why Operation Iraqi Freedom is doing badly, and why the government failed to respond to Katrina.

The Hoover scholars, agreeing with Gonzales, would give the president total control over all foreign issues. Because the war in Iraq, the expansion of China's power, and other "foreign" issues affect our security, the president must, they claim, be free of judicial restraint or congressional surveillance.

The Hoover Institute, whose board includes Richard Scaife Mel-lon, Stephen Bechtel, and Herbert Hoover III, among others, argue that the "just trust me" president is a more effective structure for a democracy. On the contrary, the Hoover Institute's argument is a model for how democracies can abandon democracy.

It brings to mind the debate within our country at its founding. Many of the Founders, while professing a passion for democracy, distrusted the "masses." Like Robert Bork, they wanted a platonic elite to govern; aspects of a monarchy pleased them. Adams suggested the chief executive's title be "His Honorable Highness, the President of the United States."

President Bush's legal defense for the surveillance program is based on his view that there is a crisis. "Therefore, give me more power," he says in effect.

Will the surveillance, the torture, and the detention, which, of course, will be controverted by the Bush administration, result in Supreme Court decisions that undercut the new congressional legislation and totally discard the president's power? Conservative justices will try to avoid cases attacking the president's surveillance system and military trial procedures. When they cannot avoid the cases, the conservative justices will pick and choose facts in particular cases to get a desired result rather than look at the overall pattern of repression.

Bush's crisis claim reminds me of the Supreme Court in *Bush v. Gore*, when the Court stated that they had to interfere with the election and overrule the Florida Supreme Court because we were in a national crisis—we couldn't elect a president at the appropriate time and place. There was no crisis. Our Constitution told us exactly how the election should be handled. The Supreme Court chose to ignore that directive for political reasons of its own.

There is no crisis today that justifies suspending the Constitution. The Bush administration has told us it does not deal with reality— it creates reality. Bush has created a legal façade allowing him to create his own world and then react to it as he chooses. Unfortunately, we are all dragged into his make-believe world with its make-believe legal system.

The Conservative court believes in Bush's nonreal world and will decide cases based on "facts" in the unreal world they both agree exists.

Thomas Jefferson, George Washington, Benjamin Franklin, and James Madison all saw the danger—they never abrogated that power to the presidency.

The president's men have articulated a new concept of the president: an executive who has unitary powers.

What does "unitary" powers mean? It means that if the president alone decides that the country is faced with what he defines as a critical problem, his authority goes unchecked.

Bush bridled when asked by a reporter if "unchecked" presidential powers were dictatorial, and angrily said, "I disagree with your view of unchecked power. There is the check of people being sworn to uphold the law, for starters. There is oversight. We're talking to Congress all the time . . . to say unchecked powers is to ascribe dictatorial powers to the President, to which I object." This disingenuous argument will be bought by a Court whose perceptions of reality and nonreality are like the president's.

Bush claims that he has congressional authority to start his own wars, preemptive or otherwise; to be the ultimate interpreter of foreign treaties; to define enemy combatants as he wishes; to detain prisoners for as long as he wishes and under such conditions as he wishes; and to continue surveillance on foreign intercept for as long as he wants.

One of the benefits of the transparency of some aspects of the Alito nomination process is that it showed how long and hard the Conservatives have thought about the "unitary" president. In Alito's earliest days with the Reagan administration, he laid out his concept of unchecked power, of inherent authority. Tracing the clear, straight line from Edwin Meese to Robert Bork to Samuel Alito to Clarence Thomas to John Yoo to Alberto Gonzales is easy. The concept of the unitary president became, long ago, a critical tenet of the Federalist Society and of the conservative wing of the Republican Party.

The new powers of the president have to come from somewhere. They come at the expense of the people, who previously exercised the power themselves through Congress.

Alito, Thomas, Scalia, and Roberts argue that if the Constitution does not specifically preclude the president's actions, he has a free hand. They claim that they are writing on a clean slate. If the Founding Fathers did not anticipate everything a president might try and do and did not prohibit it, then Bush can do it.

The Bush administration has chosen to ignore centuries of constitutional decision making that limits the president, decisions made during the Civil War, World War I, World War II, and the Korean, Vietnamese, and Cold wars. In the unlikely event that the new Supreme Court does not give this president all he wants, he will ignore those decisions as well. That is truly what a "unitary" president means. If America did not pay attention before, let it do so now.

Chapter Two

The States against the Federal Government

For us, and for Clarence Thomas, it's more impor-
tant to get it right than to maintain continuity.
—Stephen Presser (January/February 2005)

◆   ◆   ◆

Federalism is not defined in the Constitution. Long before the Constitution was drawn up, a battle was already being waged between those who wanted a strong national government and those who wanted strong state governments. Today that battle is waged over race, class, religion, money, and power. It is a battle between groups with different visions of this country and different visions of the Constitution. In the judiciary, the chief player in the battle is the Radical Right. The change in the last twenty years has been through the Rehnquist Court's efforts to change the balance toward "states' rights." The Court uses seemingly neutral language that appears only to expand and protect state sovereignty at the expense of the federal government, diminishing the powers of Congress. The contest over "states' rights" has been—and continues to be—about almost everything except whether power rests in your state capital or in Washington, D.C.

The Federalism issue is camouflage for states stepping on people's rights. The language of the debate is eye-glazing. It sounds nonpartisan to expand state power at the expense of federal power, but most often it is nothing of the sort. What really happens is that states' power is expanded and individual rights and liberties are cut back. This Court's present course of activism means seizing rights from the people. Whereas the activist New Deal Court relied on and trusted the legislature—trusted the people to make the democratic process work—the Rehnquist Court trusts neither the people nor democracy.

The Federalists, at the beginning of our history, stood for a strong federal government. Today's conservative Federalist Society uses the word in the opposite context. They are antifederalists. They seek to create a weak central government—to assert state power over the power of the federal government. The term *Federalist Society* is a clever linguistic device that is meant to confuse. For all their patriotic grandstanding, the reactionaries on the Court and the ideologues like Bork who both inspire and prod them are usurping the rights of the people. They argue that if the individual states are trying to stop the spread of killings with gun control or trying to stop rapes by giving women a day in court, the federal government need not enact additional or different legislation to achieve the same ends. But for more than two hundred years, the states and federal government each performed separate and joint functions, sometimes complementary and sometimes overlapping. The states have their own taxing power and there are areas where there is both federal and state involvement, as in education, employment laws and discrimination suits. When Congress decides that certain matters that transcend states' rights, such as in establishing a minimum wage and minimum health standards to protect workers across the land, it has the right to do so. The Federalist structure is a check on local abuses of government power in matters of race, religion, and the invasion of personal rights.

What is called "the new Federalism" is politically motivated and purposefully misnamed. The issues that Americans care most about—education, abortion, school prayer, the punishing of criminals, environmental protections—have gone from Congress to the courts for final adjudication. The political and religious obsessions of the right wing—abortion, homosexuality, pornography, and evolution—are in the courts. Pat Robertson, one of the more important political figures of the past two decades, tried to force the Republican Party to make the judiciary the Radical Right's private preserve in order to keep him, and the constituencies he led, within the Republican Party. The Republicans were determined to have battles decided in the courts they controlled and to reduce the power of a Congress they often did not control.

Right-wing Republicans see themselves as having a clear mandate to shrink the federal government while at the same time expanding the war budget. Newt Gingrich, an architect of the new Republican majority in the 1990s, put it precisely. "We are going to re-think the entire structure of American society and the entire structure of American government. This is a real revolution." President Bill Clinton agreed with Gingrich's concept when he declared that "the era of big government is over," thereby rejecting the underlying rationale of the New Deal and its courts. Most of Gingrich's "Contract with America" was passed under the Clinton administration. In late December of 2000, Justice Anthony Kennedy, sounding the same theme in *Bush v. Gore*, said the Court was reconsidering "our place in the design of the government," in changing the balance between the states and the federal government and the courts and the Constitution, because, he said, the newly placed Court cannot "admit inability to intervene when one or the other level of government has tipped the scales too far." But Gallup polls confirmed that by the 1990s, big government had replaced both big business and labor as the entity feared by most Americans.

Some commentators thought the need for a powerful central government that national crises traditionally provoke—the Civil War, the Depression, and both World Wars—would reverse this Court's weakening of the federal government after September 11. But September 11 has not had that effect The process of stripping Congress of its power by the Court and adding to the power of the executive branch continues unabated.

As the courts, with their claim to supremacy over Congress, become more involved in political matters, the pressure for more political appointments will be felt. Blocking Democratic judicial appointments and rejecting congressional acts has already become as commonplace as bottling up bills in committee. Today's Republican appointees are being held up by the Democratic-controlled Senate Judiciary Committee for appearance's sake.

The Founders of the country relied on what might be called a colonial or revolutionary model of Federalism: "revolutionary" because of the way it drew on their experience opposing centralized authority before the American Revolution and under the Articles of Confederation. Forced to explain how states could withstand the superior legal power of the national government created under the Constitution, the Federalists pointed to the realistically superior political power of the states and argued that state governments would have real rather than formal, document-driven power in any disputes with Congress.

The reliance of Alito, Scalia, and Thomas on the Founders' original intent to justify their states' rights arguments makes little sense. When today's Conservatives argue with the New Deal by pointing out how much the balance of power has shifted to the federal government, how awesome it is in size, how many new areas it deals with, how much money it has, they are correct in their facts but wrong in their conclusions. Our world is very different, even from the pre–New Deal Court that tried to cut back the federal government. Since 1937, federal expenditures have risen from 3 percent of the gross national product to 21 percent. Regulatory agencies went from 15 percent to 41, and programs receiving federal grants increased from thirty to more than six hundred. Each year the federal government transfers nearly thirty billion dollars to state and local governments.

The fact is, we have a national economy, whether it be in guns, milk, railroads, airplanes, hotels, or securities markets. To exclude the federal government from areas they have dominated since 1937 ultimately serves negative purposes—the diminution of rights and the diminution of the economic safety net and security expanded under the New Deal. The Conservative demand to use eighteenth-century standards to define today's federal balance is best answered by Thomas Jefferson. "We might as well ask a man to wear the coat which fitted him as a boy, as civilized society to remain ever under the regiment of their barbarous ancestors."

The reactionaries use the Eleventh Amendment to elevate the power states have over citizens, by forbidding citizens from suing the states over states' violations of federal law. The Eleventh Amendment provides that "the judicial power of the United States shall not be construed to extend to any suit . . . commenced against one of the States by citizens of another state [or] any foreign state." But the Eleventh Amendment's plain language only prevents a federal court from hearing a suit brought against a state by a citizen of another state or another country. The Rehnquist Court has misinterpreted the amendment's text in other significant ways. Despite the amendment's limitation to "judicial power," the Court has ruled that Congress is also powerless to subject states to lawsuits in federal court. In addition, the Court has ruled that Congress cannot require state courts to hear lawsuits challenging a state's compliance with federal law.

The Tenth Amendment was also resurrected and expanded by the Rehnquist Court and interpreted to be an independent source of judicially enforceable limits on the exercise of congressional power. The amendment states that "the powers not delegated to the United States by the Constitution, nor prohibited by it to the States, are reserved to the States respectively or the people." The plain reading of the amendment does not take away rights from the people and give those rights to state governments. To turn the Tenth Amendment into a states' rights amendment is totally unfounded. Constitutional history does not support it. The federal government is not a government of so limited power.

Congress and the Courts are necessary to protect individual freedoms. The Rehnquist Court's disregard for most of twentieth-century law through its radical reinterpretation of the Commerce Clause tries to stop the federal government from protecting black people, women, the poor, consumers, the disabled, and the aged.

Article I of the Constitution specifically gives the federal government the power to regulate "commerce . . . among the states." The first chief justice, John Marshall, recognizing the need for a strong federal government, gave the Commerce Clause a reading that permitted the New Deal Court, more than one hundred years later, to assist Congress' attempts to pull the country out of economic depression and to create the regulations and regulatory agencies we have today. Chief Justice John Marshall said in 1824 that Congress' power "may be exercised to its utmost extent, and acknowledges no limitation other than those prescribed by Congress."

But the Tenth and Eleventh amendments, the Rehnquist majority says, can stop Congress' exercise of the power to help the disadvantaged that it received from the Marshall Court, the New Deal, and Warren Courts. Congress, until the Rehnquist Court's recent decisions, freely used its commerce power to regulate not only interstate commerce but nearly any interstate activity that affects commerce. Congressional legislation to pass Social Security laws, to set minimum wage and health standards laws, to pass civil rights legislation and environmental legislation has been critical to this democracy and its growth.

Today the interpretations of the Tenth and Eleventh amendments are the keystones of the great constitutional debate over individual freedoms and states' rights.

Justice Kennedy's perception, like the perceptions of his Conservative colleagues, is that these amendments were never meant to protect the panoply of rights created by the New Deal, Warren, and early Burger Courts. The civil rights movement and the battle for better working conditions were protected by those courts. For example, the National Guard was called out to force Southern governors to keep schools open and to force bus companies to let Rosa Parks sit at the front of the bus. The courts also protected social welfare legislation.

The Supreme Court's debate on the Tenth and Eleventh amendments is framed in terms of what happened before and after the Articles of Confederation, and before and after the drafting and ratification of the Constitution. The Conservative Constitution-in-Exile finds its states' rights arguments by looking at the apparent refusal of the states to give up certain rights to form this union. They seek to apply this eighteen-century "original intent," or original meaning, to gun control laws, abortion, school integration—issues the Founders could not have imagined.

O'Connor spoke of "discerning the proper division of authority between the Federal Government and the states within a dual system of sovereignty." She and Kennedy led the Conservative Court to hold that the Roosevelt and Warren courts wrongfully expanded the federal government's power. She said, "The question is not what power the Federal Government ought to have but what powers in fact have been given by the people." Federalism properly understood, the Conservatives claim, protects state power and stops the federal government from creating and protecting rights for individuals. Justice Brennan defines Federalism in exactly the opposite way—it is "to protect individual freedom" from local or national "repressive governmental action." Today's Court majority reads the Constitution not only differently than the liberals do but differently than most twentieth-century courts.

The warring factions of this extraordinarily polarized Court see two different forms of government created by the same elements. The conservatives are fighting battles lost when the Constitution was ratified and lost again when the North won the Civil War. When our country began, the states joined to form the Union amid concerns that citizens would feel more loyalty to the federal government than to the states. These concerns were legitimate, but the advocates of a strong federal government won out. Most American law tells us—from John Marshall to William Brennan—that breaking away from a strong union is an aberration.

Immediately after the Civil War, a war fought over states' rights issues, each state citizen was given the same set of federal rights—a set of rights that would stop individual states from infringing on the rights of state citizens. The entire country ratified the Thirteenth,

Fourteenth and Fifteenth amendments, which were Congress' and the Supreme Court's emphatic way of stating that our nation was not a collection of independent states so much as a powerful union led by a federal government. For this to be true, citizens' rights had to be universal. Justice John Harlan, at the turn of the twentieth century, expressed the view early on that any violations of the Bill of Rights, if done by the federal government, were equally unlawful under the Due Process Clause of the Fourteenth Amendment if done by the states. It took years, until after World War II, in the middle of the 20th century, for his dissenting opinion to become the majority view.

Harlan's argument is that the Fourteenth Amendment, passed after the Civil War, "incorporates" the Bill of Rights to protect state citizens the same way the Bill of Rights provides protections against wrongful state actions. Without the incorporation doctrine, the Fifth Amendment right to avoid self-incrimination, the Fourth Amendment's protection against wrongful search, the Sixth Amendment's right to counsel, the Eighth Amendment's right to be free of cruel and unusual punishment, and others from the first ten amendments, would not apply to citizens in state courts; the "states rights" argument being that each state should be free to set its own standards. But in the 1947 *Adamson v. California*[23] case, the Court said that while the Fourteenth Amendment "does not draw all of the rights of the federal Bill of Rights under its protection, it does incorporate those rights that are so fundamental that they are implicit "in the concept of ordered liberty." Felix Frankfurter, writing for the majority, in a 5–4 decision, adopted a fundamental fairness test to decide which amendments should be incorporated.[24]

This so-called doctrine of "incorporation" has drawn acrimonious criticism. Meese told the bar association in 1984 that the sixty years of law supporting incorporation was wrong and correcting it was high on his agenda. Thomas, Scalia, Roberts, and Alito are dead set against the application of many of the Bill of Rights amendments against the states. So, for the first time, there are four solid votes to overturn more than sixty years of settled law. Conservatives want to take the federal judiciary, where these rights are now protected, off center stage when deciding the major social and political conflicts in our society. They achieve this by saying that some of the most important portions of the federal Bill of Rights do not apply to states and by denying citizens' rights to sue over these rights in the federal courts. Conservatives saw, correctly, that the process of incorporation is part of a process of nationalization—like the Commerce Clause, it channels power into central government at the expense of the states. But incorporation has been the settled law for half a century, and until the last few years it was inconceivable that the Court would try to strip the American people of these cherished Bill of Rights protections. Nevertheless, as Daniel Troy, a former clerk to Bork and one of the Federalist founders formerly of the Bush administration, says, "Incorporation is in play." And the Federalists have held meetings to formulate a legal strategy on how to attack this solidly decided law of the past sixty years.

Jeffrey S. Sutton, a circuit court judge nominated by Bush, has also openly called for an end to the incorporation doctrine. He briefed and argued the wrongness of it before, in an unrelated 1993 Supreme Court case. Justice Breyer found his attack hard to believe. "Are you really now saying incorporation was totally wrong?" "Yes," answered Sutton. Today there are few sacred principles in American constitutional jurisprudence.

The end of the incorporation doctrine could wreak havoc on this country. For example, Justice Thomas writes that without the incorporation doctrine, states would be free to support churches, and that the state of Utah can give funds directly to build a Mormon church or to pay a priest's salary. It would also mean that states could decide not to have jury trials in criminal cases and that states can prohibit speech that has always been protected.

Our democracy is more than the right to vote. It is more than the narrowest interpretation of the Bill of Rights. It is the right to stop the federal and state governments from invading your privacy, from denying your right to live in a secular state. It is the right to insist that the federal government protect you from racial, ethnic, and gender discrimination.

The Roberts Court will also continue the battle against the power of the people, as did the Rehnquist Court, while reinterpreting the Constitution. Its audacity is built on the audacity of the Rehnquist Court. In the last ten years, one hundred twenty-three congressional regulations were struck down; more than in all the Supreme Court's previous two hundred years. The new Court, with its new chief justice, will go further.

A number of cases you have never heard of, and which represent some of the most reprehensible moments in America's racial history, are now the decisions forming the inspiration and legal basis for today's majority on the Supreme Court. This democracy will be crippled by the Roberts–Alito Court.

Three decisions—*United States v. Cruikshank* (1876),[25] the Slaughterhouse case (1873),[26] and the Civil Rights Cases of 1883[27] (as evil and mean-spirited as the *Dred Scott* case upholding slavery and denying citizenship rights to blacks and *Plessy v. Ferguson*, which upheld racial segregation)—cited by the Rehnquist–Roberts Courts provide the basis of future decisions on issues ranging from abortion to civil liberties to race and gender persecution. These cases rewrite the history of the second half of the nineteenth century—they attempted to nullify much of the power and force of the post–Civil War amendments, the Thirteenth (banning slavery), the Fourteenth (promising citizens due process and equality), and the Fifteenth (the right to vote). They articulate the states' rights position. They were a reaction to Reconstruction—the government's attempt to eradicate slavery and to create one free country. These cases reflect the South's surge to power, effectively undercutting many of the gains of the Civil War and the legislation passed after it. The view of these nineteenth-century jurists was that the states' infringement of these new freedoms could not be attacked in a federal court. These awful race-based decisions are the foundation for the Roberts Court's decisions.

The consequences of the Rehnquist Court's states' rights and "cruel and unusual punishment" decisions are stark and tragic. After the Rehnquist Court, relying on the post-Reconstruction cases, reversed the Supreme Court's 1972 decision in the *Furman* case that capital punishment is unconstitutional, more than one thousand men and women were executed. We are the second largest executioner in the world—only Singapore is higher on a per capita basis.[28] Our execution rate is now ten prisoners per month and climbing. It took the Eleventh Circuit Court of Appeals in 2004, a conservative court sitting in Atlanta, to impose a moratorium on executions because they shared the Warren Court's view that too many men had been wrongfully convicted. The length of sentences and the severity of punishments handed out by the courts have risen dramatically since the Rehnquist Court began upholding convictions that were constitutionally invalid. The ability to prove innocence has been dramatically limited. The increase in racial violence, part of which is certainly attributed to court decisions, has led to more crime. America's prison population—at more than 2.2 million—is the largest in the world.

That Alito is for capital punishment is not surprising. But his consistent refusal to acknowledge that race intersects with the death penalty is astonishing.

Alito's refusal to acknowledge the racial world we live in was shown by his dissent in *Riley v. Taylor*,[29] the case of a black man who was convicted of murder and condemned to die by an all-white jury. He had appealed the verdict on grounds of discrimination. The appeals court reversed the conviction on grounds of racial discrimination. Alito argued that the majority was wrong in looking at the reality that within a three-year period other murder cases in the country had also been tried by all-white juries. He wrote:

> "An amateur with a pocket calculator," the majority writes, can calculate that "there is little chance of randomly selecting four consecutive all-white juries." Statistics can be very revealing—and also terribly misleading in the hands of "an

amateur with a pocket calculator." The majority's simplistic analysis treats the prospective jurors who were peremptorily challenged as if they were in effect black and white marbles in a jar from which the lawyers drew. In reality, however, these individuals had many other characteristics, and without taking those variables into account, it is simply not possible to determine whether the prosecution's strikes were based on race or something else.

The dangers in the majority's approach can be easily illustrated. Suppose we asked our "amateur with a pocket calculator" whether the American people take right- or left-handedness into account in choosing their Presidents. Although only about 10 percent of the population is left-handed, left-handers have won five of the last six presidential elections. Our "amateur with a calculator" would conclude that "there is little chance of randomly selecting" left-handers in five out of six presidential elections. But does it follow that the voters cast their ballots based on whether a candidate was right- or left-handed?

Alito's decision was insulting and odious. The Constitution does not protect the rights of left-handed people. It does protect the rights of a black man facing the death sentence from a jury that is racially biased against him.

A Roberts Court decision that allows you to look more deeply into states' rights is the very recent death penalty case *Kansas v. March*, a case upholding a Kansas statute. The statute states that if at the second part of a murder case, when deciding with whether the defendant should get the death penalty or a less severe sentence (the first part of the two part case deals with guilt or innocence), if the jury finds that the evidence against the imposition of the death penalty is equal to the evidence for the death penalty, then the death sentence is automatic. Kennedy was with the 5–4 majority—there is little doubt O'Connor would have voted the other way even though the majority tried to frame it as a states' rights case. While the basic differences between Kennedy and O'Connor will be more clearly seen when he votes against the 2007 affirmative action case and to uphold the federal ban on partial birth abortion, the Kansas case shows how strongly they disagreed on race, criminal law, and capital punishment, not only on states' rights.

Disagreeing on how to apply capital punishment is more than disagreeing on a penalty. In this case, the Court decided that the states have the last say in determining this death penalty process. It is a disagreement about how fairly the criminal justice system adjudicates, about whether the death penalty racially discriminates, and about the caliber of lawyers indigents are assigned in serious cases. It is an indication of how Kennedy will rule in other racial and criminal justice cases.

Scalia called the argument that innocent people have been executed propaganda. Nor, he said, does he care about what the rest of the world thinks of us.

Given what we all now know about capital punishment, it seems incredible that five justices of this court will allow a state to enforce a law that results in an execution when the jurors are equally divided on whether or not the defendant deserves the right to live. We know of the refusal of some states to execute because the method is a cruel and unusual one, due to the extraordinary number of death sentences reversed because of DNA and other technologies, and because it is the poor and the black who are most often executed. It was these facts that made O'Connor move from being a staunch death penalty supporter to one who was humble and cautious, skeptical of the fairness of penalty even though as she advocated states' rights. She cut and whittled away at death sentences even as she could never bring herself to say the penalty was unconstitutional. But in the Kansas case, I believe, her sense of justice would have led to a 5–4 decision the other way.

♦　　　♦　　　♦

The opening shot in attacking Congress' interpretation of the Commerce Clause and sixty years of Federalism arose from a small incident involving a high school student arrested on a minor criminal charge in Texas. That case was in many ways as significant as *Bush v. Gore*, even though it did not settle the question of who was to be the president for the next four years. *Bush v. Gore* was a high-profile affair. *United States v. Lopez* (1995)[30] and the cases that followed slipped under the radar, but in fact they will control much of our life for decades.

Alfonso Lopez, Jr., eighteen in 1992, was a senior at Edison High School in San Antonio, Texas. He planned to join the marines upon graduation. But on March 10, a mother called the school to report that Lopez had a gun. Jean Guzman, the boy's teacher, took him to the principal's office and pulled an unloaded .38-caliber gun and five bullets from his pocket. Lopez told the principal that a friend had asked him to give the gun to another friend who needed it for a "gang war." Lopez said he was paid forty dollars to deliver the gun.

Two years before this incident, Congress passed the Gun-Free School Zones Act, which made it a federal offense to possess a firearm in a school zone. Congress relied on the authority of the Commerce Clause to justify passage of the legislation as a way of stemming the rising tide of gun-related incidents in public schools. It was on this charge that a federal grand jury indicted Lopez, who had first been charged with the state crime of gun possession until agents from the Federal Bureau of Alcohol, Tobacco, Firearms and Explosives concluded that he had violated the two-year-old law. At the one-hour federal trial, Lopez's lawyer, John Carter, argued that Congress' law was unconstitutional because it held no hearings on the law when it was passed. Assistant U.S. attorney Pamela A. Mathy responded that the Commerce Clause protected the statute, and U.S. district judge H. F. Garcia accepted her argument in a one-sentence decision: "The Gun-Free School

Zone Act is a constitutional exercise of Congress' well-defined power to regulate activities in and affecting commerce and the business of elementary, middle, and high schools," he said, as it "affect[s] interstate commerce."

Lopez, who didn't have a any criminal record, expected a suspended sentence; he then planned to go on and fulfill his life's dream of becoming a marine. But the judge, concerned about guns and killings in schools, decided to make him an example. He gave Lopez a six-month jail sentence. Lopez appealed.

It seemed like an easy case. The law was clear and simple. Although the control of street crime was generally in the hands of the states, there was abundant evidence showing that school authorities and states were unable to stop the violence; the school authorities said so themselves. There was also clear evidence showing that guns in schools were interfering with the quality of education, and substantial evidence showed that our ability to educate our children affects the economy. The federal appeal was argued before a three-judge circuit court in the conservative fifth circuit. Judge Will Garwood, a Reagan appointee, and two colleagues found the law unconstitutional. When a panel of the liberal ninth circuit in a similar matter found the Gun-Free School Zones Act constitutional, the Supreme Court, seeing the conflict between two federal appeals courts, took the Lopez case.

For the past sixty years, going back to the New Deal, the Supreme Court had accepted that Congress had broad authority to regulate virtually every aspect of American life through the reach of the federal Commerce Clause. That should have been the end of the matter. In addition, the Gun-Free School Zones Act had bipartisan support. Moreover, the bombing of the Alfred P. Murrah Federal Building in Oklahoma City, while it occurred after the passage of the Gun-Free School Zones Act, had created a political environment in which both the Clinton administration and Republican congressional leaders believed that the federal government had to combat individual and group terrorism and restrict the weapons they used.

Although the National Education Association (NEA) joined the Clinton administration and various antigun groups arguing that school violence could be checked by such a law, the law's opponents, including the National Rifle Association and the conservative Cato Institute, were many and well funded. They insisted that while the goal of reducing gun violence in schools was laudable, Congress had failed to establish a national link between mere possession and actual gun violence, nor could they make a link between gun possession and interstate commerce. Such regulation, they argued in any case, properly belonged at the state and local level; it was simply beyond the power of Congress to regulate control over public schools. Worse, the Conservative groups argued, increasing federal authority over local crimes posed a threat to the states' sovereignty.

The Gun-Free School Zones Act would surely have been upheld by every Supreme Court since 1937. But, at the November 8, 1994, argument, it was clear that this Court was ready to move boldly against it, striking down a bipartisan law that a hundred senators, four hundred ninety-three representatives, the president, and four Supreme Court justices thought was appropriate.

Speaking for the administration was the solicitor general, Drew Days III, who argued that there was no reason for the Supreme Court to overrule this act of Congress. He was quickly cut off by Justice Rehnquist, who said that Congress' regulation of guns near schools had nothing to do with business between the states. When Days responded that the Court should not become involved in adjudicating this legislation, Rehnquist said the Court must, "if we were concerned that the original understandings and structural theories that underlay the Federal system have been so eroded [by this law] that the whole system is in danger."

When Scalia questioned whether legislation similar to this had been upheld, Days explained:

This Court has operated upon . . . an initial assumption . . . that Congress was given the power under the Constitution to legislate directly upon private individuals, and that there are no built-in limitations on the Constitution. But what we have in this particular act is not that bold assertion by Congress. What we have is, first of all, enough evidence to meet the test that this Court has set that Congress had a rational basis for thinking that gun possession on or near school grounds affected interstate commerce. One was the relationship between violence itself and the economic activity of the country. To the extent that there is violence in certain parts of the country, it makes it difficult for institutions to function. There is the insurance consequence. Where violence occurs, insurance burdens are shared by the entire country, not just by the locale where this particular violence occurs. It interferes in the same way that this Court found in *Heart of Atlanta Motel* with respect to the travel of persons in the face of segregation in places of public accommodations. It interferes with the willingness of people to travel to certain parts of the country.

The case Days referred to, *Heart of Atlanta Motel v. United States* (1964),[31] a landmark civil rights case, affirmed Congress' power to stop discrimination in public places on the grounds that motels, buses, and train stations were parts of interstate commerce. Because he believed it was a precedent that clearly supported his position, Days wanted to bring it to the attention of the moderate members of the Court, and he wanted the conservative members of the Court to confront it. Days understood that if the Commerce Clause argument lost here, the Rehnquist Court could reach back and cut into *Heart of Atlanta Motel*, then narrowly interpreting not only the Civil Rights Act of 1964 but also cases since then that prohibited racial and gender discrimination. Days did not want to see that precedent undone, and he hoped that painting a broader picture might persuade O'Connor and Kennedy. Days did not want to let the Court write a disingenuous opinion that would undercut *Heart of*

Atlanta Motel without mentioning it. How could mere possession be the subject of interstate commerce? Rehnquist asked.

"Well, I think, Chief Justice Rehnquist, that it is an easy step from possession to use," Days responded, "and, therefore, the fact that Congress might be concerned with possession doesn't mean that it wasn't concerned about use. And there also is sufficient evidence", he continued, "in the consideration of even the Gun-Free School Zones Act that there was heightened violence on school property by juveniles, and if one looks at the findings and records with respect to earlier legislation—for example, the Omnibus Crime Control and Safe Streets Act of 1968—Congress makes specific findings between the easy availability of firearms and the level of juvenile and youthful violence and criminality. So that the connection between possession of firearms on or near schoolyards and violence and the regulation of that possession are relationships that Congress has considered in the past, and in our estimation made perfectly good sense under the Gun-Free School Zones Act."

Scalia, O'Connor, and Rehnquist took turns attacking Days. O'Connor asked how the possession of a gun near a school could be considered interstate commerce. Days said the test was not whether Congress correctly decided it was local or interstate commerce, it was whether Congress should be free to make these judgments. At one point, when Days was explaining that Congress had decided the act was required to protect students and that this Court should not interfere with Congress' judgment, Rehnquist cut him off and, not too subtly, asked, "Can you tell me, Mr. Days, has there been anything in our recent history where it appears that Congress has not made a considered judgment?" The spectators burst into laughter. When Days said Congress acted rationally, Justice Scalia declared, "Benjamin Franklin said it was so wonderful to be a rational animal, that there is a reason for everything that one does. And if that's the test, it's all over."

John Carter, Lopez's attorney, had never before argued in the

Court or handled a case with significant constitutional issues. He found himself very far from arguing solely about guns or the Gun Control Act. As he spoke, Justice Kennedy cut in to ask rhetorical questions clearly meant to help Carter out. Carter sought to show that the area of gun control in schools was a local problem that the states could deal with. He was concerned that the federal law intruded on the states' laws in controlling states' problems. If the federal law supplanted the states, he made clear, the law must be struck down. However, if the law supplemented, or helped the states, it might be appropriate.

Stevens attacked Carter by making a statement in the form of a question and then asked Carter his view. He suggested that whether or not guns move in interstate commerce, textbooks do, the desks do, and so might the teachers. But people, he observed, "will not move to places where children are killed in schools by guns, and so if in fact the Federal Government can't do something about it, maybe the whole economy will go down the drain in a thousand obvious ways, all right." Stevens pressed on. "So that would be the argument in *Wickard v. Filburn*.[32] If some homegrown wheat affects interstate commerce, which I guess is a borderline question economically, certainly guns in schools do really, not borderline, affect commerce." Carter reiterated that the statute spoke only of possession, and that could be only within a state.

I was present in the Supreme Court that day and, with most of the other lawyers in Court, saw the significance of Justice Stevens' seemingly obscure reference to wheat and to *Wickard v. Filburn*. Decided in 1942, fifty-two years before *Lopez*, the case took congressional power to legislate under the Commerce Clause close to its outer limits. *Wickard* held that the Commerce Clause empowered Congress to regulate production of wheat grown solely for home consumption. The wheat never left the farmers' land. But it was held to be a commerce issue because home consumption by many farmers "in the aggregate," could affect interstate commerce prices.

The revisionists, in *Lopez*, won with a bitterly divided 5–4 decision, holding that the Gun-Free School Zones Act exceeded the bounds of the federal commerce power. It crossed the line from a principled to an unprincipled decision. As Justice Stephen Breyer argued in dissent, he could not understand why the majority would accept that Congress had the power to regulate the school environment by keeping it free from drugs and alcohol, but not from guns. Both economic and "police" objectives can underlie legislation, said the dissenters, and they charged that the conservatives had substituted their views of the Court for those of elected public officials. Indeed, until this time the Constitution was read by the Supreme Court to give Congress substantial latitude in Commerce Clause and Fourteenth Amendment interpretations.

While the Court's majority recognized that Congress is not as constrained as the courts are from broadening rights secured by the Fourteenth Amendment, in rejecting Days' argument Rehnquist declared "that Congress' authority under the Commerce Clause" to regulate numerous commercial activities that substantially affect interstate commerce, "is not to be interpreted as broadly as prior courts had." It was a flat rejection of Justices John Marshall and Jackson's 1942 statement that Congress, if it acted rationally, must be shown deference, and any "restraints on its exercise must proceed from political rather than judicial process."

Justice Clarence Thomas, agreeing with Rehnquist, added a strongly worded concurrence that offered his history of the commerce power, supporting the argument that the New Deal, Warren, and several Burger Court decisions were wrong in saying that the courts had to approve Congress' acts based on the Commerce Clause merely because Congress acted rationally. Justice Kennedy, also concurring with the majority, acknowledged that constitutional interpretation favored the minority's view that decisions on many matters should be left to the political branches and the people, but he said, "It does not follow, however, that in every instance the Court lacks the authority and responsibility to review Congressional attempts to alter the federal balance."

This was the first time in six decades that the Court had invalidated a congressional statute because it exceeded the scope of the Commerce Clause, or even questioned Congress' judgment as to what affects interstate commerce. In doing so, it began a steady accumulation of self-enforcing and self-perpetuating doctrines. In *Lopez*, and the later cases we will discuss next, the Rehnquist Court ignored the fact that the Court is not a legislature—and a legislature is not a court of law. They are two totally separate, independent branches of government. It's their separateness that is essential to create our form of democracy. Nor is the Court a superlegislature any more than the Founders intended the legislature to be a super judiciary. That distinction today is largely unheeded by the Court's conservatives.

Judge Alito has given us his views on *Lopez* and its progeny. He is prepared to expand its reach. *U.S. v. Rybar*[33] was a case considered in 1996 by the U.S. Court of Appeals for the third Circuit, a federal appeals court that has jurisdiction over Pennsylvania, Delaware, the U.S. Virgin Islands, and Judge Alito's home state of New Jersey.

Alito argued in a sole dissenting opinion that the federal ban on the possession of fully automatic repeating machine guns—a law that has been on the books in some form since 1934—is unconstitutional. The *Rybar* case involved a gun dealer, Raymond Rybar, who unlawfully possessed a "Chinese Type 54, 7.62-millimeter submachine gun" and a "U.S. Military M-3, .45 caliber submachine gun." In his dissent, Alito argued that Congress may have no power to regulate "the simple possession of a firearm," as this "is not 'economic' or 'commercial activity'".

The two appeals judges who formed the majority in the *Rybar* case dismissed Alito's dissent in harsh terms. Noting that Alito's opinion would require that Congress make specific findings as to a link between possessing a machine gun and its effect on interstate commerce, the majority said that "making such a demand of Congress or the Executive runs counter to the deference that the judiciary owes to its two coordinate branches of government, a basic tenet of the constitutional separation of powers." The law, the majority wrote, did not require Congress or the executive branch "to play Show and Tell with the federal courts at the peril of invalidation of a Congressional statute."

All but one of the other federal appeals courts to have considered the law in the wake of *United States v. Lopez* have agreed with the *Rybar* majority and not with Alito. The one court that arguably disagreed with the *Rybar* majority (based on slightly different facts) later had its judgment vacated by the Supreme Court. The courts in these cases have overwhelmingly rejected Alito's cramped view of Congress' lawmaking authority—and his overinflated view of the power of judges to strike down laws. These many decisions represent a consensus—to which Alito apparently does not subscribe—that Congress can enact laws limiting the possession and transfer of dangerous weapons and thereby protect public safety.

Alfonso Lopez and the events of his case were unknown to the general public. The next gun case to come before the Supreme Court was famous before it got to the Court. It arose from John W. Hinckley Jr.'s attempt to kill Ronald Reagan. At 1:30 PM on March 30, 1981, the young gunman stepped forward from a crowd of television reporters and fired six shots from a Rohm R6-14 revolver, striking the president and three other people, including press secretary James Brady. All of Hinckley's victims survived, although Brady suffered terrible head wounds and a broken spine. He has been in a wheelchair ever since. Immediately following his hospital release, Brady began lobbying for a gun-control bill. When Hinckley's trial began, his obsession with guns, killing, and stalking people resulted in a jury finding him not guilty by reason of insanity.

Hinckley was the poster boy for gun control. A college dropout and malcontent, he purchased his first gun, a .38 caliber pistol, in 1979, and attempted to kill himself by playing Russian roulette. On antidepressants and tranquilizers, the following year he bought the exploding bullets he used to shoot Reagan. He is well remembered for stalking actress Jodie Foster; less vividly recalled are two 1980 incidents involving President Carter. In one, Hinckley attended a Carter campaign appearance, but left his gun collection, three handguns and two rifles, in his hotel room. When Hinckley flew to Nashville during another of Carter's campaign stops, he was arrested after airport security detected handguns in his suitcase. The guns were taken, and Hinckley was fined $62.50. Later, though, he bought two more .22-caliber pistols. On the morning of the Reagan's assassination attempt, he wrote Foster that he was going to kill President Reagan. A few hours later, he nearly succeeded.

Congress, faced with this close call and a history of gun-generated violence with which the states seemed unable to cope, held extensive hearings, considered the danger, and sought to remedy it. The long, tortured congressional history of the Brady Bill evidenced that Congress recognized the evil early on, but until Clinton's election, it did not have a sympathetic Congress and gun-control president ready to fight the power of NRA lobbyists. On November 24, 1993, after ten years of heated debate and evidence showing that the states alone could not contend with the problem because of the enormous interstate commerce traffic in guns, the Brady legislation was passed by a Democratic Congress. The statute, in addition to providing a waiting period of five days to purchase a gun, requires local law enforcement to conduct background checks on potential buyers. At the time of the vote, a CNN/USA Today Gallup Poll showed that 81 percent of Americans supported gun registration, and that 89 percent favored mandatory safety training for handgun purchasers.

As soon as the bill was passed, two sheriffs, Jay Printz of Ravalli County, Montana, and Richard Mack, of Graham County, Arizona, backed by the gun lobby, filed suit in federal court challenging the law on the grounds that the federal government did not have the power to order state officials to help administer a gun-registration law.

The appeals court dismissed the sheriffs' case, *Printz v. United States*,[34] but in 1997 another bitterly divided Supreme Court, aligned exactly as it had been in *United States v. Lopez*, continued the practice of striking down federal laws. The Brady law was unconstitutional, Justice Scalia said, because the federal government did not have the right or power to order state officials to help administer a federal law, for this would break down the separation between the federal and state governments. Scalia based his decision on his "historical understanding and practice, in the structure of the Constitution, and in the jurisprudence of the court." Uncertainty is not part of Scalia's jurisprudence. His argument, never made in two hundred years of constitutional history, was pulled out of thin air; it is described by Professor Kermit Hall, a Supreme Court scholar at North Carolina State University, as "one of the most remarkable assertions by the Court in favor of State authority in the history of the nation." The Court was using states' rights as a smokescreen for the right-wing goal of minimizing gun control.

Justice Thomas decision was as stunning as Scalia's. Although the issue was not before the Court, the justice volunteered his lengthy historical view of the right to bear arms, covered by the Second Amendment. While saying that a definite understanding of the Second Amendment must wait for another day, he clearly believed every citizen had a right to a gun. Thomas was sending a message to the lower courts. He rejected the argument that only an authorized "militia" could bear arms to protect the state, and he based his decision on the rediscovered Tenth Amendment that limits Congress' power and expands the states' power. Thomas' dicta made the position presentable enough so that within two years, for the first time in our history, a lower federal court found that the Second Amendment gave every citizen the right to own a gun, a ruling that was then affirmed by a conservative circuit court. A tenet of conservative jurisprudence is that you do not rule on, or even speak to, issues that are not before the Court. A hallmark of Scalia's and Thomas' jurisprudence is that they do exactly that.

The dissenters' arguments were impassioned. Stevens and Souter denounced as wrong the majority's reading of American history and of constitutional documents as establishing dual sovereignty, with the states protected from such federal intervention. They referred to the text of the Constitution and the Federalist papers, in which Alexander Hamilton said that, under the Constitution, state officials could become "auxiliaries" to the federal government, obligated to help carry out law enforcement. This text, the dissent said, very specifically justified the use of state offices to help apply the Brady law. Justice Breyer, in fact, went further, noting that state aid to enforce federal regulation had always been an integral part of the law. He pointed out that the federal government had the option of having federal employees in the states carry out the federal law, and he said doing so would be seen as more of an intervention than using state employees. Yet no case made the argument better than John W. Hinckley. Without the Brady Bill's provisions, there might not be a record of what he had done elsewhere. Only a federal program could have tracked him.

Yes, continued Souter, the Constitution did seek to distinguish between interstate commerce and local commerce. But, as the New Deal Court recognized, the line is often blurred, and inflexible distinctions between what is local and what is national make no sense in modern times. He therefore distinguished three basic principles required to interpret the Commerce Clause: first, that Congress can reach local activities; second, that when deciding if commerce is "affected" (permitting federal legislation), the Court must look at cumulative acts, not single acts; and third, that the judgment of Congress is entitled to the substantial deference the Constitution provides—it should be up to the people, through the electoral process, and not the courts, to determine if Congress has made the wrong political judgments about issues affecting the nation's health, safety, and welfare.

Having none of this, the five-member bloc, in their *Lopez* and *Printz* decisions, rejected much of Justice John Marshall's opinion in *Gibbons v. Ogden* (1824),[35] an iconic case in our history. The opinion in *Gibbons* continued Marshall's attempt to create a unified national government. It had its own drama. Daniel Webster, one of America's greatest lawyers, argued before Marshall, America's greatest jurist, on one of the most important legal issues in our democracy. It seemed like an ordinary case—not likely to be given attention by John Marshall. Webster's client, Thomas Gibbons, held a federal license to run boats between New Jersey and Manhattan. Robert Fulton, considered the inventor of the steamboat, had a conflicting license issued by New York State over the same waters.

Marshall asked simple factual questions to arrive at one of the Court's greatest cases. Does the federal license give its holder greater rights than state license does? Does the federal government or the state government control the boats that go between states? Does the federal government or the state government control passage over interstate waterways, and, implicitly, highways? Marshall, after seizing the case to further express his strong nationalistic views, persuaded the other justices to join in a unanimous 6–0 decision.

His answer, that federal government controlled matters of interstate commerce, and that the Commerce Clause of the Constitution was to be interpreted expansively, was the accepted jurisprudence for one hundred sixty years, until the advent of the Rehnquist Court. Then Justice Clarence Thomas said that Marshall had defined the Commerce Clause and federal rights too broadly to protect presidents from assassination attempts by future Hinckleys. By not overruling the case, Thomas sought to honor precedent and, at the same time, change the case's holding.

But John Paul Stevens, in claiming that the Brady law was valid, said it was irrelevant whether Scalia could find authority in the documents that preceded the Constitution; whether or not the gun laws in *Lopez* or *Printz* were appropriate in 1789 is not the question. Congress decided they are necessary now. He paid homage to the past; he quoted Chief Justice John Marshall in the *Gibbons* case: "The power over commerce with foreign nations, and among the several states is vested in Congress as absolute[ly] as it would be in a single government."

Stevens' reasoning, following a century and a half of precedent, was the same as Marshall's. If different states created their own rules of commerce, the United States would become like separate sovereignties, each potentially in conflict with another. The states could tariff one anothers' goods; they could maintain armies to settle border disputes. The right of states to be totally sovereign over their own citizens could reduce the federal government to a meaningless entity. There would not be a national Social Security system, minimum wage laws, or national environmental regulations. In 1842 Marshall anticipated the centuries ahead. Without his interpretation, we would not have a standing army capable of defending the country; we would not have a federal government that could deal with the nation's environment.

In 1997, four years before the World Trade Center tragedy, Stevens was aware of the future consequences of the majority's decision. He said in the *Printz* case that the "threat of an international terrorist may require a national response before federal personnel can be made available to respond. Is there anything [in the Constitution] that forbids the enlistment of state officials to make that response effective?" We saw how critical it was during Hurricane Katrina that a "competent" federal government be free to coordinate a national response to disaster. Cutting a competent federal government out of the process is exactly the wrong thing to do. It leads to confusion, lack of responsibility, and ultimate chaos. We saw in Katrina not only an inefficient federal government, but also a vague and ambiguous division of power between the states and the federal government. The federal government, the *Printz* case tells us, could not "commandeer" state personnel—federal officials could not tell state employees what to do. This made a coordinated effort far more difficult.

The *Lopez* and *Printz* decisions spurred the Court's conservative justices to start attacking Congress' many other attempts to deal with economic and social problems. Even after September 11, 2001, the gun lobby and the right wing continue to press their agenda, even though it is against law enforcement interests and is clearly against the interests of the American people. Attorney General Ashcroft, a vocal opponent of both the laws attacked in *Lopez* and *Printz* during his tenure as a Missouri senator, refused to let the Justice Department turn over the FBI records showing whether any of the twelve hundred people it detained after September 11 owned guns. The FBI–Ashcroft fight became public on December 6, 2001, when, after two months of failed negotiations, the FBI claimed the attorney general was hampering the war against terrorism. Despite unfavorable media coverage, Ashcroft did not back down, claiming that doing so would violate the privacy rights of gun holders. But no one ever said that gun holders have the right to keep their ownership private—on the contrary, the Justice Department kept such records with the knowledge of gun owners. The *Printz* opinion, precluding federal officials from cooperating with state officials for gun-control purposes, severely inhibits our war against terrorism. The states alone cannot stop guns from flowing over state borders. Congress could help the fight by specifically writing legislation that would give the federal government power to direct state agencies. The question is whether the Court would act against this new legislation as it did in Brady. If it does, then it is all up to the federal government—a task it cannot do by itself.

◆　　　◆　　　◆

We look further to the precedents the Rehnquist Court gives the Roberts Court. On September 13, 1994, President Clinton signed into law the Violence Against Women Act. This act made gender-motivated violent acts a civil rights violation and gave the victim the right to file a damage suit for money damages in the federal courts. Congress was giving women the same kind of beneficial legislation that had been given to racial groups.

Nine days after the bill's signing, Christy Brzonkala, a Virginia Polytechnic Institute freshman, at school less than two weeks, attended a party at which the alcohol flowed freely. Thirty minutes into the party, she was gang–raped by football players. Antonio Morrison raped her, then James Crawford, and then Morrison again; they each weighed more than two hundred pounds. Each said they were not using contraceptives. Before he left, Morrison warned, "You better not have any fucking diseases." "I was in shock and blanked out," Brzonkala reported. Emotionally shattered, she returned to her room, sat in the bathtub for hours, and told no one about the incident. Over the next weeks, she stopped going to classes, refused to leave her dorm room, and attempted suicide. Several months later, in an April phone call to her parents, Christy blurted out the truth. Nine months and one suicide attempt after the attack, she reported the rapes to the university. They did nothing.

She was told not to go to the district attorney, that it would be bad for the school, and that, in any event, the state of Virginia would not prosecute because she had waited so long to tell anyone. The university, Christy was told, would take care of it. She agreed, and dropped out of school.

She was advised to file charges under the university's sexual assault policy. Morrison's friends who testified heard him brag that his method with women was to get them drunk and then force sex. Following a May 1996 hearing, Morrison, the star linebacker, was suspended for a year; charges against Crawford were dropped. Morrison appealed and lost. Christy thought that was the end of it.

But when school started, the football team needed Morrison. The school dean contacted Christy and said they had used the wrong policy for the hearing and that another hearing would be held. After the second hearing, school officials decided that Morrison suspension's would be "deferred" until after he graduated. He was found guilty only of "using abusive language," not rape. Morrison's crime was linguistic—it was the use of the word *fuck* while talking to Christy. The school never told her of the decision; Christy "accidentally" heard it when she learned Morrison was playing again. It turned out Morrison appealed the second conviction and it was reversed.

Christy learned that the head football coach had intervened—he needed Morrison for the year.

Virginia refused to notify the police or file criminal charges, claiming no jury would believe Christy's claim because too much time had passed. Rape is a felony punishable in Virginia by a sentence of five years to life.

In December 1996, Christy Brzonkala filed a lawsuit under the Violence Against Women Act in the Virginia federal court seeking damages from Morrison and Crawford, the two men who raped her, as well as an injunction forcing Virginia Tech to develop a more effective hearing process to prosecute future sexual assault cases. Christy's case was exactly what the new law was aimed at.

Six years later the Supreme Court, in a 5–4 decision, *Morrison v. United States*,[36] threw out Christy's claim, saying that Congress had no power to punish private violence motivated by gender. The argument from twenty-four states that rape victims could not get fair trials in their state courts did not move the justices.

Christy's decision becomes one of the most important building blocks for future Roberts Court's rulings. The majority opinion was built on Reconstruction era biases and Court decisions more than a hundred years old.

Christy Brzonkala's fate was linked to that of the more than two hundred blacks murdered in Colfax, Louisiana, in 1873, for defending their right to vote. The Supreme Court, in the *Morrison* case, relying on precedent, referred to an earlier Supreme Court case, *United States v. Cruikshank* (1875), that arose from the attempted criminal prosecution of the Colfax murderers.

The Colfax murders occurred on April 13, 1873. It was the bloodiest single instance of racial violence in the United States after the Civil War. The White League, a paramilitary group intent on securing white rule in Louisiana, shot it out with Louisiana's almost all-black state militia. According to John G. Lewis, a black educator and legislator in Louisiana, blacks tried to defend their rights, with the result that "on Easter Sunday of 1873, when the sun went down that night, it went down on the corpses of two hundred and eighty negroes." Only three members of the White League died. Nearly half of the blacks were murdered in cold blood after they had already surrendered.

The White League, like the Ku Klux Klan, attacked white Republicans as well as blacks. While the worst violence occurred in Colfax, other killings were sparked in Coushatta, when the White League murdered six Republicans, and in New Orleans, when thirty blacks were killed and one hundred more wounded. The Civil War had not ended in Louisiana—or in a host of other states. The violence was in reaction to the North's attempts at Reconstruction—to put together a freer country.

The federal government at trial convicted only three whites for the Colfax murders. But in *Cruikshank,* the Court, on states' rights grounds, declared that they had been convicted unconstitutionally.

The *Cruikshank* Court said Congress had no power to punish racist violence by private citizens, thereby encouraging nearly one hundred years of Klan terrorism. Decades later, the Warren Court and Congress, with a different view of the federal government's power, said Congress did have that power.

But in the 1880s, Republicans gave up on their attempt to spread freedom, knowing that the cause was hopeless without federal enforcement power. Federal troops were soon withdrawn. It would be almost a century before troops had to be brought back so blacks could again vote and go to Southern schools.

The Supreme Court decisions in the 1880s directly flew in the face of a Congress that, immediately after the Civil War, tried to get the country to honor its fifty-two-word preamble to the Constitution and the Declaration of Independence. In passing the Thirteenth, Fourteenth, and Fifteenth Amendments, Congress said the federal government must defend civil rights. The losing Southern states could not be expected or trusted to do the job.

According to the *Cruikshank* Court, the Fourteenth Amendment "adds nothing to the rights of one citizen against another." This contradicts the country's history as well as constitutional history. It flies in the face of logic. If it did not give citizens, blacks and whites, additional rights, why was it passed? Congress could not protect violence against blacks when blacks attempted to vote. Justices of the Roosevelt and Warren courts thought they put that case to rest. The Rehnquist Court's fights over states' rights brought it back to the logic of the nineteenth century courts. Although Drew Days did not mention it in his *Lopez* argument, most Americans would be surprised to learn that Congress had previously banned segregation in private inns, restaurants, and transportation as early as 1875, let alone that a congressional majority demanded mandatory desegregation of public schools eighty years before *Brown v. Board of Education*. When Strom Thurmond unsuccessfully filibustered the Civil Rights Act of 1964, he was blocking legislation that Congress had thoroughly considered and passed one hundred years before.

The much-maligned and misused concept of precedent, *stare decisis*, threw us back more than one hundred years when Rehnquist said in the *Morrison* case:

> The force of the doctrine of stare decisis behind these decisions stems not only from the length of time they have been on the books, but also from the insight attributable to the Members of the Court at that time [who] obviously had intimate knowledge and familiarity with the events surrounding the adoption of the Fourteenth Amendment.

Rehnquist knew the facts leading up to Colfax and *Cruikshank*, as did Louisiana, evidenced by a monument, erected in 1950, which read:

> On this site occurred the Colfax Riot in which three white men and 150 Negroes were slain. This event on April 13, 1873 marked the end of carpetbag misrule in the South.

> ◆ ◆ ◆

> Erected to the Memory of the Heroes Who Fell in the Colfax Riot Fighting for White Supremacy, April 13, 1873.

Cruikshank was a momentous case and a turning point in our history. The federal government's drive to break white supremacy was put to an end in 1883. Federal troops were withdrawn from the South. The civil rights laws were not enforced and became meaningless.

In the Civil Rights Cases in 1883, the Court held the Civil Rights Act of 1875 unconstitutional because Congress did not have the power to ban racial discrimination because it made blacks "the special favorite of the law." The present Court uses that precedent to enhance states' rights. The Supreme Court, in 1883, said "individual invasion of individual rights" is not protected by the Fourteenth Amendment. "It would be running the slavery argument into the ground," the Court said, "to make the 14th Amendment apply to every act of discrimination which a person may seem fit to make." Justice Harlan dissented. He asked whether Congress' purpose was only to remove the institution of slavery and "remit the race held in bondage, to the several states for such protection, in the civil rights, necessarily growing out of freedoms, as those states in their discretion chose to provide." No, he answered, slavery rested on inferiority and every vestige of that inferiority must be wiped out. The programs that Harlan envisioned, Bork says, were "reverse discrimination, passed out of hostility to whites."

Congress' vision was destroyed by justices who eviscerated some of the most fundamental gains made during and after the Civil War. The Thirteenth, Fourteenth and Fifteenth amendments, which attempted to create a legacy of freedom, liberty, and equal protection, instead left a legacy of lynching, segregation, and white supremacy.

Rehnquist's Court evoked the post–Civil War court, as it discarded congressional legislation and judicial decisions meant to further carry out Lincoln's dream of equality. Relying on post–Dred Scott decisions, it struck down parts of not only the Violence Against Women Act, but the Americans with Disabilities Act, the Age Discrimination in Employment Act, and the Religious Freedom Restoration Act. Alito and Roberts, sitting as circuit court judges before their appointment, were part of the swelling conservative movement that followed, in lockstep, the Rehnquist Court's path. Together they have laid a foundation for the Roberts Court to immediately reject any congressional legislation that seeks to expand the rights of women, racial minorities, the aged, and those who oppose the establishment of religion.

Today's conservatives argue that the new Court reflects the swing in electoral politics—that the people are getting what they voted for. But in the *Morrison* case the Court paid no attention to the elected officials in Congress or to the president. They found the Violence Against Women Act was not justified because interstate commerce was not involved. The dissent quoted from Congress' finding said the states needed help both to give women a chance to have at least a partial redress for being victims of rape and to stop the economic consequences of crimes against women:

> Partial estimates show that violent crime against women costs this country at least 3 billion—not million, but billion—dollars a year. . . . Estimates suggest that we spend $5 to $10 billion a year on health care, criminal justice, and other social costs of domestic violence. Three out of four American women will be victims of violent crimes sometime during their life. . . . Violence is the leading cause of injuries to women ages 15 to 44. . . . As many as 50 percent of homeless women and children are fleeing domestic violence. . . . Between 2,000 and 4,000 women die every year from [domestic] abuse. . . . Arrest rates may be as low as 1 for every 100 domestic assaults . . .

O'Connor and Kennedy were in the majority. And even as we point out how Alito's appointment dramatically affects the Court, we should be mindful of how conservative O'Connor was on most issues.

It is important to keep O'Connor's perspective in mind to show that the conservatives' attack on her and Kennedy as liberal traitors helped obscure the conservatism of these justices. As Christy

Brzonkala's lawyer Julie Goldscheid began her oral argument in *Morrison v. United State* mind on January 11, 2000, the question on her mind was whether O'Connor's interest in protecting women would overcome her strong belief in states' rights and her disdain for Congress. Goldscheid started her argument by summing up the nearly uncontroverted evidence Congress had reviewed when passing the bill. Calling gender-based violence "one of the most persistent barriers to women's full equality and free participation in the economy," she went on to detail the four-year bipartisan study that found it "deters women's travel interstate, restricts women's choice of jobs and ability to perform those jobs, reduces national productivity, and increases medical and other costs." The effect was pervasive and compelling; most dramatic was the evidence Congress heard from the victims of spousal abuse, "whose batterers kept their partners from working, who wouldn't let them leave home if they did work, or who inflicted visible injuries so that [the abuse victims] were afraid to go to work or were physically unable to show up."

After her opening statement, Goldscheid was attacked by the five judges. Normally the four justices who might agree with her would have come to her aid and thrown some softball questions. But the majority did not stop the attack long enough for the other justices to have a chance. And Goldscheid never again had time to give full answers.

Seth Waxman, representing the United States and prepared to argue on Goldscheid's side that the law was constitutional, was next. He was optimistic when he started, but less so when he finished, after Scalia asked if the states that supported the legislation were the states that had the most sexual abuse. Waxman responded that it was not Congress' intention "to deal with the States as bad actors." Congress' finding revealed that federal courts are often not much better. When Scalia asked if Congress had any evidence to show that the states were discriminating against women who filed criminal rape charges, Waxman pointed to the states' briefs admitting that discrimination.

It was now Michael Rossman's turn representing Morrison. Rossman argued that the act's intention was to supplant state law and that the federal government has no jurisdiction over crimes occurring within a state. Justice Breyer, after pointing out that there were federal as well as state drug laws, asked Rossman if his "view is that if it turns out that, to use one of the Government's examples, people are in their own houses cooking up biological warfare or it turns out that in their own fireplaces, they pollute the air in a way that will, through global warming, swamp the East Coast—or, you know, use any of their other imaginative examples—Congress is powerless to act?"

Rossman started to answer, but Breyer cut in: "Well, you see my point. My point is that there are many, many, many instances of non-commercial activity, when you collect them all together, that could have overwhelming effects on interstate commerce. And so I want to know if you think in any of those myriads of examples—I won't be too far-fetched—the Congress is powerless to act simply because the cause of the major economic impact is itself not economic?"

Justice Ginsburg asked Rossman if he was challenging Congress' conclusions concerning the impact of rape on the national economy. Rossman said those findings were "broader than the aim of the statute." Ginsburg then asked if there was a distinction between the Violence Against Women Act and the Civil Rights Act: "We have so many parallel legislations in public accommodations, laws, employment, and discrimination. We don't say that that's a traditional area for the States just because they got there first, which they did. In both areas there was State legislation before Federal. So, if you can have harmonious legislation for public accommodations, for employment, then why not here?"

Rossman tried to distinguish the Violence Against Women Act from the 1964 Civil Rights law. He did the opposite of what Days did in *Lopez*. "I take it we've moved back to the Commerce Clause, Justice Ginsburg. And I think the answer to your question is: because this isn't commerce. The reason that there was harmonious legislation on both the Federal and State level in the examples that you described is that Congress is regulating commerce. This is not commerce. This is violence. This is interpersonal violence, the kind of thing the States have always had the exclusive province of regulating since the start of our country."

Before Congress passed the Violence Against Women Act, it did hold at least nine extensive hearings specifically related to the issue over a six-year period of time. Congress concluded that the testimony before them showed that the incidence of rape had risen four times as fast as the total national crime rate over the previous ten years; that one hundred twenty-five thousand college women "can expect to be raped during this—or any—year"; that 41 percent of state judges surveyed believe that state juries give sexual assault victims less credibility than other crime victims; that an individual who commits rape "has only about four chances in one hundred of being arrested, prosecuted, and found guilty of any offense in the State Court"; and that almost 50 percent of rape victims "lose their jobs or are forced to quit because of the crime's severity."

Five months later, in May 2000, the Court decided the case. The factual record, the Court majority said, "is not enough to find the statute Constitutional." Rape did not have sufficient economic effects to allow the federal government to step in. Goldscheid's preargument analysis was correct; if she could not get O'Connor's vote, Christy Brzonkala would lose. She did not get O'Connor's vote and lost 5–4.

Chief Justice Rehnquist, who wrote the *Morrison* majority opinion, said the federal government did not justify its interfering in the states' legal process and that the people should look to the states to protect them. It was another instance of this Court's rewriting of American law. The building blocks of the American democracy were not the people, Rehnquist said, but the states, which were the authentic organs of democratic government. Thus, from a practical standpoint, according to Larry Kramer, a constitutional law expert who teaches at New York University Law School, the Court's *Morrison* explanation means that "any possibility of using the Commerce Clause to regulate what the Court defines [as] non-commercial appears doomed."

Justice Souter disagreed strenuously with Rehnquist's conclusions, fearing the Court would use *Morrison* to reverse prior cases. Alarmed, he wrote, "We live in a Nation knit together by two centuries of scientific, technological, commercial, and environmental change. Those changes, taken together, mean that virtually every kind of activity, no matter how local, genuinely can affect commerce, or its conditions, outside the State." Justice Breyer's dissent, joined by Justices Stevens, Souter, and Ginsburg, quoted from essential parts of Congress' voluminous findings.

Justice Breyer protested that the majority's casual disregard for Congress upset the separation of powers established in the Constitution and made the Court superior to the people's elected body. He stated that the majority, "through its evidentiary demands, its nondeferential review, and its failure to distinguish between judicial and legislative constitutional competencies, improperly invades a power that the Constitution assigns to Congress."

Breyer's remarks in the *Morrison* oral argument evoked John Marshall's concerns and turned out to be prescient. If the federal government's power was limited to the extent that it could not stop attacks on women because of existing state laws, he asked, how could it stop terrorists from developing biological weapons because of existing state laws. Clearly, he said, if the states could not deal with national problems, it was up to the federal government. Gun control, violence against women, and the crisis that flows from September 11 all demand a level of national coordination and expertise that only the federal government possesses. Federal officials, Breyer made clear in his remarks in the *Morrison* case, are better equipped to fight national problems. Through his questions, he urged, at argument, that the Supreme Court's Federalism decisions should not be used to prevent Congress from enlisting state and local officials to fight terrorism.

Congress' capacity to protect women from violence and discrimination is a critical element in the defense of civil rights. The Court and the country feels differently about the cause, effect, and present harm of racial discrimination as compared to discrimination against women. It is not as serious, does not cause harm and does not require remedial laws, the conservatives tell us.

We speak of slavery as if it ended one hundred years ago, even as we accept that the effects of slavery dominate our present landscape. But with discrimination against women it is different. We know women got the right to vote only in 1920, less than a hundred years ago—long after blacks were extensively given that right. Women were prohibited from holding political offices by state and federal law, from having certain professions and jobs, from buying or selling property, and from keeping their earnings. Women could not get legal protection from abusive husbands, a concept that still pervades much of America's legal atmosphere. The Violence Against Women Act was Congress' attempt to rectify some of those past failures.

When the Supreme Court, in *Morrison,* had the chance to stop private acts of violence against women, they knew that laws passed by Congress had given African Americans that protection. But the Rehnquist majority opposed those laws. They saw civil rights legislation as having been wrongfully forced on the South by the federal government. The Court signaled its desire to resist those laws and strike down laws similar to these in the civil rights cases of 1883. Justices Rehnquist, Scalia, and Thomas all chillingly questioned the constitutionality of the Civil Rights Act as previously justified by the Commerce Clause and the Fourteenth Amendment. But before they took such a drastic step, they waited until they had a better case.

The states were the champions of the Violence Against Women Act. It was their representatives who asked Congress to pass the law. State representatives testified without any substantial opposition and gave statistics to Congress. In the early 1990s, even the states recognized the importance of the federal government's intervention in cases where women were abused. Twenty-one states said that women did not get equal justice in their state systems and that they needed the federal courts. They recognized their inability to deal effectively with the problem and pledged their cooperation with federal authorities.

Not one state opposed the law. The states were not arguing states' rights—only the majority of the Supreme Court was.

The Court has also tried other ways to undercut Congress and deny as "new" the rights granted by the Warren Court to racial minorities. Instead of only relying on their interpretation of the Thirteenth Amendment, they began to rely on the Eleventh Amendment, which in certain circumstances prohibits suits against the states.

♦   ♦   ♦

In 1995, Patricia Garrett was diagnosed with breast cancer. Fifty-five years old and the nursing director at a University of Alabama hospital, she had a lumpectomy and underwent chemotherapy. Then, like many people who are treated for cancer, she tried to keep working. But Garrett, who worked in a division handling high-risk pregnancies, says she was pressured by her boss to quit and then was demoted. She later testified that a colleague had told her the boss didn't like "sick people" and tried to get rid of them. "I loved to work," Garrett says now. "It was so demoralizing. To just be told to go home was terrible."

Milton Ash, also of Alabama, was a prison guard who had asthma. Assigned to work in an asbestos area, he asked to be moved to another location where he could still perform the same work. The state refused and fired him. Ash's and Garrett's separate lawsuits seeking money damages under the Americans with Disabilities Act were soon after joined.[37] Their briefs to the high court argued that the history of this nation's treatment of people with disabilities has been previously described by Congress as grotesque.

As civil rights laws showed, often the most effective way of stopping an illegal action and of making sure it doesn't happen again is to allow money damages. Garrett and Ash said: "The fact is, society's vital quest for equality, integration, and dignity of the disabled has never been about money damages. . . . To the extent the disabled have ever asked for anything more than the government already provides all citizens, it has always been about the forward-looking objective of removing barriers to access, not the backward-looking objective" of damage lawsuits.

In a highly unusual bipartisan act, the GOP and Democratic congressional leaders who wrote the Americans with Disabilities law asked for permission to file a brief on behalf of the claimants and against the state of Alabama. The Court permitted it. Then, former president George Bush, for whom the ADA represented a major accomplishment of his administration, also asked to file a brief; his request, too, was granted. Bush's brief argued that before the ADA, laws protecting the disabled were enacted in a piecemeal fashion. He explained that the goal of the law was to cover "all aspects of American life, including our workplaces, our communities and our schools, and other public services."

Alabama argued that even though Section 5 of the Fourteenth Amendment authorizes Congress to enforce rights guaranteed therein by "appropriate legislation," of which the Americans with Disabilities Act would be an appropriate example, the Eleventh Amendment protects the state from unreasonable interference in its business by the federal government, and stops the use of the Fourteenth Amendment enforcement process. Garrett and Ash lost.

The *Lopez* claim, that the evidence given to Congress was not sufficient when it passed the gun law, could not be made here. Congress, both with respect to the aged and disabled, held extensive hearings to see if there was massive state discrimination over a period of years. In fashioning its ADA legislation, Congress held thirteen hearings in Washington, created a task force that held additional hearings in all fifty states, and took testimony from thousands of witnesses. At least three hundred acts of alleged discrimination by the states were documented. Congress found that discrimination and maltreatment against the disabled was so widespread that it pervaded every aspect of our society, and that private companies as well as state and local governments were all responsible. The act was passed by the legislature specifically to stop that nationwide discrimination.

Michael Gottesman, now a Georgetown University law professor, was an experienced litigator who had argued nineteen cases before the Supreme Court. He knew when he was asked to represent Pat Garrett and Milton Ash that he had a difficult road ahead. A year earlier, the Court, in yet another 5–4 ruling, had voted to dismiss the complaint of a Florida State University physics professor, J. Daniel Kimel, in an age-bias suit against the university. The Court said it is constitutional for the state to discriminate against the aged if the state has a rational reason for the discrimination, even if it "is probably not true that those reasons are valid in the majority of cases." In addition, prior to *Garrett,* in six decisions after 1993, the conservatives also ruled in a string of decisions, over angry dissents by the other justices, that damage suits against a state are barred by the Eleventh Amendment.

Gottesman's concern that these decisions and the *Kimel v. Florida Board of Regents*[38] rationale might cover his case was justified. The Supreme Court, indeed, relied on its decision against Kimel in its 5–4 vote: disabled people like Garrett and Ash could not sue a state in any court to enforce a right created by a federal statute. Rehnquist and O'Connor found that the Eleventh Amendment trumped the enforcement clause of the Fourteenth Amendment. The Court said that the Fourteenth Amendment—asserting that no state may "deny to any person the equal protection of the laws" and that "the laws of the United States shall be the supreme law of the land. . . the laws of any state to the contrary notwithstanding"—were not violated. Nor did the Court find that states are required to make special accommodations for the disabled. "They could quite hardheadedly—and perhaps hardheartedly—hold to job-qualification requirements which do not make allowance for the disabled," said Rehnquist. Moving in for the kill, he added that even if all the statistics did show a pattern of discrimination, Congress hadn't proved that the discrimination was "irrational." He brazenly brushed aside all Congress had heard and saw and all the conclusions it had reached. Disingenuously, the chief justice said, Congress had put together only "minimal evidence of unconstitutional state discrimination." This conclusion, denigrating Congress as being incapable of evaluating what it heard, and rejecting its judgment, brings us back to the early twentieth century, when the Court refused to allow Congress to decide if child labor laws were needed. With this opinion, the five conservatives substituted their judgment for that of the senators and representatives of Congress who had passed the bill and of the president who had signed it.

Souter disagreed. The Eleventh Amendment, adopted in 1794 and enacted to stop the states from being bankrupted with suits over debts from the Revolutionary War, he explained, "is inapplicable to the claims of Garrett and Ash." Rather, that amendment merely denies federal courts the authority to hear suits against a state by residents of another state. The conservative majority has, however, interpreted the amendment to incorporate the ancient and now-discredited notion that "the king can do no wrong." As a result of the Rehnquist Court, Souter continued, "State governments do not have to pay their victims when the states do what Congress has prohibited." No matter how egregious the violation, Souter said, the state can now disregard the Fourteenth Amendment and discriminate because of the new, wrongful use of the Eleventh Amendment.

As a consequence of the *Garrett* and *Kimel* cases, many of the federal statutes protecting the aged and disabled have been thrown into the wastebasket. States can now violate congressionally created rights for the elderly, pregnant women, the mentally disabled, the mentally ill, and others with impunity, for they know they won't have to pay anything if they are sued. Hypercritically, O'Connor claims the laws were vague because they were not as carefully written as a group of law professors might have written the statutes. But for the past two hundred years, congressmen, after compromise and negotiations, were the ones to write laws, not law professors.

♦   ♦   ♦

Dred Scott[39] was important not only for what it held, but also because it showed the North that war was inevitable. In 1857, it was the only case in the eighty years of pre–Civil War constitutional history in which the Supreme Court limited congressional power in any significant way. What Justice Roger Taney, the chief justice in the *Dred Scott* case, started, Chief Justice William Rehnquist, one hundred years later, brought to a new level. The conservative-dominated Taney Court knew the political consequences of its act. Benjamin Curtis, an underappreciated jurist, one of the dissenting justices, himself a slaveholder, resigned over the decision. When the federal government continued to support slave interests, the Court did not interfere.

Before the Civil War ended, Congress passed the Thirteenth Amendment, banning slavery. It said Congress should enforce abolition with "appropriate legislation." Congress intended to both end slavery and make blacks citizens (overruling *Dred Scott*), with the federal government obligated to guarantee the rights of citizenship.

The Fourteenth Amendment's principal purpose was to make the Thirteenth Amendment and the Civil Rights Act a reality. The congressional history at that time shows that Congress also wanted the Fourteenth Amendment to enforce the Bill of Rights against the states. Congress adopted the Fourteenth Amendment at the same time they passed the Civil Rights Act of 1866, also as a prohibition on the states. These clauses were now designed to be self-executing.

◆　　　◆　　　◆

On May 28, 2002, the Supreme Court, in another 5–4 decision citing nineteenth century states' rights laws, said that sovereign immunity meant that federal agencies cannot hold hearings in a proceeding brought by a private party claiming injury against a state. The Court in *Federal Maritime Commission v. South Carolina State Port Authority*,[40] with O'Connor and Kennedy in the majority, started to whittle away at the power of administrative agencies, again on the grounds of states' rights. We will see the day when a state violating your federal rights will be nearly totally immune before administrative agencies that were created during the New Deal days, as well as before the federal courts.

The clash between the Rehnquist–Roberts bloc and the moderate members of the Court over whether citizens can sue federal and state government officials over violations of their constitutional rights is of great meaning. The difference is more than the interpretation of specific statutes or constitutional clauses, or questions of who has standing to sue. It is based on two very different views of our democracy, on how the government is to be run, and on what values shape the Constitution.

Conservatives believe that the government cannot run if its managers, police officials, and welfare agencies are constantly defending themselves in court. The government was created by the Constitution to be run by those elected officials, but the conservatives argue that if each discretionary act by an official could lead to a constitutional claim, the government would come to a halt. Within this context, Roberts, Alito, Scalia, Thomas, and often Kennedy see many sexual and racial harassment suits as frivolous. The Supreme Court's basic purpose, they believe, is to resolve disputes that have significant impact and are of broad general concern.

The liberal view assumes that the people should hold the government accountable under the Constitution. When a citizen's rights are trampled on, citizens have the right to sue welfare officials, prison officials, and all manner of public employees accused of deliberate rights violations.

President Bush, in his January 31, 2006, State of the Union speech, railed against activist Courts. But the president and conservative media have consistently urged the present Court to become even more activist, striking down laws that impinge on big business and bring on multimillion-dollar punitive-damage awards against oil polluters and tobacco companies. It is a course upon which the present Court, and the one to follow, are already set: The *Wall Street Journal* applauded the Supreme Court's May 14, 2001, opinion that said appellate courts were not bound by a jury's ruling on punitive damages, that the judges could look anew at the record and were relatively free to set aside people's verdicts. With future appointees likely to be antigovernment, free-market ideologues sympathetic to business interest, this decision is but a taste of things to come.

Rehnquist, during the Warren Court period, railed that the least dangerous branch, the judicial, was becoming the most dangerous branch, and that the Constitution's separation of powers would be frustrated by the Court, an unelected, undemocratic elite. It was his own dark fantasy, since as chief justice that is exactly what his Court became and what it did.

◆   ◆   ◆

We have seen the states' failed attempts to make religion an essential part of the state government. The states' attempts to protect white privilege have been far more successful. When the time the Constitution was signed, every state except Massachusetts permitted slavery. Article I, Section 9, of the Constitution makes clear that the slave trade cannot be abolished before 1808. It did not say it can then be abolished—the South would not have joined the Union if it had.

When Benjamin Franklin and Quaker abolitionists petitioned the House of Representatives in 1790 to end slavery, both the North and the South refused to comply. A compromise resolution read, "The Congress shall have no authority to interfere with the emancipation of the slaves, or in the treatment of them within any of the States; it remaining with the several States alone to provide any regulation therein, which humanity and true policy may require."

James Madison and Thomas Jefferson, himself a slaveholder, did not oppose the compromise. They accepted the resolution as necessary to keep the Union together. Madison, trying to put the best face on it, said that the Constitution made it unconstitutional to pass a law abolishing slavery. This was not true.

The Declaration of Independence and the Constitution, among the most imaginative documents ever written, are both deeply stained by the cancer of slavery. Our Founding Fathers' "self-evident truths" were anything but when they dealt with race. The fifty-two word preamble is the clearest, most passionate statement of the reasons for a democracy. But fifty-five members of the Constitutional Convention were elite property owners, not necessarily representative of the noble image meant to be conveyed by "We the People." In reality, the preamble for many was hypocrisy and agreed to because of opposition. The Declaration of Independence and the Constitution, spellbinding orations of democracy, also solidified the slave system for nearly the next hundred years. The United States was one of the last western nations to abolish slavery.

The Supreme Court, from 1873 until the 1930s dismantled the Civil War amendments passed to enact equality and equal protection. The New Deal and Warren Courts reversed the earlier Courts. But the strong racism inherent in the proslavery spirit was reinvigorated by the Rehnquist Court, which was determined to deny blacks and other minorities an education, freedom, and the right to a meaningful vote. The Rehnquist Court laid a good foundation for the Roberts Court to bring intolerance to new levels.

Nathan Newman and J.J. Gass, two constitutional lawyers at the New York University Brennan Center for Justice, as well as other scholars point out that this Court's race jurisprudence, including affirmative action and school separation, is based on a sleight of hand. Conservatives saw *Brown* as one of the worst cases ever decided, creating the racial turmoil that lead to the civil rights movement. Chief Justice Rehnquist ordered a school integration case back to the trial court, observing that the Court "should consider that many goals of its quality education plan already have been attained." The leading school integration cases, *Brown*, *Green*, and *Swann*, he said no longer truly dealt with today's reality. The Court must "restore state and local authorities to the control of a school system that is operating in compliance with the Constitution." By that he meant the Court should get out of the interpretation business and let the communities be free of judicial restraint. Rehnquist believed that whether or not the schools were integrated was not the main issue. If the white exodus to the suburbs helped lead to more segregated schools than existed at the time of *Brown*, there was nothing the courts could do about it. And even if the segregation were caused by Southern resistance, he said, it was now time to leave the school systems alone. Unlike Justice Ginsburg, who looked at Missouri's forty-two years of opposition to integrated schools and insisted the state had an obligation to do something about it, Rehnquist refused even to see the states' successful resistance. His opinion gave the states a blank check to have separate and unequal school systems.

The conservatives in this and other cases have adopted a new meaning of the Fourteenth Amendment. Totally disregarding how it came to life, the Court now interprets it to apply to both blacks and whites. "Racial discrimination" is barred; "equal protection" for "any person" is guaranteed. The Court's refusal to look at the facts, past and present, and claim instead to rely on "logic" is to ignore history to get the result they want, a separated society.

In *Missouri v. Jenkins*,[41] the Rehnquist Court said one could not distinguish whether resistance to segregation had created all-black and all-white schools, or whether demographic factors were to blame. The Rehnquist Court also did not find evidence that school desegregation had any beneficial effects on students. In looking at the past, the Court said *Brown v. Board of Education* did not help integration. But the studies indicate otherwise—that when *Brown* was being enforced in the 1960s and 1970s it had a profound impact on segregation.

Courts, although they have neither an army nor money, can have great effect. A July 1, 2001, report, "Schools More Separate: Consequences of a Decade of Resegregation," by Harvard University's Civil Rights Project, describes a return to segregation even in the face of growing support for integration. The most important reasons for the reverse shift, the study concluded, were the Rehnquist Court's limiting and reversing of desegregation orders, along with sharp reductions in federal funding, a decrease in political support for desegregation in schools and housing, and demographic changes.

The Harvard study, which analyzed educational and census data, found that 78 percent of black children attended predominantly minority schools in the 1998–99 academic year, dramatically up from 66 percent just a few years before. Minorities were most likely to attend school with whites in the South, although integration was also unraveling most quickly in the South.

The report also said that more evidence exists now than did at the time of *Brown* that desegregated schools both improve test scores and dramatically change the lives of students and that more schools today are isolated by both race and poverty and are in no way even remotely equal. Because of the "dramatic reversal of *Brown's* spirit by the Rehnquist Courts, there was little the Clinton administration did do to reverse the demise of integration. . . . There has been little or no positive political leadership on this issue for a generation . . . and the courts have made a dramatic turn around in decisions about desegregated schools. . . . Citizens in some communities, such as Charlotte, N.C., have elected school boards committed to integration only to have their will blocked by a federal court forbidding any conscious effort to achieve or maintain segregation," states the report. There is still a good deal of *Brown*-inspired litigation throughout the country. More than two hundred consent orders are being enforced (twenty-six in Alabama), and in 2001, a Louisiana judge in Fayetteville, Arkansas, took control of the schools after he learned that a school board had intentionally disobeyed an order. Although the Legal Defense Fund has as many lawyers involved in the cases today as it did fifteen years ago, the federal government is no longer as active as before.

James Madison warned, "If a majority be united by a common interest, the rights of the minority will be insecure." The tyranny of the majority requires safeguards to protect "one part of the society against the injustice of the other part." Majority rule and democracy are not the same thing. What is good for the 51 percent majority is not necessarily good for everyone. People of color can improve their lives only through their political power. Over the years, poll taxes, literacy tests, all-white primaries, grandfather clauses, and violence surrounding elections have led to the disenfranchisement of minorities. The disenfranchisement of blacks in Florida by the violence and obstruction that surfaced in *Bush v. Gore* in 2001 occurs regularly in the South. The NAACP keeps voluminous records of years past, and in one of my previous books I described some of the ways blacks were stopped from voting, including being beaten up, having their cars ticketed on their way to the polls, and being threatened with the loss of either welfare or jobs. Although the Fifteenth Amendment, ratified on February 3, 1870, prohibited the denial of every citizen's right to vote "on account of race, color, or previous condition of servitude," it is not yet fully operative.

♦   ♦   ♦

The Supreme Court case that most directly affected the lives of all Americans was *Baker v. Carr,* a 6–3[42] 1959 decision that attempted to give us one man–one vote and meaning to the word "equality." At his confirmation hearing, Alito said he was against it. I believe it to be the most important case of the twentieth century, the very foundation of our democracy.

Conservatives believe the Court should not take cases that seek to enforce *Baker.*

In *Baker,* the Supreme Court said it was a violation of the Fourteenth Amendment's Equal Protection Clause to make one person's vote count less than another's. It was an attack on racist legislatures and entrenched powers that suppressed minority rights. *Baker v. Carr* has been touted as a landmark that has withstood challenge for forty-five years. But its enforcement was ignored by the Rehnquist Court and will be ignored by the Roberts Court.

Baker, more than any other Supreme Court case, dramatically changed the political landscape—it tried to empower blacks equally to whites, it tried to stop gerrymandering, it tried to give new candidates a chance against incumbents, it tried to create equality between rural and urban voters. The case is the logical conclusion to the end of slavery—to the Thirteenth, Fourteenth, and Fifteenth amendments, *Brown*, and the Civil Rights Movement.

Because so much attention was focused on other matters at the Roberts and Alito hearings, their views on *Baker* were lost in the shuffle.

The Warren Court, at the height of its power and influence in 1962, decided to move on from school segregation to the protection of the black vote. Both the South and the North were interested in minimizing the black vote and creating racially unbalanced districts, so that large numbers of blacks would have no representation at all. Democratic and Republican incumbents carved up districts so they could not lose elections.

The minority of the Warren Court, headed by Justice Felix Frankfurter, did not want to take the *Baker* case, saying the legislature, not the courts, as responsible for deciding apportionment cases. They said that the courts had no legal standards to apply to political issues and that our Constitution did not provide a judicial remedy for every wrongful exercise of legislative powers. It is not our job, Frankfurter said, to get involved in battles over the allocation of power within a state.

The Conservative court can easily end one man–one vote without directly overruling it. Both Roberts and Alito find cases such as these "non-justifiable."

By narrowing its docket, the Rehnquist Court refused to review blatant gerrymandering cases without giving any reasons or letting us see a dramatic signal. That's why the issue had so little resonance during the nomination process. The case stands, but its application is nearly dead. Since *Baker v. Carr* (1959), legislatures have carved up electoral districts to protect incumbents and to deny minority votes.

The Roberts Court will do at least the same—it need not reverse *Baker* to finally kill it.

Baker v. Carr fits into the Warren Court's attempts to eliminate racial discrimination in voting and to protect minorities from being overrun by majority rule. The Voting Rights Act and *Baker v. Carr* helped Congress and the Court make the black and Hispanic vote count as much as the white vote. The Warren Court decisions and the Voting Rights Act immediately doubled the number of black and Hispanic majority districts.

There were political repercussions. The new voters were primarily Democrats. The Rehnquist Court uses the color-blind test and the language of reverse discrimination to disenfranchise minority voters, to the benefit of the Republican Party.

Kennedy and the conservative majority also see this as a states' rights issue. Let the states have the sole power to elect its representatives, free of Court involvement. Today's Court does not want to get embroiled in the issues decided by the Warren Court—they say they do not want to burden the court system with overseeing schools, voting booths, and jobs. They see a satisfied majority, a white group that feels it has already done too much for blacks and Hispanics. In "reverse discrimination" Thomas, Bork, and Scalia see the lessening of white Republican power and going against the country's majority. Pervading all these decisions is the thought that we have now achieved equality, an America without racism—and an America defined only by the vision of the majorities, a concept that Madison found so dangerous.

After the Warren Court passed into history, the Burger Court, after the 1980 Reagan landslide, failed to find racial discrimination in voting when African Americans, who composed more than a third of the population of Mobile, Alabama, challenged an at-large electoral scheme that had resulted in an all-white city commission and a white mayor. The Burger Court said, "The Constitution does not entail the right to have Negro candidates elected" and denied that "their freedom to vote has been denied or abridged by anyone." The

Court ruled that although blacks may enjoy the right to vote, that does not necessarily include the right to govern. This justifies gerrymandering no matter how outrageous.

A more recent case concerns the districts of representatives Eva Clayton and Mel Watt, both Democrats elected in 1997 and the first blacks ever elected to Congress from North Carolina. Their districts were newly drawn after the 1990 census to meet federal standards designed to increase the chances of minority candidates.

Under the guidelines of the 1965 Voting Rights Act and the directive of the elder Bush's Department of Justice, North Carolina doubled its number of black and Hispanic majority districts from twenty-six to fifty-two. Of these new districts, however, none had an odder history and a stranger shape than the Twelfth, which Representative Watt served. Except for a few bulges and detours, the Twelfth Congressional District ran along Interstate 85 for about one hundred sixty miles, from Durham to Gastonia; in some instances, the district was no wider than the interstate highway that it followed. North Carolina initially had been gerrymandered to keep blacks out of office, but the Department of Justice said two districts must be created so that the state's 22 percent African American population be sufficiently represented in Congress.

Even after North Carolina's redistricting, the majority white population continued to control ten of the twelve districts, while it constituted only 70 percent of the state's population. But Ruth Shaw, a white Democrat, and four other residents of her district, brought suit against North Carolina and the United States in *Shaw v. Hunt*,[43] claiming the redrawing of districts for the benefit of black voters violated the Equal Protection Clause because the districts had been divided by race and whites were proportionally underrepresented. Such racial redistricting, they argued, discriminated against whites and insulted blacks because it implied that they could not work together. As a result, the plan threatened to balkanize North Carolina into competing racial factions and entrench racial-bloc voting. It was precisely such gerrymandering, Shaw said, that discriminated against blacks in the South during the first half of the twentieth century and led to the Voting Rights Act.

The Democratic plaintiffs, however, were haunted by another political reality. By consolidating the black vote, a process called "max black," which had historically been Democratic, the Republican Party was better able to make inroads in "bleached" white districts. The federal government and the state of North Carolina argued that they had done in the Twelfth District exactly what the Voting Rights Act required—used race to establish districts with majority black voting blocs where there had been voting discrimination. Even though white voters had now lost one historically white district, the government argued, blacks were still disproportionately underrepresented in Congress. The court of appeals agreed: such redistricting was appropriate because of North Carolina's long history of discrimination in creating voting districts. After the appeals court said that if racial gerrymandering were not permitted, North Carolina would never have an African American congressman, the case went to the Supreme Court.

In a 5–4 decision reversing the lower court, the Supreme Court held that the Voting Rights Act did not allow for race-based districting. Invoking the language of individual rights, Justice O'Connor, writing for the majority, said voters had a right to participate in a color-blind election. "It is unsettling," O'Connor continued, "how closely the North Carolina plan resembles the most egregious racial gerrymanders of the past," and it "bears an uncomfortable resemblance to political apartheid." The Warren Court had said that "preference for pleasingly shaped districts" should not be used to justify the denial of voting rights for blacks. But O'Connor rejected the Warren Court's reason and criticized the odd shape of the Twelfth District, whose residents "may have little in common with one another but the color of their skin." O'Connor said that racial classification can lead only to larger social harms, such as the balkanization and politicization of racial groups. She and the majority said that the state must show a compelling interest that required it to treat some of its citizens differently than others based on race in order to find this, or any future redistricting plan, acceptable—a test she understood the state could not meet.

Justice Byron R. White, on his last day in the Court, disagreed that white voters in North Carolina had been hurt by the redistricting plan. The benefit of the Equal Protection Clause of the Fourteenth Amendment belonged on the side of the minority voters. The state's effort to get at proportionality in voting could not, he said, violate the Fourteenth Amendment.

Then, in an April 2001 decision, Justice O'Connor justified a different position as she switched sides. The 5–4 vote this time was won by the moderates. In another North Carolina case, *Easley v. Cromartie*,[44] she concluded that politics, not race, was the predominant factor in drawing the districts. The swing vote for the Right in the *Shaw* case, she now became the swing vote for the moderate bloc, holding that it was permissible for district lines to be drawn along race lines, if that was not the sole motivation. She claimed she was not contradicting herself. Some commentators described her vote as part of the *Bush v. Gore* aftermath: here she swings deliberately toward the moderates and liberals. Justice O'Connor now acknowledged that gerrymandering on racial grounds is also gerrymandering on political grounds, because the black Southern vote is predominantly Democratic. Her view is that the Constitution generally forbids the government from making decisions based on race, but there is no such legal bar on making decisions based on political or partisan grounds. Therefore, shifting African-American voters into a new district to create a Democratic stronghold is appropriate if it is a political decision.

Justice Breyer, writing as part of the majority, emphasized that because African Americans in the state register and vote Democratic more than 95 percent of the time, it was hard to distinguish a legislature's effort to create a majority black district from a legislature's effort to create a safe Democratic one. And because white registered Democrats more frequently vote Republican than

African American registered Democrats do, a legislature trying to secure a safe Democratic seat could plausibly include more heavily African American precincts for political, not racial, reasons. "Race in this case correlates closely with political behavior," Justice Breyer concluded, reasoning that judges should therefore give legislatures leeway to balance racial and political considerations without assuming one was predominant.

Justice Thomas, the strongest opponent of race-based decision making, wrote the opinion for the four dissenters: "Racial gerrymandering offends the Constitution whether the motive is malicious or benign and it is not an excuse that the legislature merely may have drawn the district based on the stereotype that blacks are reliable Democratic voters."

While blacks vote 95 percent Democratic, white voters are more split. Thus, by reducing the number of blacks in an area, the Republicans will win; by putting more blacks in contested areas with a previously white majority, Democrats can win. While a very small percentage of blacks will, given the choice, vote against a black Democrat, a substantial percentage of white voters will vote for black candidates. An Emory College study published in the *Emory Law Journal* found that in many states, including Southern states, black congressional candidates "always got at least one white vote in five." Professor Charles Bullock III of the University of Georgia, the coauthor of the Emory study, said, "The white electorate is increasingly willing to vote for black candidates."

After the April 2001 decision, courts in both the South and the North began to uphold racial redistricting, calling it partisan redistricting when the legislators' motive was to create partisan redistricting. Racial redistricting, according to the Rehnquist Court, violates the Fourteenth Amendment, but partisan redistricting does not. O'Conner changed labels to make permissible what previously was impermissible.

The political nature of voting cases was best shown in a 2002 Mississippi case. Justice Scalia, showing disregard for judicial ethics and affirming his commitment to bullying politics rather than the law, rejected an emergency appeal in a voting rights case in Mississippi.

Mississippi, losing one of its five seats in Congress, redistricted the state. Both the Justice Department and a trial judge approved a plan that would favor the Democrat incumbent Ronnie Shows rather than the Republican incumbent Charles Pickering, Jr. Ashcroft intervened, and the Justice Department reversed itself. Shows appealed to a three-judge Republican court, which included Pickering's father, that reversed the trial court. When Shows sought an emergency appeal to the Supreme Court, Scalia denied it.

The Court's reluctance to follow *Baker v. Carr* to its logical conclusion—to do all it can to enforce one man–one vote—expanded when it refused in 2006 to set aside nearly all of Tom Delay's Texas congressional partisan redistricting. We are now told partisan redistricting, an evil the *Baker v. Carr* suit was aiming at, is too complex an issue for the Court. The creation of an unfair electoral landscape, partisan redistricting, and the protection of incumbents was given a boost when the Court said the redistricting could be done any time the legislature wants to do it. Although four hundred thirty-five seats are up for reelection every other year, only thirty to forty seats are truly contested, because the party in power has gerrymandered the district for its convenience. The Court knows, as the *Baker v. Carr* Court knew, that the politicians certainly will not reject partisan redistricting and incumbent protection. If this Supreme Court does not even attempt it, it is perpetuated for decades to come. It is unlikely that there will be a Court in the next twenty-five years that will try to create a fair electoral landscape.

A painstaking review of Bork's, Roberts', Scalia's, Thomas' and Alito's cases show that they all seek to minimize the restrictions of the Bill of Rights, extend state power at the expense of federal power, and destroy the separation of church and state.

Roberts and Alito have consistently been to the right of the Court in these three areas. In several decisions in the last three years, O'Connor, along with the moderates, voted against the Roberts-

Alito-Bork-Scalia-Thomas view of how democracy should be, what the powers of our presidents should be, and how voting rights cases should be decided. With the appointments of Alito and Roberts, these decisions will go the other way.

With state governments barred after the Civil War from officially disenfranchising blacks, private groups did their best to supply the deficiency. The Ku Klux Klan, organized in Tennessee in 1866, became the model. In the 1868 election, the Klan's suppression of turnout led to conservative Democratic victories in Georgia and Louisiana. The violence convinced even moderates that explicitly guaranteeing blacks' right to vote was the only way to ensure that civil rights would be protected. Thus, a new federal amendment to forbid racial discrimination in voting was ratified in 1870. As the drafter of the Fifteenth Amendment, Massachusetts Republican George Boutwell, explained, "With the right of voting, everything a man ought to have or enjoy of civil rights comes to him. Without that right he is nothing." The former abolitionist leader Wendell Phillips wrote: "A man with a ballot in his hand is the master of the situation. He defines all his other rights and what is not now given him, he takes."

The probusiness, antilabor period of the late nineteenth century continued into the early twentieth. The logic was the same. Federal courts regularly struck down laws regulating subjects like labor relations and food packaging on the grounds that they violated the Fourteenth Amendment's Due Process Clause. The highest New York court invalidated a New York statute prohibiting bakery employees from working more than sixty hours per week. As historian Eric Foner observed, "The federal courts . . . retained the greatly expanded jurisdiction born of Reconstruction; they increasingly employed it, however, to protect corporations from local regulation."

The Congress that wrote the Fourteenth Amendment and passed the civil rights laws that the Court struck down surely had intimate knowledge and familiarity with the events surrounding the adoption of the Fourteenth Amendment, but the Rehnquist Court does not mention them. One of the arguments of the originalists was that we must look at what Congress intended when they wrote the Constitution. But we must also look then at the intent of those who passed the Thirteenth, Fourteenth and Fifteenth Amendments. Scalia, Alito, and Thomas are selective originalists taking what they like and disregarding what does not agree with their views.

Thus far, most antidiscrimination laws have survived challenges, but a familiar bloc of justices has unmistakably embarked on a program of restricting federal civil rights legislation. The renewed attack on Congress is the work of supposed "originalists" lauded for their "judicial restraint" (or, as President Bush puts it in citing Justices Scalia and Thomas as models for his own judicial appointments, not "legislating from the bench"). But the Court's states' rights bloc rarely attempts to defend its interpretation by analyzing historical sources, such as the congressional debates or the legislation passed. Compare this with the genuflection given to the records of the Philadelphia convention, the *Federalist,* and founding-generation statutes like the Judiciary Act of 1789 in construing provisions of the 1787 Constitution. When it comes to the post–Civil War Amendments, the Court cites long-discredited decisions of its antiequality predecessors rather than seeking anything approximating the "original understanding." As for "judicial restraint" and declining to "legislate from the bench," the Rehnquist Court has struck down federal statutes at a pace unprecedented in the Court's history.

Newman and Gass, writing for the Brennan Center at New York University Law School, make the point that the claim of states' rights jurisprudence, based on an appeal to an originalist legitimacy, succeeds through racism and public ignorance. Only those who have forgotten the Klan's court-abetted assault on Reconstruction can accept the Rehnquist Court's superficial version of history. The antidiscrimination movement must fight the Roberts Court and help restore the public's memory of the reasons for the Thirteenth, Fourteenth, and Fifteenth amendments. Distorting the history of Reconstruction and the new amendments was a deliberate and sustained project of racist historians and legal scholars in the late nineteenth and early twentieth centuries; it will take a deliberate and sustained effort to correct the rewriting of the past by the Rehnquist-Roberts Court.

While the worst revisionist history has been removed from textbooks, it has been replaced mostly by silence. Teachers mention America's powerful nineteenth century voices for slavery and Reconstruction in passing, if at all. In most American schools, it is as if history stopped at the end of the Civil War and did not resume until the Gilded Age and the emergence of populism near the end of the century.

Even the Civil War battlefields maintained by the National Park Service mentioned nothing about slavery until very recently. Of hundreds of Civil War monuments, only two or three include any representation of black soldiers. Americans can visit historical sites like Gettysburg without learning much about why people went to war and what became of Lincoln's speech calling for a new birth of freedom.

The history of the Rehnquist Court will be the model for the Roberts Court. First the Rehnquist Court strikes down a law passed by Congress. Then Congress passes a new law to fix the defects in the old one the Court found objectionable. Next, the Supreme Court strikes down that law. Between our elected legislatures and the Supreme Court rages a war to an extent never seen before. Today, separation of powers exists only conceptually. The Court overrules the Congress nearly whenever it wishes.

The ultimate hypocrisy of the Right's attack on Federalism was seen in Bush's defeated assault on doctor-assisted suicide under Oregon's Death with Dignity Act, overwhelmingly passed by Oregon voters during a 1997 referendum. Bush placed the Drug Enforcement Administration between Oregon physicians and their dying patients. Ashcroft announced he would make it a federal crime for a doctor or patient to collaborate in assisted suicide and that the doctor's license would be revoked.

Commenting on the attorney general's action, Oregon senator Ron Wyden, a Democrat, said: "They've tossed the ballots of Oregon voters in the trash can. They're frustrated by the inconvenience of the democratic process." The Oregon law said that the state must be free to do what it wants in this area, relying on the state's rights just laid down by the Rehnquist Court. On November 13, 2001, a federal judge issued a four-month temporary restraining order and then later a permanent injunction stopping Ashcroft in his tracks. On January 20, 2006, the Supreme Court, with O'Connor writing the decision, upheld the Oregon law. Roberts, Scalia, and Thomas claimed the federal drug laws authority overrode states rights. The liberal majority upheld the state claims.

Critics said Oregon would become a suicide state, with people flocking in to end their misery. It has proven not to be true.

The conservatives are in a quandary. They are prepared to uphold states' rights but not if the states' laws appear immoral. It is here that the battle within the Republican Party rages—those who see family values as the sole issue or those who have a broader view and do not want to see the Republicans impaled on a dubious morality. With gay marriage, other assisted suicide cases, and *Roe v. Wade* facing the Rehnquist Court, if the justices are consistent they will let the states do what they want. But Scalia, Thomas, Roberts, and Alito already indicated they will vote against those laws.

In *Gonzales v. Raich* (June 6, 2005),[45] the Bush Administration lost its argument that federal drug laws preempted California's medical marijuana law, claiming federal power to regulate a health measure the state thought essential. Justice O'Connor criticized the Bush administration for upholding federal power against state power in the *Raich* case—federal power, she said, was being improperly employed for conservative political policy ends.

The conservatives' pending Federal Marriage Amendment also runs against the states' rights argument. The immediate response by Conservatives to Massachusetts' 2003 *Goodridge* decision,[46] legalizing gay marriage, was to explore every federal means of regulating marriage that exists. But this, as Professor Marci Hamilton, a former O'Connor clerk, argued, is a family law issue, and in this area the states—not the federal government—are the relevant, proper sovereigns.

The Conservatives' attempt to make gay rights a federal issue through a constitutional amendment excluding same-sex arrangements would make very clear the hypocrisy of the states' rights arguments. The federal government has no business in this area. States' rights to control family law issues has never seriously been challenged.

◆　　　◆　　　◆

Roe v. Wade was decided in 1973. Since then there have been more than forty million abortions in the United States. The women's movement, the Supreme Court's privacy cases, as well as other cultural and social forces all contributed to the 1973 decision. One hundred years prior to *Roe v. Wade*, a married woman could not normally own or control her property or enter contractual agreements. If she worked outside her home, her husband legally owned her wages. When Myra Bradwell was denied admission to the bar in 1873, she appealed, but her petition to the Supreme Court was denied. Justice Joseph Bradley's concurring opinion explained why: "The Constitution of the family organization which is founded on the divine ordinance, as well as in the nature of things, indicates the domestic sphere as that which properly belongs to the domain and functions of womanhood."

As recently as 1948, Justice Felix Frankfurter, writing an opinion for the Court, said that a law prohibiting the employment of women bartenders unless they were related to a male bar owner was appropriate so that men could look after the morals of their wives or daughters.

The opening the Rehnquist-O'Connor Court left in *Roe v. Wade* is the stuff of nightmares. Alito made an important distinction when he conceded *Roe* was precedent but said it was not settled law. It can, he believes, be overturned precedent because the law is unsettled. In *Planned Parenthood v. Casey*,[47] the Supreme Court said it retained "the essential holdings" of *Roe v. Wade,* notwithstanding substantial "reservations" that some of the justices had that the case had been decided properly. Alito and Roberts both seemed to suggest that their commitment to precedent was the kind that would permit the Court to keep *Roe v. Wade* in name and yet make it increasingly difficult for many Americans to benefit from its protection. The Court could stop nearly all abortions in most states even as they paid homage to *Roe.*

Casey was thought to preserve *Roe* forever, but in *Casey,* only three of the nine judges said *Roe* had been properly decided. Six did not say *Roe* was correct. Three of the six said it was wrongly decided. The other three said they had substantial reservations about whether *Roe* was right or wrong. When we are told that the *Casey* case, twenty years after *Roe,* affirmed the heart and soul of *Roe* and left the landmark case firmly etched into law, it is misleading. Neither Alito nor Roberts will feel constrained by *Casey* when abortion issues come before them.

The Roberts Court's first abortion decision in a New Hampshire case made the fragility of *Roe* very clear.

New Hampshire's Parental Notification Act prohibited doctors from performing an abortion on a minor until forty-eight hours after written notice of the abortion is delivered to her parents or guardians. The lower federal court struck down the law because it interfered with rights granted in *Roe v. Wade.* The statute did not permit an adequate waiver of the forty-eight-hour notification if the woman's health is at stake.

The statute required that the doctor state the abortion was "necessary." The lower court found this to thwart *Roe v. Wade* because it required the doctor to render an opinion with "impossible precision." The First Circuit Court of Appeals, one of the best appellate courts in the country, said that the life exception was "intolerably vague" and forced doctors to "gamble with their patients' lives" by barring them from performing abortions without notice until they were certain that death was imminent.

The Supreme Court, in its 9–0 opinion, stated that the circuit court's decision, while wrong, was understandable as it was based on a previous Supreme Court case, *Stenberg v. Carhart*,[48] the case that held Nebraska's Partial Birth Abortion Act unconstitutional because it did not say that if the woman's health required it then the partial birth abortion would be appropriate.

Why then did the Supreme Court not affirm on the basis of *Stenberg?*

It was Justice O'Connor's last abortion decision. Out of deference to her, and in light of what would happen in the 2006–2007 term, the Court allowed O'Connor to have her way. The Supreme Court knew that *Stenberg* was soon to be reversed. *Stenberg* was a 5–4 decision. Alito replaces O'Connor. Justice Kennedy, who was in the minority in *Stenberg*, will be in the majority, and state laws permitting partial–birth abortions will then be prohibited. (On November 8, 2006 the federal ban on partial birth abortions was argued in *Gonzalez v. Planned Parenthood* and *Gonzalez v. Cathart*. The Court can in those cases avoid a head-on collision with Stenberg.) And then, when the Parental Notification Act comes up to the Supreme Court, the Court will accept the placing of such obstacles to a teenager's attempt to get an abortion, strangling her right to do so. The conservatives decided not to slap O'Connor in the face in her last days on the bench. Now that she has left, a great deal of her work, in abortion and other areas, will be undone.

Do you describe the New Hampshire case as a reversal or a modification of *Roe?* It depends on the agenda and belief system of who's doing the describing.

Forty-four states now have parental notification laws. Some of the notification laws, even though they seem to have health exceptions (like the New Hampshire law) are formidable obstacles to abortions. These laws generally allow a minor to avoid telling a parent if she can convince a judge that she would face abuse from her parents, or that she is mature enough to make the decision on her own. Her right to an abortion then depends on the state or federal judge she appears before.

But the federal bench is now stacked with conservative judges. All but three of the twelve circuit courts are controlled by conservatives. By 2008, at least two more appeals courts may be conservative. And a large majority of federal trial judges are conservative. It is unlikely that they will find in a teenager's favor, and it is unlikely that they will be sympathetic to doctors who will perform these abortions.

Abortion for even a small number of Americans hangs by a slender thread. The Hyde Amendment, which bars federal Medicaid funds from being used for abortion, strikes directly at the poor. The Fourth Circuit, in *Greenville Women's Clinic v. Bryand*,[49] in a 2–1 decision in 1999, approved a rigorous bundle of requirements on clinics, ranging from zoning restrictions and insurance requirements to the extensive and expensive training of clinic workers and the width of clinic doorways. These regulations have made it so difficult for doctors that few in the states governed by the circuit court will perform abortions. The Fourth Circuit, with a 45 percent minority population—one of the poorest in the nation—succeeded with that decision in increasing the number of back-alley abortions and deaths. The very conservative court overruled the trial judge who found the procedures irrational and crafted mainly to discourage the procedure. That law stood up when the full Fourth Circuit affirmed it, and the statute is now a model for new statutes being passed around the country.

Many states, including Ohio and Georgia, are now trying to pass statutes that would outlaw abortion except when bringing a pregnancy to term would threaten a woman's life or put her physical health in danger of "substantial permanent impairment." Previously, in cases of rape or incest, women can have an abortion even if that standard is not met. The *Roe* case said doctors could consider "all factors . . . relevant to the well-being of the patient, including emotional and psychological health." Laws like Ohio's and Georgia's may be upheld by Kennedy and the Supreme Court. The doctors, in all but a few cases, are put in an impossible situation by those laws. We can't expect them to perform at their own risk.

Abortions are currently unavailable in many states that have already imposed regulations so burdensome on "abortion clinics" that the clinics cannot function. Those licensing requirements will spread, as will putting pressure on women seeking abortion. The Supreme Court will certainly uphold regulations requiring those women to first view ultrasound images of their fetuses and discuss the pain the aborted fetus will feel.

Fourteen states presently have laws criminalizing abortion—a "small" modification can result in "murder-type" sentences on doctors.

The result will look very much like the Red state–Blue state political map. The Red states would criminalize it, the Blue states would not. While not as divisive as slavery was in 1860, abortion rights would be the most polarizing event since then.

A recent Supreme Court case made that clear. The Supreme Court, on January 2006, refused to affirm a federal appeals court decision that said that the New Hampshire Parental Notification Act was unconstitutional.

Why?

Politics, pure and simple. Politics with a capital *P*. More subtle, perhaps, than *Bush v. Gore*, but politics nonetheless.

The Supreme Court judges have a commitment to maintaining the facade that theirs is a nonpolitical institution with extraordinary collegiality and agreement between the judges that this country is governed by an objective rule of law. We saw that commitment very recently as the small eruptions after *Bush v. Gore* were quickly papered over. Justice Ginsburg's criticism of the *Bush v. Gore* court and Day O'Connor's statements indicating her distress when she thought Gore had won are, according to these justices, aberrations of the past.

Since *Bush v. Gore*, many of the justices have written books and appeared on television and in the print media trying to show collegiality. Justice Breyer's recent book, *Activate Liberty: Interpreting Our Democratic Constitution*, is a paean to the institutional role of the Court. Today's justices have refused to acknowledge what many former Supreme Court justices have acknowledged, the divisive role politics plays in the Court.

Why did the pro-choice judges not write an opinion and express their view that the Parental Notification Act was unconstitutional? For the same reasons that the liberal judges did not continue to attack the Supreme Court after *Bush v. Gore*. They saw it as a losing battle and one that would only make clear that the Court makes decisions primarily along political and cultural fault lines.

The press gave us no real analysis of the New Hampshire case. Sound bites on cases are not enough. Too many cases get overlooked and those that do not are often misreported. A bit more detail than the media gives us is required, but only a very few Americans are really interested.

Justice O'Connor's analysis of *Roe v. Wade*—as in *Planned Parenthood v. Casey*—is more of a states' rights argument than a pro-choice argument. Recognizing the right for a woman to choose whether to have an abortion, she is willing to permit the states to regulate abortion in many ways—unless a state's regulation places an "undue" or substantial burden on the right to choose. The right persists, but the state's power to care for its citizens' health and welfare is quite broad—except when it begins to seriously infringe on the exercise of the right.

The *Casey* decision reaffirmed *Roe* in 1992—but only with the help of Justices Kennedy and O'Connor's crucial swing votes. The undue burden standard has, as Professor Marci Hamilton points out, left room for the states to heavily regulate—if not nearly eliminate—abortions.

The result is a wide variety of abortion regulation in the United States. Overturning *Roe*, as it now stands, will not result in a large shift in abortion policy for those states that would ban it by law since they have already effectively banned it by practice.

After *Casey*, the Evangelicals focused their attack on so-called partial-birth abortions, a term that has high emotional impact. In fact, they were attacking the safest medical procedures available, used in first-and occasionally second-and third-trimester abortions. Grisly pictures and stories of such abortions were sent to members of Congress, which in turn twice tried to pass laws making it a serious crime. President Clinton vetoed those bills, driving the Right-to-Lifers to lobby the states, many of which adopted these criminal bans. Then, in 1999, Dr. Leroy Carhart sought, in *Stenberg v. Carhart*, to challenge a Nebraska law that made performing partial-birth abortions— defined as "a procedure in which the doctor delivers vaginally, a living unborn child, before intentionally killing the child"—a felony punishable by up to twenty years in prison, a fine of $25,000, and revocation of the doctor's license. In fact, the statute was intentionally vague and could be applied to the safest first-and second-trimester procedures. It put physicians at constant risk of criminal prosecution, making abortions less accessible. The lower court and appeals court held the Nebraska law unconstitutional, and Justice Breyer, writing for a five-justice majority, agreed, for the Nebraska law permitted the misnamed partial-birth abortion if the mother's life was at stake. Today five justices are solid for reversal.

Let's look more closely at the partial birth abortion case since it tells us a great deal about Kennedy. Donald Stenberg, the named defendant and the attorney general of Nebraska, presented his case on April 20, 2000. His first sentence stopped his argument—he loudly declared that partial-birth abortion "borders on infanticide." The moderate members of the Court jumped on that rhetoric, pointing out there are criminal laws for killing infants, and there can be no infanticide until there is an infant. "Have you read *Roe v. Wade?*" Justice Blackmun asked. Stenberg said he had. Justice Scalia jumped in to help Stenberg; permitting the killing of a fetus, he observed, "can coerce public perception to other forms of killing fetuses or children outside the womb, right?" Yes, agreed Stenberg, that is what he meant.

His opponent argued that, "The Nebraska statute seeks to eliminate the central principle of Roe and Casey. It seeks to reverse the supremacy of women's health over fetal interests throughout pregnancy." He said that if the doctor decides to use a particular procedure that is the safest for the mother, then he should be permitted to do it.

And, indeed, it was on these points that Breyer's opinion focused. He said that *Casey* held that laws "designed to further the state's interest in fetal life" are unconstitutional if they place an undue burden on the woman's decision prior to "fetal viability." Casey prohibits laws having the "purpose or effect of placing a substantial obstacle in the path of a woman seeking an abortion of a nonviable fetus." Breyer concluded that the Nebraska statute is such an obstacle because of its vagueness. He rejected Nebraska's argument that the legislature intended to ban only Dilation & Curettage procedures. In reviewing the medical evidence, Breyer cited the rulings of other federal courts that had reached similar conclusions.

Stenberg could have been lost and yet *Roe* saved it. But it would have been another deep wound. Kennedy, voting in the minority, said that if the procedure was offensive to one's conscience (as this was to his), then it could not be used, even if it were the safest abortion procedure. From there to a state statute that prohibits, on moral grounds, the safest procedure, is but a short step. And with Alito replacing O'Connor, Kennedy swings into the majority.

Bork attacked my view that the Rehnquist Court undercut *Roe v. Wade*. Far from eviscerating the right to abortion, the Rehnquist Court, Bork says, protected that right so fiercely that in *Stenberg v. Carhart*, it struck down Nebraska's prohibition of partial-birth abortions in a way that may well doom all such statutes in the future. The language of Justice Kennedy in *Stenberg*, while far more measured, evinces the same passion and views as Bork.

On the same day as *Stenberg*, the Court vacated the Seventh Circuit Court of Appeals' ruling in *Hope Clinic v. Ryan*,[50] upholding the Illinois and Wisconsin partial-birth abortion bans, sending the case back to the Seventh Circuit to be reconsidered in light of the Court's decision in *Stenberg*. Federal courts since have struck down the nineteen remaining bans that have been challenged. Bans enacted in eleven states—Georgia, Indiana, Kansas, Mississippi, North Dakota, Ohio, Oklahoma, South Carolina, South Dakota, Tennessee, and Utah—are currently enforceable, but only three (Utah, Ohio, and Kansas) would likely survive the Court's *Stenberg* ruling since they include a health exception. But with *Stenberg* soon to be reversed (if the Court deals directly with that issue), the law will change dramatically.

On February 3, 2002, the Justice Department asked a federal appeals court to review an Ohio ban on the procedure. The Ohio law passed the month before the *Stenberg* decision will reverse it. When the federal judge struck down the Ohio procedure, he said the health exception did not ensure that physicians would provide the best procedure. Ohio appealed, and the government jumped in.

It is rare for the Justice Department to intervene in a state abortion dispute in a lower U.S. court rather than wait for a showdown at the Supreme Court. Not since 1992, when the first President Bush was in office, has the White House backed an abortion restriction in court. The Court declined to take the case.

The Supreme Court in the 2007–2008 term will, if it gets to the merits, reverse *Stenberg v. Carhart*, and will find the Partial-Birth Abortion Act of 2003 unconstitutional. Alito will become the swing vote. Justice Kennedy, who previously voted to uphold the act on the grounds that a partial–birth abortion shocked his conscience, will be in the majority. Any illusion that Justice Kennedy would step into Justice O'Connor's "swing position" will be shattered.

A recent study found that 94 percent of the counties in the Midwest and 91 percent in the South had no abortion provider. Thirty-four percent of all women in the U.S. live in counties that do not have one. That is the situation with *Roe v. Wade*.

Some states are way beyond Ohio's and Georgia's efforts to stop abortions. South Dakota's new law, the most sweeping anti-abortion law passed since *Roe v. Wade*, permits an abortion in which rape and incest are involved only if the mother's life is at stake. If the mother's life is not at stake, then she must bear the child. But by the time the South Dakota law arrives in the Supreme Court, the probabilities are that two of the present liberal justices will be gone. Justice Stevens is eighty-five and the next oldest judge is Justice Ginsburg. If they are replaced by conservatives, a slightly softer law like South Dakota's will become the model for other states.

The decision in the partial-birth abortion case coming up next term and a South Dakota-type law give us a window into the next twenty-five years of Supreme Court decisions. The original anti-abortion plan to eviscerate the present law in small ways—by parental notification rules, waiting periods before abortions, and enormous financial and paperwork requirements for clinics, will soon become unnecessary.

We are seeing an expanded attack on *Roe v. Wade* through endless restrictions, even though the polls show a reversal will cost the Republicans votes. Encouraged, conservatives will also start to make a frontal attack on some of the other significant decisions of Roosevelt's New Deal Court and the Warren Court.

President Clinton twice vetoed bills calling for a federal ban on "partial-birth" abortions. The White House's support of Ohio's law could lead other states to write laws matching Ohio's. In the brief it filed with the U.S. Court of Appeals for the Sixth Circuit, the Justice Department justified its intervention because President Bush supports a federal ban. The same week, the Bush administration announced to the twenty-ninth annual Conservative Political Action Conference that a child would now become eligible for coverage under the Children's Health Insurance Program at conception. The crowd erupted in cheers.

Representative Henry A. Waxman, a California Democrat, argued that the administration could have broadened coverage to pregnant

women by many other means and that the new rule was not a serious policy effort but "an ideological statement" aimed at pleasing
the administration's conservative base. But, it's even more dangerous. There will be new legislation and regulations in different social
services areas, passed by the federal and state governments, which
establish that the unborn fetus at conception has rights that are different from, and perhaps superior to, the rights of the mother.

Justice Scalia wants courts and legislatures to set out rules that
will make life simple for courts and litigants. He says judges merely
"find" or "discover" the law and do not ever make it. In a 1990 case,
he said, "to hold a governmental act to be unconstitutional is not to
announce that we forbid it, but that the Constitution forbids it."
Justice Edward White, attacking Scalia, said, "Even though the justice is not naive enough (nor does he think the Framers were naive
enough) to be unaware that judges in a real sense make law, he suggests that judges (in an unreal sense, I suppose) should never concede that they do no more than discover it, hence suggesting that
there are citizens who are naive enough to believe them."

Scalia explains the contradiction between believing in judicial
restraint while arguing for the easy overturning of precedent, by
saying, "I do not care how analytically consistent with analogous
precedents such a holding might be, nor how socially desirable in
a judge's view." This refusal to adhere to precedent contradicts what
he has previously written elsewhere and decided in at least one concurring opinion.

While the legislature can be criticized for not producing clear
statutes, Scalia's attempted restructuring of our government is not
the answer. Scalia's willingness to overrule Congress and treat it
like a low-level trial court is based on his belief that congressional
laws are more a reflection of lobbyists and politics than of the will
of the people. In this, he was joined by O'Connor, the only justice
who had been a legislator prior to being on the Court. Together,
they rejected reliance on legislative history and legislative fact-finding. Their approach, when reviewing legislation, was solely to inter-

pret the words; since words are open to interpretation, the justices have enormous latitude.

Scalia draws a distinction between "original meaning" and "original intent." He claims to look at the words of the Constitution, not at the intent in the Framers' minds. Original meaning, he says, permitted the possibility of an evolving Constitution. An original intentionist would say that a provision means today exactly what it meant in 1789; if flogging were permissible then, it would be permissible now. In other words, the "Constitution is not meant to be elastic," and a court of nine judges cannot fill it up with whatever content the current times "seem" to require.

Scalia's argument for being an originalist is elegantly justified—"Our Constitution is a covenant running from the first generation of Americans to us and then to future generations. It is a coherent succession. Each generation must learn anew that the Constitution's written terms embody ideas and aspirations that must survive more ages than one." Drawn to originalism because it mandates a "rock-solid unchanging Constitution," Scalia's voice, thus far, is still a minority one; the Supreme Court does not have four other members who conceptually agree with him. But one more conservative member gives the conservative Court a substantial "originalist" bloc—one that may pull other conservative judges along. The right of privacy, which forms the foundation for the abortion cases, has been rejected in every case that the conservatives on the Roberts Court have considered it.

The Supreme Court's second privacy and search warrant case, *Herdson v. Michigan*, reached the same conclusion as the first. The privacy claim was again rejected. But *Herdson*'s holding was far broader, rejecting legal concepts that predated the Constitution and reached back to fourteenth-century British law. For centuries, it has always been understood that police can't just break into a house. For fifty years, here and in England, there has been an exclusionary rule that says if police with a search warrant rush into house without a warrant or without knocking and announcing they are police officers, then prosecutor cannot use the illegally seized evidence in trial.

The four dissenters said that the Court's decision rejected ninety years of precedent and all but repealed the rule that protected the privacy and dignity of people in their homes. As important as the privacy issue is that the Roberts Court specifically reversed the Warren, Burger, and Rehnquist courts' holdings that illegally seized evidence cannot be admitted into trial. The reason is not hard to understand. To allow police to do it would encourage police to violate constitutional protections to get evidence.

The Rehnquist Court, because of O'Connor, repeatedly said illegally seized evidence is not admissible. The *Herdson v. Michigan* case was first argued while O'Connor was on the bench and then set for reargument after Alito came. At the original hearing, O'Connor, consistent with her earlier rulings, evinced sympathy for the defendants' position. "Is there no policy of protecting the homeowner a little bit and the sanctity of the home from this immediate entry?" she asked.

Kennedy joined the conservatives while also paying homage to the preexisting law. "The continued operation of the exclusioning rule is not in doubt," he said. He was correct—it was not in doubt because it had been breached. He also disingenuously said, "It bears repeating that it is a serious matter if law enforcement officers violate the sanctity of the home by ignoring the requisites of lawful entry." But not sufficiently serious, it seems, as to uphold the privacy right. Privacy, the right to be left alone and to be free of government intrusion, whether it comes up in criminal or abortion areas, is very different now than when O'Connor was on the bench. We shall see that right severly narrowed now that Alito is on the Court and Kennedy is the swing vote.

Herdson v. Michigan established the new "Don't Bother to Knock Rule," a rule that says illegally seized evidence can now be admitted. Kennedy's majority opinion disregards principles that date back both to thirteenth-century England and to 1914 in the United States. So much for precedent.

Justice Scalia said upholding the prior cases that upheld the exclusionary rule "would be forcing the public today to pay for the sins and inadequacies of a legal regime that existed almost half a century ago." The police, he said, are not as they once were—they now do not violate people's rights on the same scale as before in part because they are better trained and have more sophisticated technologies. This logic reduces the value of precedent to nearly nothing.

Scalia's decision shows the hypocrisy of his "originalist" position that you do not take into consideration evolving times. Breyer correctly said Scalia's argument is one "this Court until now has consistently rejected."

In 2006 the Roberts Court was faced with an appeal for a murder conviction in which the death row inmate Paul House claimed that modern DNA testing, which was not available at the time of his 1986 conviction, showed he was innocent. Roberts, Scalia, and Thomas voted to uphold the 1986 conviction. Alito was not on the bench when the case was argued. Kennedy, joining the liberals, wrote the 5–3 majority opinion, finding that the DNA evidence excluded House as the source of semen on Carolyn Muncey, the murder victim. Commentators used the case to emphasize a conservative defeat.

But the decision was narrowly written, a bloodless, technical decision. It again made me aware that it had now been nearly two decades since there had been a powerful, humane, passionate liberal voice on the Court. Justices Brennan or Marshall would have written this decision with feeling and outrage. Even if they were only one voice in a dissent, at least there would be some ringing voice for justice. America sorely misses that voice.

House is of minimal precedent. The Court sent the case back to the lower court. House can still be executed. The precedent does not cover the next DNA case that comes to the Court. The semen proved to be not House's, but Muncey's husband's, who had confessed to his wife's murder. Kennedy also claimed the prosecution was sloppy with most of the evidence in the case. The only connection at trial between House and the murder was the semen. At the trial the jury heard that House tried to commit suicide—the state said because he knew he was guilty.

Notwithstanding all of those "errors," a trial that was a mockery of justice and that saw an innocent man jailed for decades, three justices were prepared to see House die.

Chapter Three

The Federal Government against the People

Let's do away with the SEC.
—The Federalist Society newsletter (2002)

◆   ◆   ◆

How could fifty years of law, including much of today's legal architecture, be undone?

Consider that, after the preamble, the first sentence of the Constitution says, "All legislative powers herein granted shall be vested in a Congress of the United States."

The Roosevelt and Warren courts believed this sentence permitted Congress to enact laws to set up federal agencies, such as the Federal Trade Commission, the Securities and Exchange Commission, and the Environmental Protection Administration. Because Congress delegated the power to them, these agencies could create laws, rules, and regulations to regulate American commerce and protect Americans.

The conservatives, who controlled the Court before 1937, when the Roosevelt Court began, believed that this first sentence did not permit Congress to delegate lawmaking authority to others and that the agencies in place since 1937 were not permitted and were unconstitutional. According to the nondelegation theory, Congress may regulate only laws binding on the federal government, not on private citizens or state or local governments.

In 2001, Judge Douglas H. Ginsberg of the Federal Appeals Court in Washington, pointing out that nondelegation theory was the law before the Roosevelt Court, says the memory of this doctrine "banished for standing in opposition to unlimited government, is kept alive by a few scholars who labor on in the hope of a resurrection, a second coming of the Constitutional liberty—even if perhaps not in their own lifetimes"—Bork's Constitution in exile.

Bork would return us to the pre–Roosevelt Court. Congress would not regulate child labor, could not set maximum hours or minimum wages, and would have no power to regulate the environment or to try to stop antitrust cartels.

Conservatives are correct when they assume that legislators vote "partly on the basis of how their vote will look to the public rather than whether it helps the public." Judge Douglas H. Ginsberg argued that from the legislators' perspective, a publicly perceived benefit that outweighs a publicly perceived cost is a bargain—regardless of whether the real cost outweighs the real benefit. This model, Ginsburg argues, does not depend on public stupidity in order to explain legislative action, however. Rather, it distinguishes between sophisticated, concentrated interests, that are unlikely to be fooled, and the general public, which doesn't pay attention because the stakes are small for any one individual. Hence, he concludes, the agencies, rather than benefit the public, harm them.

David Schoenbrod, a conservative scholar, has extended Judge Ginsberg's insight to a breathtakingly simple conclusion: the Supreme Court should declare unconstitutional "any statute in which Congress delegates any power to another body, whether agency or court, to decide what conduct [is] prohibited." His alternative solution would require that any regulation imposed by any agency in excess of "a specified amount, say a hundred million dollars, not take effect unless affirmatively approved by both Houses of Congress—of course, the lower the threshold, the better." His solution would destroy the agencies, provide a rich new area for lobbyists, and establish another source of illegal income to Congressmen. It would also make U.S. and foreign corporations virtually a law unto themselves.

The law is seen as an obstacle to free marketers, except when it provides remedies for default and makes the country safe for capitalism. The Federalist Society several years ago sponsored a panel in Chicago called "Rolling Back the New Deal: Judicial Review of Economic Regulations." The panel featured, among other speakers, the University of Chicago Law School Professor Richard Epstein. The program brochure said, "Since the New Deal, the Supreme Court has taken a hands-off approach to economic regulations. If an economic regulation had any rational basis, it was generally deemed constitutional. Now however . . . the Court has begun to look more closely at legislation to determine if it unconstitutionally takes property from businesses or individuals. If a law requires a business to pay for activities that occurred long ago, the retroactive liability may violate the Takings Clause of the Fifth Amendment."

The Takings Clause provides, "[N]or shall private property be taken for public use, without just compensation." According to Epstein, that one sentence covers virtually any governmental "interference" with an owner's right to possess, use, and dispose of property. That one sentence says a great deal, but whether it can be put to the radical use that Epstein wants rests in the hands of our nine justices. Traditionally called the power of eminent domain, this clause allows the government to physically take one's property, even under protest, for a public use—a park, a hospital, a dam, a public highway—in exchange for just compensation.

The discussion that evening articulated both the Right's desire for deregulation and the legal argument that supports it. The desire to protect the free-market business ethic has been turned into an article of faith. Even though the Enron bankruptcy and the damage it has done to all Americans can be traced to deregulation, the Right still pushes its agenda before the courts and the legislature.

This panel and others like it brought together the chief theorists of the reactionary movement, as they announced their view of how law in the economic sphere had changed over the past twenty years and would continue to change over the next twenty years. They claimed that five- and six-year-old Rehnquist Court decisions eviscerating congressional power are now treated as "settled law," and that the body of new law gives the Supreme Court the building blocks to "deregulate society and restore property rights to its proper place." Professor Epstein and the New Federalists pointed out that the Supreme Court majority is incrementally and relentlessly moving forward. Although The Court established its supremacy in limiting individual freedoms and rolled back much of the Warren and Burger Court's advances, Epstein still found the Court lacking because so much of the New Deal law was still on the books. The deregulation of business—in part achieved by striking down federal child labor, minimum wage, and maximum hour laws—was essential to reap the benefits of the free market. Epstein's free-market views extend into every area of the law—from approving voucher programs, financial aid to parochial schools because it gives parents "choice" and it reduces public school monopolies, to claiming that desegregation should end because the costs are too high and the method too invested with governmental control. His positions, not all yet accepted, are the harbinger of the future. What Epstein urges is nothing less than the wholesale betrayal of the constitutional values most of us believe in.

Epstein's panel resurrected legal and political arguments successfully made between 1890 and 1916. That period is known in legal culture as the *Lochner* era. To evoke it is to evoke a time long past, a time of strikes and sweatshops, low wages and long hours, tenement living and economic tumult. The federal and state cases that came down during this time reflected the benefits and costs created by the industrial revolution. With money flowing into capital expansion, the Court was prepared to accept the brutal price of that growth.

In 1895, as a result of new progressive forces and the beginning of unionism, New York State passed legislation to regulate sanitary conditions as well as to reform working conditions and reduce work hours. Ten years later, the Supreme Court, in the 5–4 *Lochner v. New York* decision, invalidated the New York regulation. Justice Rufus Peckham said that New York's attempt to regulate hours of labor in bakeries "necessarily interfered with the right of contract between the employer and the employee." Denying there were valuable economic reasons for the state regulations, Peckham held that the liberty protected by the Fourteenth Amendment included the right to purchase and sell labor. Any statute interfering with it would be invalid "unless there are circumstances which exclude that right"—slavery being one such circumstance. *Lochner* stands for the judiciary thwarting the will of its elected officials. The case is an example of a Court asserting its supremacy over the legislature and undermining the legislature's constitutional responsibility to respond to economic and social problems. When given a chance, the Rehnquist Court now asserts that same authority to help big business at the expense of the people.

Lochner, the case we saw referenced a half-century later by Hugo Black in *Griswold v. Connecticut*, is well-known for its two dissents by Justices Oliver Wendell Holmes and John Harlan. As the latter argued, the New York legislature had sound reasoning for the passage of the law:

> The labor of the bakers is among the hardest and most laborious imaginable, because it has to be performed under conditions injurious to the health of those engaged in it. It is hard, very hard work, not only because it requires a great deal of physical exertion in an overheated workshop and during unreasonably long hours, but [also because the] constant inhaling of flour dust causes inflammation of the lungs and of the bronchial tubes [and the] long hours of toil to which all bakers are subjected produce rheumatism, cramps, and swollen legs. [Nearly] all bakers are pale-faced and of more delicate health than the workers of other crafts . . . they seldom live over their fiftieth year.

Yet with the exact same information that Harlan had before him, Peckham reached the exact opposite factual conclusion. "It is manifest to us that the [law here] has no such direct relation to and no substantial effect upon the health of the employees as to justify us in regarding the section as really a health law."

Justice Holmes' famous dissent started with one of the most memorable passages in American legal writing. "The Fourteenth Amendment does not enact Mr. Herbert Spencer's Social Statistics. A constitution is not intended to embody a particular economic theory, whether of paternalism and the organic relation of the citizen to the State or of laissez faire. It is made for people of fundamentally differing views, and the accident of our finding certain opinions natural and familiar or novel and even shocking ought not to conclude our judgment upon the question whether statutes embodying them conflict with the Constitution of the United States. General propositions do not decide concrete cases. The decision will depend on a judgment or intuition more subtle than any articulate major premise."

For many years thereafter the Supreme Court, because of the *Lochner* rationale, continued to reject state wage and safety laws. The child labor legislation, also declared unconstitutional, was seen by the 5–4 majority in *Hammer v. Dagenhart* (1918)[51] as something that could put an end to "all freedom of commerce . . . and thus our system of government [would] be practically destroyed." It is the logic of Scalia, Rehnquist, and Thomas: that government ought not interfere with the free market; that the benefits of the free market will flow down to the employees; and that there is a greater danger from regulation than from potentially abusive employers. Governmental paternalism is the great danger.

But if any side could be charged with "interference," it would be *Lochner* and *Hammer*, the dissenters said, where the Court substituted its views over those of elected officials. Indeed, the Court, headed until the Great Depression by Chief Justice (and former president) William Howard Taft, invalidated state and federal regulatory laws in greater numbers than any previous Court until the Rehnquist Court. The free market was made freer. Taft's Court created new rights for the benefit of business so that it would be unhampered by the government. The right of contract, not found in the Constitution, was established by this conservative Court, in the same way, today's right-wing conservative jurists argue, that the Roosevelt, Warren, and early Burger Courts created many rights not found in the Constitution.

In truth, even before 1932, the Supreme Court was starting to shift from its role as a protector of business. The New Deal Court did not discover, and was not the first Court to try to protect, individual rights against business interests. Some Court decisions in the late 1920s were critical of the extent to which the legal system was protecting laissez-faire capitalism at the expense of individual rights.

When, after Franklin D. Roosevelt's election, the Democrats began to experiment with national economic regulation, the Supreme Court responded in 1934 and 1935 by striking down much of the New Deal. After Roosevelt's 1936 landslide reelection, the President denounced the Court for imposing its own views of laissez-faire economics for those of the people, and he sought ways to remove the Court as an obstacle. The Court was composed of aged railroad lawyers and business executives. Roosevelt proposed in 1937 to expand the court if any of the existing justices remained on the bench after the age of seventy, in order to dilute the power of the "nine old men" who were stopping progress. Even though the court-packing plan failed in the Senate, the political pressure forced the justices to remove themselves as obstacles to the New Deal. The Court's "switch in time saved nine," as it changed from a posture of judicial activism to one of judicial restraint, giving the president and Congress broad deference to regulate the economy in an increasingly interdependent world.

But it was not until 1941, in *United States v. Darby Lumber*,[52] that the Supreme Court, in a 9–0 decision, upheld Congress' right to set minimum wages and maximum hours for all employees who worked on goods shipped in interstate commerce. This was when, finally, *Hammer*, the child labor law case, was totally rejected. Justice Harlan F. Stone invoked "the powerful and now classic dissent of Mr. Justice Holmes," in the *Lochner* case, to uphold Congress' nearly unreviewable power to interpret the Commerce Clause.

Epstein claims that the "Marxist view" that "minimum wage laws, for example, can boost the least fortunate workers' share of the gain to a larger, and more just, proportion" is wrong. Instead, he says, minimum wage laws for adults and children "induce some employers to reduce their work forces, others to change non-wage terms of the contract. It will narrow the gap between lower and higher skilled employees and thus reduce workers' incentives to invest in their own human capital. The higher the minimum wage, the more likely that some firms will exit from the market."

His concern, and the concern of today's right-wing jurists, is to value property rights over personal rights. One of the most important cases in the New Deal's judicial revolution, *United States v. Carolene*,[53] decided in 1938, is, according to Epstein, wrong. *Carolene* established a different and higher level of protection for personal rights than for property rights. *Carolene*, the underpinning for the next sixty years of law, is today being rejected by much of this Court and will firmly be entombed if one or two more right-wing jurists are appointed.

Justice Stone, who later became chief justice, wrote the opinion in *Carolene* upholding a federal law, justified by the Commerce Clause, prohibiting the shipment of "filled" milk (skim milk mixed with non-milk fats) as an exercise of its national police power to protect the citizens of all states. Refuting the minority argument that Congress did not have the authority to expand the Commerce Clause to achieve that result, Stone said laws "affecting ordinary commercial transactions" were to be presumed constitutional and struck down only if lacking "some rational basis within the knowledge and experience of the legislators." He added his famous "first freedoms" footnote, suggesting that there may be a stronger case for holding a law unconstitutional if the laws are aimed at the political process, at free speech, religion, or privacy, in which case "they are subjected to more exacting judicial scrutiny" than laws dealing only with economic matters.

Because of the *Carolene* case and other New Deal court decisions, American law since 1938 has been to allow Congress to decide what is right and wrong for the country on economic matters, with respect given to the judicial system as the government branch charged with protecting individual rights against federal or state intrusion. It has been an understanding uninterrupted until 1996; the Supreme Court had not struck down one congressional regulation. Since then, the present Court majority, through a variety of new constitutional strategies and the reinterpretation of old established principles, has virtually consigned this important New Deal legacy to mothballs. The concepts behind *Lochner* are being resurrected, and *Carolene* has been firmly, though not explicitly, rejected. The test going forward is what is best for the free market and not what is best for the people.

One argument for the preferred freedoms doctrine is that some rights, such as free speech, are higher on the ladder of rights our Constitution gives us. We cannot be a free people without the Court's aggressive protection of our freedom of speech, press, and religion, but we can be a free people without the Courts zealous protection of our economic rights. The Bill of Rights explicitly contains political rights, while many economic rights rest on creative interpretations of the due process clause. In this way, the Constitution justifies a greater protection of personal rights than economic rights.

Professor Gary Lawson of Boston University, writing in the 1994 *Harvard Law Review*, speaking for himself and a large body of conservative scholars, says: "The post–New Deal administrative state is unconstitutional." He has no difficulty overruling *Carolene*. The judiciary is the sole interpreter of the Constitution, he believes, and there is no need to defer to Congressional fact-finding or conclusions, both of which are irrelevant. Precedent, he writes, is in general not required by the law. Because judicial deference need not be paid to judicial meaning, nearly any case can be overruled. Lawson, as well as voluminous conservative literature and certain appellate judges, justify the resurrection of *Lochner* and *Hammer*, validate the attack on the post–1937 Court, and support Epstein, as well as the decisions in *Lopez*, *Kimmel*, and *Garret*.

Since 1986, Rehnquist, Scalia, and Thomas, whenever they can, return to the logic of *Hammer* and *Lochner*. The 1938 Fair Labor Standards Act (FLSA), which set minimum wage and maximum hours standards, was the last major piece of New Deal social legislation. The act was expanded in 1974 to include state and local governments; but in 1976, a 5–4 decision, *National League of Cities v. Usery*,[54] the Supreme Court struck down that wage extension for encroaching on the states' "traditional functions and their ability to function effectively." Writing in dissent, Justice Brennan declared that the Court was overreaching, ignoring a carefully considered decision of Congress. Calling it a "catastrophic judicial body blow at Congress['] power under the Commerce Clause," he pointed out that the logic of the Court could undo much of the New Deal achievement. He saw it as the rehabilitation of *Lochner*.

But then the Court swung. Nine years later, in 1985, another 5–4 decision, the *Garcia v. San Antonio Metropolitan Transit Authority*,[55] overruled *Usery*. States, the Court now said, were not immune from following national overtime and minimum wage requirements. Garcia, the appellant, would henceforth receive his overtime pay because one of the majority justices in *Garcia*, Harry Blackmun, who'd voted with the *Usery* majority, had changed his mind. Like a Ping-Pong ball being paddled back and forth, the law can be changed repeatedly. Blackmun is long gone, and today's Court is different. If a case close to *Usery* and *Garcia* comes to the Court now, the result will be the same as *Usery*, with the likelihood of an unequivocal resurrection of *Lochner*.

Both sides in *Lopez v. United States*, *Printz v. United States*, and *Morrison v. United States* referred in their briefs to *Wickard v. Fil-*

burn, the 9–0 1942 Supreme Court case. Justice Stevens mentioned the 1942 case during oral arguments in *Lopez*. The *Wickard* reference in those arguments, evoking the long-ago struggle to give Congress the power necessary to help govern the country, reminds us that the line defining interstate commerce is often difficult to draw. Congress and the Roosevelt Court recognized that formal, previous distinctions were not helpful, and that it was more important to look at the reality of each situation.

The *Wickard* case of 1942 turned out to be the Court's high-water mark of its expansive view of Congress' ability to determine the limits of the Commerce Clause. It best indicates how completely the Supreme Court had come around in agreeing that federal intrusion is necessary for the country to function. Reading *Wickard* in the context of *Lopez* and *Morrison* shows how a legal system such as ours, built on precedent, develops and operates. The history of the Commerce Clause in this century is book-ended by a $120 fine imposed in the *Wickard* case and by Christy Brzonkala's failed damage claim.

The specific question in *Wickard* was whether Congress' Agricultural Act seeking to enforce wheat quotas could be applied, under the Commerce Clause, to wheat that never left the farm and supposedly never went into interstate commerce. This was the same legal principle as in the *Lopez*, *Printz*, and *Morrison* cases. Is the activity involved in interstate commerce? Does it affect interstate commerce in a substantial way, or is it purely or primarily a local matter? In deciding *Wickard*, the court had to look at the same part of the Constitution the Warren Court looked at when it upheld the constitutionality of the Civil Rights Act of 1964 and the Rehnquist Court looked at in deciding *Lopez* and *Printz*.

When Roscoe Filburn's challenge of his $120 fine reached the Court in 1942, it was a body that had been dramatically restructured by President Roosevelt's new appointments. Had the case gotten to the Court in the early 1930s, Filburn would have won; the Court would have concluded that Congress interpreted the Commerce Clause too widely. Instead, the entire Court agreed that Filburn's tiny two hundred thirty-nine bushels of wheat consumed but not marketed still had an effect upon interstate commerce and thus could be regulated. In the early 1940s, more than 20 percent of all the wheat grown in the country never left the farm. By consuming their own grain, Filburn and thousands of farmers like him affected the overall demand and market price of wheat. Since their actions taken together clearly had an impact on interstate commerce they were, the Court agreed, subject to federal regulation.

The 9–0 ruling in *Wickard* rejected formality in the interpretation of the Commerce Clause and deferred to Congress' view of reality. *Wickard*, *Lopez*, and *Morrison*, more than a half-century apart, talk to one another and to us. Judge Souter, referring to *Wickard* in the *Morrison* case, said that the five conservative judges' attempt to circumscribe the commerce power "can only be seen as a revival of similar efforts that led to near tragedy for the Court."

Christy Brzonkala's lawyer and the government lawyers in *Lopez* and *Printz*, as well as the Court's dissenting judges, believed *Wickard* set the contours for the law. If you could regulate home-grown and home-consumed wheat because it affected interstate commerce and therefore the nation, so, too, could you uphold federal laws that give a raped woman a claim for damages and one that penalized gun possession near a school. But when the composition of the Court changed in the early 1990s, with Brennan and Marshall gone and Clarence Thomas present, the Court started to relentlessly strike down congressional laws using the Commerce Clause to protect the personal rights of individuals.

The majority decision in *Lopez* told us that the Court was rethinking all of the Commerce Clause cases and preferred freedoms cases decided by the New Deal Court. For the first time, it told us, starkly and most clearly, that any federal legislation, whether about guns or child labor, would be examined very closely—and that if Congress passed maximum hours and minimum wage laws, such as existed in the *Usery* case, the Court would now rule as it had then. *Garcia* would be a dead letter. As Justice Stevens said, the present

Court's logic "would undermine most of [the Court's] post–New Deal Commerce clause jurisprudence."

At the same time that Reagan became president, the Chicago School of Economics, along with the University of Chicago's School of Law, gave rise to the law and economics movement, providing a new rationale for limits on legislative decision making. That conservative movement is today one of the most powerful forces in changing the law's direction and completing the legal revolution. Interestingly, it involves the application of economics to an ever-increasing range of legal fields. Free-market legal theory seeks to empty legal doctrine of socially binding moral content and aspirations by reinstating the primacy of the individual or business, who must be free to do whatever it, he, or she wants, unless it, he, or she is paid for any legal constraints put on that freedom by the government. In other words, if the government wants to regulate, it will have to pay such a heavy price that it will be encouraged or, in fact, forced, to deregulate.

Richard Posner is the seminal influence in the law and economics movement. Few jurists have been more important and, for many valid reasons, more respected, than he. A graduate of Harvard Law School, a clerk for Justice Brennan, a law professor at Stanford and then at the University of Chicago, he was then appointed in 1981 by Ronald Reagan to the U.S. Court of Appeals for the Seventh Circuit. Because Posner has written so much, has been so provocative, and is over sixty, it is unlikely he is a candidate for the Supreme Court. Posner's relentless decisions and prolific writings dominate the circuit court he sits on, which has jurisdiction over Illinois, Michigan, Indiana, and Wisconsin. Indeed, the Supreme Court and some circuit courts have in a number of cases referred to his economic analysis of law, giving it added legitimacy.

The Posnerian analysis supports the New Right in areas besides pure economics. His is a worldview that admittedly "manifests a conservative political bias." In his scheme, capital punishment has a deterrent effect, legislation designed to protect consumers frequently ends up hurting them, no-fault automobile insurance is probably inefficient, and securities regulation may be a waste of time.

The Roberts Court will seek to reject much of the law developed after 1937. Posner's ideas will be one of the new Court's foundations. In his book, *Economic Analysis of the Law* (1993), Posner says, "The pre–New Deal Courts were on solid ground when [they] refused to enforce agreements to join unions, enjoined picketing, and enforced yellow dog contracts." Posner says that health, welfare, and safety laws enacted by the state and federal governments are not necessary because "the employer has a selfish interest in providing the optimal level of worker health and safety." Posner argues that the employer will look out best for his workers' benefits; that paternal employers rather than a paternal government will lead to efficiency and wealth for all and is achieved best by the invisible hand of Adam Smith. The administrative state is to be dispensed with, as are all safety nets like Social Security and subsidies. This new Court agrees.

The goal of law, as of economics, is efficiency; and efficiency is defined as wealth maximization. The law should intervene, Posner tells us, "to reprehend only that which is inefficient," and even then the law's role should be limited since the "market punishes inefficiency faster and better than the machinery of the law." To Posner, the New Deal Court's rulings "were attempts to suppress competition under the guise of promoting the general welfare." The acceptance of this doctrine would result, as Posner rightly says, in a "seismic constitutional change."

Because all legal rights have costs, he articulates and promotes a cost-benefit analysis of the law. Posner's cost-benefit analysis has had remarkable success in tort law and is now being applied to constitutional law. Its strategy is to ask the courts to decide cases on an economic basis—to put a dollar figure on the cost to society of protecting individual rights and then to ask if it is worth it. He and Epstein agree that large amounts of money should not be spent on desegregation efforts, or on propping up the public school system by denying governmental monies to parochial schools that precludes them from competing. Posner even looked at the decision in *Bush v. Gore* (of which he approved) through a cost-benefit analysis and determined that the Supreme Court was correct largely because, had the Supreme Court not quickly rushed in, the costs of the imminent constitutional crisis would have been greater. He argues for the constitutionality of the Patriot Act using a cost-benefit analysis: individual rights "should be curtailed to the extent that the benefits in greater security outweigh the costs in reduced liberty."

Posner's cost-benefit analysis reduces law to dollars and cents. If the financial benefits of regulation are exceeded by its costs, then there should be no regulation. He says that if requiring low emissions standards or other environmental protections outweigh cost-benefit analysis, then environmental protection laws should not be upheld. He argues that air quality is not a value to be used when considering the validity of environmental law.

Posner applies his efficiency standards to argue that juries are an unnecessary expense because judges preside at both nonjury and jury trials. He recalls fondly the income tax cases of the nineteenth century, when the Supreme Court ruled invalid the 1894 federal income tax law. He wants the free market to triumph over regulation. For the Chicago School of Economics, the law's role should be limited, and Posner himself has done much to translate his market theories into legal doctrine.

Posner's analysis of the law is of a kind with his other empirical studies. To him, all aspects of life are on a balance sheet. He has argued that a higher proportion of black women than white women are fat because the supply of eligible black men is limited, thus black women find the likelihood of profiting from attaining an elegant figure too small to compensate for the costs of dieting.

The right wing in legal thinking supports the right wing in the economic arena. Political and economic argument has been transformed into constitutional argument, and the battle over economics and the future of the administrative state has moved into the courts and away from Congress.

Like his former colleague at the University of Chicago Law School, Richard Epstein sees a half-century of protective regulation as harming friends and helping enemies. Laura Ingalls Wilder's book, *Little House on the Prairie*, Epstein claims, shows that "the children in the factories were certainly not as well off as we would like, but they were probably better off than they would have been back on the farm, or than if they had been left in the city without any opportunity to sell their labor. Their families had voted to leave the farm or the old country with their feet, as a matter of life and death." Laws limiting child labor should be reversed because they may well have been misguided initiatives that inflicted harm upon the very persons they were ostensibly intended to benefit.

Supreme Court judges' decisions often mask their true bias—but by looking at the scholars that the Conservative school relies on we can illuminate the hidden text. Some of Epstein's harshest rhetoric is directed against welfare and government entitlement programs. He, like Posner, has been deeply critical of the humanity driving *Goldberg v. Kelly* (1970),[56] a 6–3 Supreme Court decision, called by Justice Brennan one of his most important cases, "the opening shot in the modern due process revolution." Today, that case—little-known except to legal specialists—has been undercut by procedural obstacles. Brennan, in *Goldberg*, found that welfare benefits could not be terminated without giving the recipient a chance to oppose that termination. Prior to that decision, welfare recipients were arbitrarily cut off from aid, often for no reason at all—and usually just to reduce the cost of welfare.

In the *Goldberg* majority opinion, Justice Brennan described what happened after two of the five plaintiffs had their benefits terminated:

> Angela Velez and her four young children were evicted for nonpayment of rent and all forced to live in one small room of a relative's already crowded apartment. The children had

little to eat during the four months it took the Department to correct its [termination] error. Esther Lett and her four children at once began to live on the handouts of impoverished neighbors; within two weeks all five required hospital treatment because of the inadequacy of their diet. Soon after, Esther Lett fainted in a welfare center while seeking an emergency food payment of $15 to feed herself and her family for three days.

The amount of monies to be gained by the Velez and Lett families were trivial as compared to the cost of the hearing. Due process be damned, say Epstein and Posner. By Posnerian logic, the costs and injustices of the hearings required by due process can be judged solely by a cost analysis. If the cost of the injustices are less than the cost of obtaining justice, the hearing should be cut back or ended.

Prior to *Goldberg v. Kelly*, a case in which I was one of the lawyers representing the plaintiffs, due process was required only where personal or property rights were adversely affected by governmental action. Brennan extended that due process right to anyone who had a "statutory entitlement" to benefits, and said the decision can be seen as expressing the importance of attention to the concrete human realities at stake in governmental conduct. From this perspective, *Goldberg* can be seen as injecting common sense into a system mired in abstraction, as can another Supreme Court case, *King v. Smith*,[57] which I argued in 1968. That case said that the welfare benefits of single mothers and their children had been wrongfully denied under an Alabama statute aimed at punishing women for having extramarital relationships. Finding that the state had disregarded the economic needs of the children, the Court here, as in *Goldberg*, attempted to protect the vulnerable from the unregulated free market. These cases draw the harshest anger from Epstein.

The Supreme Court, a prime player in effecting a transition from the free market to the safety net times of the New Deal, is now trying to turn the country back toward the laissez-faire state. A few more

conservative justices on the court and the fight will be over. As one federal court said, "Of the three fundamental principles which underlie
government, and for which the government exists, the protection of
life, liberty, and property, the chief of these is property."

Richard Pipes, now a professor at Harvard and formerly a Reagan National Security Council advisor, supports Epstein's analysis
and commitment to property rights over personal rights. "The
assault on property rights is not always apparent," he says, "because
it is carried out in the name of the common good—an elastic concept, defined by those whose interest it serves." For instance, Pipes
asserts that minimum wage laws do not "bring wage earners the
material benefits which is their purpose"; rather they outprice "the
labor of persons with little education, especially black youths, making some of them unemployable, and thus, unintentionally, [dis-
criminate] against them." As he writes in *Property and Freedom*:

> Thus the modern government not only "redistributes" the pos-
> sessions of its citizens, it also regulates their use. It invokes
> environmental laws to limit the use of land and housing. It
> interferes with the freedom of contract by . . . enforcing
> "affirmative action" hiring practices. It imposes rent con-
> trols. It interferes with virtually every aspect of business, pun-
> ishing any action that looks like price-fixing, setting rates for
> public utilities, preventing the formation of trusts, regulating
> communications and transport, pressuring banks to lend to
> designated neighborhoods, and so on.

Pipes says, "The right of property in and of itself does not guarantee civil rights and liberties. But historically speaking, it has been
the single most effective device for ensuring both, because it creates
an autonomous sphere in which, by mutual consent, neither the
state nor society can encroach: By drawing a line between the public and the private, it makes the owner co-sovereign, as it were.
Hence, it is arguably more important than the right to vote."

Professor Bernard Siegan, the rejected Reagan appointee to a federal court of appeals judgeship, has written extensively in the law and economics area. Without property rights, he says, the Framers knew personal rights would have no meaning and would be devoid of practical content. Until nearly half a century ago, he points out, property predominated in the trilogy of rights protected by the Constitution.

According to Professor Siegan, the Court should sit as a super legislature. If a law is based upon what the judge considers an unsound economic theory, the judge should, Siegan believes, hold the law contrary to due process. Siegan concludes: "Judicial withdrawal from the protection of economic activity violates" the Constitution: "The evidence is very persuasive that *Lochner* was a legitimate interpretation. . . . Full rehabilitation may be in order"— and that means unregulated markets.

Newt Gingrich may be gone, but his legacy is with us today. The Contract with America, endorsed by the majority of Americans in 1994, contained a clause calling for compensation of property owners whenever government regulations reduced their value. The resulting Private Property Rights Bill, passed by the House of Representatives in March 1995, called for compensation if government actions caused a property's worth to decline by 10 percent or more. The proposal has not as yet been enacted into law, although a bill with those provisions is submitted each year. But what Congress refuses to do through legislation, the Court may do through decisions. This would dramatically escalate the shift from the poor to the wealthy.

The doctrine relied on by both Epstein and the Court's reactionary members, "that a regulation on the use of land may cause a taking of property," comes from a 1922 decision—*Pennsylvania Coal Co. v. Mahon*[58]—striking down a Pennsylvania statute that prohibited the mining of coal from underground land owned by the coal company. Justice Holmes said that a land-use regulation can become a taking if it went "too far" in restricting the use of land and thereby diminished its value.

Holmes' decision, rarely cited after 1922, is now incorrectly cited as the foundation for Epstein's argument. Even the Burger Court, contrary to Epstein and some present members of the Rehnquist Court, said: "The denial of one's traditional property right does not always amount to a taking. At least where an owner possesses a full 'bundle' of property rights, the destruction of one 'strand' of the bundle is not a taking because the aggregate must be viewed in its entirety."

Indeed, the Fifth Amendment is one of the best known and most celebrated amendments, woven into the fabric of American history. Thousands of cases have interpreted it. The Supreme Court has many times referred to the Fifth Amendment, but rarely to the eminent domain clause. It is not a surprise that few have paid attention to this last, nearly lost clause.

The Meese Justice Department laid the groundwork for Gingrich's justification of the Takings Clause's use through a number of important measures. They convened conferences on "economic liberties" to discuss the strategies for reinvigorating the clause; they drafted a takings executive order, requiring government decision-makers to "evaluate carefully the effect of their administrative, regulatory, and legislative actions on constitutionally protected property rights"; and, most important, they helped appoint takings activists to spots on the three federal courts—the Supreme Court, the Circuit Court of Appeals for the District of Columbia, and the Court of Federal Claims—that mainly control the direction of federal takings law.

This Takings Project is long-term and still gathering momentum. Several right-wing foundations have fueled intensive programs to further takings cases. At least twelve active organizations, with combined budgets in excess of $15 million, litigate such cases on behalf of developers. The Federalist Society and others recruit and train an army of private practitioners to assist in shepherding these cases through the legal system. And groups such as the Foundation for Research on Economics and the Environment (FREE) host all expenses paid seminars in resort locations for federal judges, educating them in how to strike down environmental protections in takings cases.

There could be something to be said for the Takings Clause if we were all just recently removed from a state of nature. Certainly, long ago, if we owned adjoining pieces of land and mine was saddled with governmental regulations, your land would be more valuable. But today, if I buy a business or a piece of land, the market in nearly every transaction has already discounted the restriction the new owner faces. If I buy acres of land near the sea, which prohibits me from build-ing a factory or restricts me to building a small private house, the price I pay will reflect that. To suggest that our forefathers, in enact-ing the Takings Clause, believed that if the government sets up land-use regulations or environmental controls the owner should be fully compensated for his loss finds very little authority.

There is almost no constitutional history of the Takings Clause. The federal Bill of Rights, along with the Fifth Amendment and the Takings Clause, was the work of James Madison. His draft, shown to the House of Representatives on June 8, 1789, was the basis for the amendments passed by the First Congress. The Tak-ings Clause then read: "No person shall . . . be obliged to relin-quish his property, where it may be necessary for public use, without a just compensation." Reading the clause, it seems clear Madison intended that it apply only to the direct, physical taking of property for public use, not for cases in which the owner still keeps it, even though it is hampered by regulation.

Miller v. Schoene,[59] decided by the Supreme Court in 1928, is a case that ignites Epstein's fury and puts his argument in its best light. Rust-infected red cedar trees in Oregon threatened to destroy neigh-boring apple orchards by contamination. Apple growing was a major part of the state's economy, and Oregon had a statute permitting the destruction of infected trees that could wipe out other farmers. As a consequence, the red cedar trees were cut, the apple industry was saved, and the owner of the infected trees was not compensated even though he totally lost his property. So far as the cedar tree owner was concerned, Epstein says it was no different than losing his trees through eminent domain, and therefore he should be paid.

The unanimous *Miller v. Schoene* decision, written by Justice Harlan F. Stone, Epstein tells us, "is wholly inconsistent with any theory of property rights. . . . In the absence of any wrong by the owner of the cedar trees, the decision not to compensate is nothing more than authorization to transfer property illicitly from one class of citizens to another, as the owner of the cedar trees is left with neither the thing nor its value, when he has done no wrong."

But this decision is logical. The state took the property under its legitimate police power to protect the welfare of the people. Every regulation gives preference to governmental interest over the right of the property owner. Justices Scalia, O'Connor, Thomas, and Rehnquist approve of much of Epstein's argument; Kennedy is not yet there. One or two more justices can make for a solid majority view that will see regulation and taking as synonymous. How far the new conservatives will take the Epstein argument is still unclear.

Taxation, Epstein tells us, is taking. "With a tax, the government takes property in the narrowest sense of the term, ending up with ownership and possession of that which was once in private hands." Thus, all taxes and subsidies, which provide the government with the wherewithal to guarantee every part of the safety net—public schools, public transportation, minimum health and social security standards, even unemployment benefits and workers' compensation—are takings that require compensation.

As Bernard Schwartz, a former law professor at New York University, has said, Epstein's conception of the Takings Clause would effect the most radical change in public law that has ever taken place. "The Takings Clause would become the center of a new constitutional cosmology, with its rays protecting property to a hitherto unheard-of extent. Property rights would be immunized against the police power and redistributive taxation. Public power would be reduced to a power to proceed by purchase."

Various opinions in the five recent cases from the Supreme

Court agree with Epstein's concept that "takings" and "regulations" may be synonymous.

In the 1987 case *First Lutheran Church v. Los Angeles County*,[60] Chief Justice Rehnquist speaking for the Court said a regulation can amount to a taking requiring the owner to be paid even if the regulation is withdrawn after a successful court challenge. The First English Evangelical Lutheran Church of Glendale owned buildings destroyed by floods, but an ordinance prohibited the rebuilding on the flood plain area where the church had been. Following a successful Court challenge, the ordinance was withdrawn. The church was permitted to rebuild—and the Supreme Court said that holding up the rebuilding required the government to pay a compensation.

And in a 1988 California case, *Pennel v. City of San Jose*,[61] Justice Scalia applied the Takings Clause to rent control. Although the majority of the Court decided not to decide the case because it was premature, Scalia, joined by Justice O'Connor, dissented, stating that they would decide and would hold that the Takings Clause was violated. In his opinion, Scalia agreed with the landowner that the hardship provision underlying rent guidelines is aimed at the problem of poor tenants, and that landlords are being compelled to subsidize those who cannot pay reasonable rents. Scalia declared that rent regulation is being used "to establish a welfare program, privately funded by those landlords who happen to have 'hardship' tenants." Scalia's logic applies to every part of the safety net and calls into question all economic regulation that affects wealth transfers, including other comparable regulatory measures, such as those providing for price control and wage and hour regulation.

A high point in the Radical Right's revision of taking laws and their attack on government regulation was in the *Lucas v. South Carolina*[62] 1992 case.

David H. Lucas paid $975,000 for two lots of land along the South Carolina coast. In twenty of the forty years prior to the time Lucas bought the land, all or part of the land was part of the beach, and so was flooded twice daily by the ebb and flow of the tide.

Between 1963 and 1973 the shoreline extended one hundred to one hundred fifty feet onto Lucas's plots.

Lucas knew when he bought the land that it had been underwater for a long period of time and that for many years prior to the date of purchase, both the federal and South Carolina governments had been seeking to protect the beach from erosion. Nonetheless, when the state refused him permission to build on the land, he claimed the land was wrongfully taken from him.

The Supreme Court agreed in a 6–3 decision. Scalia wrote the opinion of the Court. Agreeing with him were Thomas, Rehnquist, O'Connor, Kennedy, and White. Blackmun, Stevens, and Souter dissented. Scalia rejected the claim that South Carolina had the power to prevent, without compensating Lucas fully, the use of property the state found harmful to the coastline. Again, relying on Justice Holmes' decision in the *Pennsylvania Coal*[63] case, Scalia said South Carolina had rendered Lucas' land valueless, and thus he was entitled to compensation.

Blackmun's dissent contradicted Scalia's history of the Takings Clause. Relying on *Miller v. Schoene*, the 1928 case that justified the burning of some trees to save others, Blackmun claimed that Holmes' 1922 decision had been consistently taken out of context to form the basis for Scalia's takings theory. Holmes, said Blackmun, regarded economic injury as only one factor to be used in evaluating if there was a taking. Holmes did not say that once an economic injury occurred the landowner must be paid the full value of the damage.

Stevens argued that the Lucas case showed again that the majority was returning to the *Lochner* era—that laws of Congress and the state of South Carolina were being rejected because the Court was substituting its own judgment on what was the best way to protect the environment. Later in the *Lake Tahoe Preservation v. Lake Tahoe Regional Planning* case Scalia, Thomas, and Rehnquist lost when they tried to extend Lucas to cover an instance in which landowners were temporarily blocked from building developments along the Nevada lake.

The next case, *Dolan v. City of Tigard* (1994),[64] shows how Epstein's theories became even more firmly embedded in American jurisprudence after Clarence Thomas joined the Court. Frances Dolan owned an electrical and plumbing supply store in the central business district of Tigard, Oregon, a Portland suburb. Business was good. She asked the Tigard City Planning Commission for permission to more than double the size of her building. They agreed to give her permission if she gave one strip of her land to the city for bicycle and pedestrian use and another piece of the land, which was on a flood plain, to the city so it could better protect itself against floods. Dolan sued to allow her to build and to require the city to pay for any land it took. The Land Use Appeal Board, the Oregon trial court, and the Oregon Supreme Court all decided against her.

Rehnquist, writing for a 5–4 majority, ruled in her favor. In reversing three prior decisions, he dusted off the Takings Clause, saying it "was as much a part of the Bill of Rights as the First and the Fourth Amendments" and should not "be relegated to the status of a poor relation." Economic liberties are worth at least as much protection as personal liberties, he says. Any diminution of property values requires as much protection as any diminution of personal rights; thus, in battles between landowners and the government's "takings," the government loses.

Stevens and Souter, in dissent, said this decision was predicated upon a radical departure from the law, weakening in crucial ways the government's ability to protect its citizens. The dissenters warned that the unrestrained majority could now crack down on minimum wage and maximum hour legislation by reaching back to the *Lochner* result through a Takings Clause theory.

Another high-water mark in the Court's use of the Takings Clause was in 1998, when Justice O'Connor's swing opinion in the *Eastern Enterprises v. Apfel*[65] case was based on Epstein's view of the clause's intent. The roots of this case reach back to the 1940s, when labor and management were at odds and Harry Truman seized the coal mines in order to keep them running. Shortly thereafter, the disputes were settled and agreements between the unions and the owners were entered into.

Eastern, a very successful coal company that began in 1946, agreed to give health benefits to its miners. By 1965 the corporation called Eastern had stopped mining coal, but its wholly owned subsidiary continued making substantial profits until 1987. Eastern owned the holding company for twenty-two years, took 100 percent of the profits of the coal mining operation as they did before ($100 million from 1965 to 1987), shared offices with the holding company, and had the same officers, indicating clearly that it was only a corporate façade paper company that Eastern owners were using to try to insulate themselves from liability.

The case arose when the company challenged a 1992 federal statute requiring coal operators to retroactively provide health benefits for miners. The question before the Supreme Court in 1998 was how to interpret those contracts—the first of which was finalized in 1946—when so much time and history had intervened.

The Supreme Court argument took place on March 4, 1998. After reviewing the history of the contracts and labor struggles, Peter Buscemi, arguing on behalf of the miners, said, "I think it's easy in the midst of the argument to lose sight of the human dimension in the problem." Under questioning, he rejected Scalia's argument that Eastern's liability should be passed to the consumer: "Neither fairness nor justice should permit Eastern to avoid all financial responsibility for its coal industry retirees and to have these costs shouldered by the general public." Fourteen hundred employees and spouses would be covered if the Court ruled against Eastern, although no hard numbers were known on the total cost to Eastern.

Eastern argued that the Supreme Court could not "pierce the corporate veil"; namely, the fact that they sold the mining company to one of their own subsidiaries cut the company's liability off in 1965, the date of the transfer, even though the subsidiary continued to operate the mine and make substantial profits. Additionally, Eastern claimed that to make them pay the miners' benefits would so diminish the company's value that the government must reimburse it.

Justice O'Connor observed during the argument that "Eastern sold the coal mining company to a wholly owned subsidiary . . . and then there was cross management. I mean some of the same managers were also managers of the subsidiary corporation." She then asked if the original coal mining company had agreed, as a condition of the transfer, to repay the subsidiary if a court found that the subsidiary must pay the miners' benefits. Eastern's counsel tried to avoid the question. O'Connor pursued it, and the attorney finally answered yes, the original coal mining company would bear the entire burden, for it had agreed, as part of the sale, to indemnify the parent. These answers should have persuaded O'Connor to go along with the moderates. She looked behind the corporate structure and saw that it was form over substance. But it was not to be so.

The case was decided with the usual 5–4 split. The coal miners lost; the corporation won. Justice O'Connor's separate opinion in Eastern refused to require the company to pay the unpaid benefits, claiming any order to require Eastern to pay substantial monies, between $50 to $100 million, would be wrongfully "taking" the company's money: You cannot ask a company, she said, that stopped doing business in 1965 to pay thirty years of benefits more than thirty years later. O'Connor describes her test for implementing the Takings Clause. One must look at the financial impact on the company and the extent to which the regulation interferes with the company's expected profits.

Eastern, once you look at reality and pierce the corporate veil, was a profitable company operating until 1987, and was trying to renege on an agreement that gave it substantial profits. Justice Breyer said the coal company earned substantial profits until 1987: "For many years Eastern benefited from the labor of those miners. Eastern helped to create conditions that led the miners to expect continued health care benefits for themselves and their families after they retired." Justice Stevens saw that the sickness and early deaths of coal miners led to an understanding that the miners would put themselves at risk in exchange for lifetime benefits. The coal company had gone through quite a bit of corporate manipulation, he cited, not all driven by the desire to get rid of the miners, but having that effect anyway.

The moderates did not emphasize the cost to the 1965 company—the company they were writing about was making profits in 1987. The way the majority and minority saw facts differently helped justify their very different decisions. The extent to which the different-fact finders deviate from a "true" reading of the record tells the reader how result-oriented the decision is. Previous to the *Eastern* case, five federal circuit courts that had looked at the issues similar to those presented in this case had all decided against the position taken by Eastern.

In their *Eastern* dissent, the four minority justices claimed the Takings Clause was totally inappropriate, applying only when the government physically takes over property; the clause was never intended to reallocate funds of two private warring parties. The government itself took nothing in this case, they noted, and yet the Court was striking down a congressional act, passed after extensive hearings. Congress said in passing the law, that "retired coal miners have legitimate expectations of health care benefits; that was the promise they received during their working lives and that is how they planned their retirement years. That commitment should be honored." Echoes of *Lochner* and *Hammer* could be heard in the Court's decision.

Most important, the dissenters concluded that the Takings Clause could drastically alter the constitutional landscape by giving greater recognition to economic rights. An expansive reading of the clause, warned Justice Breyer, could be raised whenever the government assessed taxes or imposed any burden on certain parties.

Conservatives are for the use of eminent domain to limit the government and expand corporate powers. One of the few areas that elicited Alito's passion was when eminent domain was being used against commercial power for a true public good. Alito's view is that the majority of the Supreme Court was wrong when it allowed officials in New London, Connecticut, to condemn homes for the "public purpose" of developing a blighted area to provide jobs and taxes. After the 2005 *Kelo v. New London*[66] decision, federal and state legislatures saw a rush of statutes aimed at stopping government officials from taking land for such public purposes.

Few cases show the conservatives' elevation of private property over the community's interest more than the 5–4 *Kelo* decision. The conservatives lost when Kennedy, who did not join the opinion of the four liberal justices, nonetheless joined the decision. His narrow, reluctant opinion will go the other way if the facts are slightly different.

Justice Thomas said that public necessity, as in the redevelopment in Connecticut, falls below "the sacred and inviolate rights of private property." He quoted the Takings Clause, "nor shall private property be taken for public use, without just compensation"; and said public benefit does not mean public use.

That decision, coupled with reports of abuses in places like the predominantly African American community of Riviera Beach, Florida, where plans called for replacing thousands of homes with upscale condos, has prompted an onslaught of legislation, both federal and state.

In November, the House of Representatives approved a bill by F. James Sensenbrenner, Jr., a Republican of Wisconsin, that would penalize government agencies for using condemnation powers for private projects by denying them economic development funds for two years. Legislation has been introduced in twenty-seven states, and more is coming, said Larry Morandi, the director of the environment, energy, and transportation programs of the National Conference of State Legislatures.

In California, where eminent domain can be used only in urban areas—and only when there is substantial evidence of blight—four ballot initiatives have been filed with the state attorney general's office to further limit condemnation, said John F. Shirey, the executive director of the California Redevelopment Association, a trade group.

The outcry has given heart to property-rights advocates. "We lost the Supreme Court case, but we're ultimately going to win in changing the way that eminent domain is going to be used in this country," said Dana Berliner, a senior attorney for the Institute for Justice, the most prominent conservative advocacy group.

But around the country, developers and city officials say weakening or destroying the power to condemn property will seriously undermine efforts to rehabilitate decaying cities and might even hinder the rebuilding of New Orleans. Without eminent domain, the Inner Harbor, which played an essential role in Baltimore's success in building its tourist industry, could not have been redeveloped, said Ralph S. Tyler, the city solicitor.

"What you're seeing is a coherent attack by the right on the power of eminent domain," said Richard L. Brodsky, a New York State assemblyman from Westchester County.

Since June, three states have passed bills banning the use of eminent domain for economic development. Michigan lawmakers have approved a constitutional amendment, subject to a popular vote. The Supreme Court has fueled "takings" activism in the past fifteen years by ruling in favor of developers and other property owners in an unbroken string of cases. Although these rulings are relatively narrow, they reflect an untoward eagerness to overcome procedural obstacles in order to uphold takings claims.

◆　　　◆　　　◆

Alito was involved in a case, a 10–1 decision, that makes perfectly clear how he and his Supreme Court colleagues will try to undermine the fight against racial and gender discrimination. Alito was the single dissenter. The entire sitting bench of the Third Circuit was voting against him. Conservative judges as well as liberal judges excoriated Alito.

Barbara Sheridan, a head captain at the Hotel DuPont, said she was fired because she complained of sexual harassment. A jury agreed and awarded her substantial damages.

After Sheridan complained, the hotel started to keep meticulous records on her that were not kept on other employees. They recorded, over a six-month period, every time she was a minute late. They went to people she dealt with and recorded only the negative remarks.

Alito wanted to do more than deny Barbara Sheridan her day in court. He wanted to change the burden of proof in Civil Rights discrimination cases—make the employee prove racial, gender, or age discrimination rather than placing the burden on the company to prove they had a valid reason for firing her. That seemingly small procedural change would reverse the result in well over 90 percent of discrimination suits.

The ten-member Court would not go along with Alito's view of the facts or law; they found DuPont's testimony fraudulent, and unanimously said Alito's view of the law would make race, gender, disability, or age antidiscrimination statutes meaningless. Judge Doris Sloviter, writing for the ten, said all believed, as did the jury, the testimony given by a DuPont employee that, after Sheridan complained, DuPont said they would watch her like a "hawk" and a "dog," and that they did.

In the second Alito case, Beryl Bray, an African American Marriott employee, said she was denied a promotion to director of services because of her race. The majority of the court denied the hotel's motion to dismiss the case, saying the case should be decided by a local jury. Alito, after waxing poetic about the value of the Civil Rights Act and our country's commitment to equality, decided her case should be dismissed because, unlike all the other trial and appellate judges, he did not believe her testimony.

The Marriott Hotel, defending their decision to give a white woman the job, like DuPont, gave reasons in court they did not give at the time the employee was passed over.

The majority of the court looked at the overall picture—Bray, they said, had been promoted several times by Marriott, was a star, and had done well at the interview.

Alito chose to believe Marriott's argument that there was no interview and that her post-complaint record, which Bray said was fabricated, showed she should not have the job; he disregarded that Marriott had hired an outsider, ignoring its practice of hiring from within, and that Marriott had admitted that the reasons for firing her were very different than the ones they gave her.

Alito's decision, the majority said, "ignores the sad reality that racial animus" had "warped" Marriott's testimony. Decisions of Rehnquist, Roberts, Thomas, and Scalia use the same technique to deny individuals' civil rights.

In case after case, in jury selections, in sentencing, in discrimination cases, these judges do not see "conscious racial bias" or gender bias where their colleagues do. It is impossible to look at abortion cases without considering race and gender issues. Yet this is exactly what this group of four judges does in case after case.

In both Barbara Sheridan's case and Beryl Bray's, there were two separate versions of what happened. The majority in both cases was willing to accept a jury's view—Alito said no, I, a single appellate judge, decided against both women. He paid only lip service to precedent.

Alito's discrimination laws are applied to disability cases as well. He routinely denies benefits by ignoring what Congress intended to do and narrowly interpreting statutes meant to benefit the disabled.

Robert Bork's legal view, that the value of precedent is overstated, is shared by many of his conservative and liberal colleagues. All cases depend on the facts, and the facts that the different judges select as the most relevant and believable determine the outcome. Nearly every case is factually different from any other—nearly any case can be distinguished. That is why O'Connor's legacy will be so short—nearly all the cases she decided were so fact-based that they are hardly precedent for the next case that comes along. That is why *Brown v. Board of Education* stands, why school segregation still exists, and why the NAACP no longer bothers to file school segregation cases. It is the same reason, after *Baker v. Carr*, one man–one vote is not yet a reality. Every gerrymandering legislature acts differently. Alito, like most other judges, selects the facts to get the result he wants.

Nine judges' different views of the "facts" may well persuade the reader of this book that there is no truth in facts. Rashomon is evident wherever there is a factual controversy in the Courts. Alito looking at the same facts in the *Bray* and *Sheridan* cases saw totally different truths than the other judges on his circuit court.

Bork believes his conservative interpretation will stop the new immorality of our nation. Because one "can hardly have foreseen that passionate intensity, uncoupled from morality, would destroy the fabric of Western culture. The rough beast of decadence, a long time in gestation, having reached its maturity in the last three decades, now sends us slouching toward our new home, not Bethlehem but Gomorrah." The Court has five Mass-going Catholics, more than at any time in our history. They share a Borkian view. The Court's past decisions, they say, that have led us into immorality.

Roberts, Scalia, Alito, and Thomas want to return to what in their view was the Court's Golden Age, before *Brown v. Board of Education*, before *Roe v. Wade*, before the Senate passed the Civil Rights Act, and before the Roosevelt Court established minimum wages and maximum hours and created agencies to regulate corporate America. They join Bork in the quest for their Holy Grail—the "Constitution in exile."

Alito, in opposition to his fellow judges, wanted to reverse the jury finding and dismiss Bray's case—he chose to accept the employer's version of the facts rather than the employee's. He chose Marriot's reasons for firing Bray that were never told to her before she lost her job, but were later, in Court, offered as rationale. Nonetheless, he praised the law she was suing under, noted it was a great advance and should be easily applied.

Judge Alito has also taken a narrow view of the federal government's responsibility to protect the health and safety of its citizens. As a lawyer in the Reagan administration, Alito recommended that President Reagan veto a piece of legislation that protected consumers against fraud in the auto industry, the Truth in Mileage Act of 1986. In a memo, Alito wrote that he believed "this bill should be vetoed because is [sic] violates the principles of federalism." He urged that President Reagan use this language to veto the bill: "It is the states and not the federal government, that are charged with protecting the health, safety and welfare of their citizens." If this extreme view became the law of the land, it would endanger many critical protections in the areas of job safety, civil rights, environmental protection, and consumer protection, to name a few.

Alito's views of the relationship between the state and its employees, as clearly stated in recent cases, speak to the ages before the New Deal Court. In *Chittister v. Department of Community and Economic Development*, 226 F.3d 223 (Third Circuit, 2000),[67] Judge Alito held that Congress did not have the authority to give the country's five million state employees the right to sue their employers for damages for violating the Family and Medical Leave Act's guarantee of personal unpaid sick leave. Alito tried to strike down a law Congress enacted to provide assistance to Americans at critical periods in their lives—when a worker or family member is ill.

That decision was out of the then-mainstream. In *Nevada Dept. of Human Resources v. Hibbs*, 538 U.S. 721 (2003),[68] the Supreme Court reached the opposite conclusion from Alito's: It found that state employees can enforce their rights under the part of the law requiring employers to provide for family leave. The court held Congress empowered to enact family leave legislation to "dismantle persisting gender-based barriers to women in the workplace." That will now change.

In a worker safety case, *RNS Services v. Secretary of Labor*,[69] Alito dissented from his Third Circuit colleagues in holding that a group of workers was not covered under mine safety laws. The Third Circuit majority court found that a mining services company was violating safety laws under the Federal Mine Safety and Health Act. The court rejected the company claim that it was not covered by mining safety laws, seeking to narrow application of the law to mines, not coal processing plants associated with such mines. Alito, in dissent, argued that the facility should be excluded from those mining safety regulations.

The onslaught on the New Deal years continued when on June 24, 2006, the formerly liberal, now Republican-dominated Circuit Court of Appeals in the District of Columbia Court said in *Phillips v. S.E.C.* that the Securities and Exchange Commission did not have the right to regulate hedge funds, a rapidly growing industry with more than $1.1 trillion of assets.

Christopher Cox, the Republican S.E.C. chairman, said the commission would review the issue but stopped short of indicating that it would continue to seek authority over hedge funds.

"The S.E.C. takes seriously its responsibility to make rules in accordance with our governing laws," Cox said in a statement. "The court's finding, that despite the commission's investor protection objective its rule is arbitrary and in violation of law, requires that going forward we re-evaluate the agency's approach to hedge fund activity."

He said the commission would "use the court's decision as a spur to improvement in both our rule making process and the effectiveness of our programs to protect investors, maintain fair and orderly markets, and promote capital formation."

As hedge funds have grown, and as some have collapsed amid fraud or because they took excessive risk-taking, pressures to regulate them responsibly have also grown. The regulatory law was passed by the then-Democratic commission, over the opposing votes of the two Republicans. Conservatives, including Christopher Byron, applauded the ruling, and said that this case showed why the S.E.C. should be shut down. They create such confusion, Byron said; the S.E.C. does not know what to do with hedge funds and can't regulate them. The now-Republican-dominated S.E.C. will not appeal the decision overruling its own Commission's rule, a highly unusual event.

Byron calls the S.E.C. "a poorly led, bureaucratic anachronism from the New Deal that lacks a mission." It had three heads under Bush, and, as Byron points out, it has been marked under Bush by revolving door leadership, staff defections, and poor morale. There are many different ways of making the S.E.C. ineffective.

The Supreme Court can also limit personal rights and protect economic interests by preventing an individual from going to court to sue. "Standing," the right to stand in court for a constitutional violation, is not just a mere technicality; it goes to the heart of the Constitution. If you don't meet the legal requirements for standing, you can't sue. For plaintiffs to satisfy the standing requirements and get into court, they must prove they have suffered a real injury; that the injury is the result of an act forbidden by law; and that the court can provide relief. What this means is that if I don't have a remedy—a place to enforce a right given to you by law—then you don't have the right. It's that simple.

The Warren Court opened the doors to the courthouse, expanding access to the federal courts because it saw that the state courts were not enforcing Constitutional rights. Justice Douglas was in favor of giving the widest access to "private attorney generals" to challenge laws the people believed were unconstitutional rather than to wait, often in vain, for elected officials to do so. Expanding standing would dramatically change the kinds of cases the federal courts would hear.

In a 1968 Warren Court decision, *Flast v. Cohen,*[70] the Court held by 8–1 that under limited circumstances taxpayers could sue in federal courts to challenge federal spending. Even though the plaintiffs suffered no economic harm, the concept of opening the courts to citizens for limited purposes brought nearly all nine Supreme Court justices together. Two years later, with only the change of chief justices, Burger replacing Warren, the Court upheld and expanded *Flast*, giving standing to anyone who claimed an actual injury to some recognized interest, be it economic, environmental, aesthetic, or otherwise.

At last, children denied access to schools had access to federal courts to enforce their rights to attend integrated schools. Demonstrators denied the right to assemble went to federal courts to protect their right to do so. But after Rehnquist and Powell replaced Black and Harlan, the Court clamped down and began to close the courthouse door. In 1974, the Court in a 5–4 decision that recognized the new conservative power, refused to allow a taxpayer to make public the CIA's expenditures because the taxpayer "is seeking to employ a federal court as a forum in which to air his generalized grievances about the conduct of government." Justice Burger, who wrote the majority opinion, and Justice Powell, who wrote a concurring opinion, blasted *Flast*.

The Court, through a variety of legal strategies, including standing, joined the elder Bush's support of corporate interests that attack the environment. The limitation on standing is especially significant in environmental protection cases, where the question of who has been injured by the pollutant companies is directly relevant to who can challenge them in Court. Justices Rehnquist, Scalia, Kennedy, O'Connor, and Thomas have already used their positions as part of 5–4 majorities to undermine the ability of citizen groups to bring lawsuits in their efforts to enforce environmental protections. It is a major weapon. In the recent environmental case, *Friends of the Earth v. Laidlaw*,[71] we can see how a court adopting the dissenting views of Scalia and Thomas would weaken or nullify some important environmental laws. Here, a waste disposal company repeatedly released toxic pollutants, including mercury, into a river in South Carolina, a direct violation of the company's permit to operate a wastewater treatment plant. The trial found that Laidlaw had violated the mercury limits on 489 occasions between 1987 and 1995.

But the Supreme Court majority opinion refused to authorize citizen lawsuits to enforce the antipollution law that the company was charged with violating. Scalia and Thomas, ridiculing the dissent, first argued that there was no proof that the illegal release of mercury and other pollutants into the waterway actually harmed the environment. They also claimed that citizen suits should not be allowed at all, that only the individuals damaged could bring suit.

Individuals, of course, rarely have the resources to sue large corporations. And yet, when they do, the individual challenging the government is routinely denied standing. These cases do not even get to the Supreme Court, for the Court denies review. The nearly physical revulsion many conservatives feel for environmental groups and values, and their reflex to protect business being encroached upon, threaten to wipe out all the gains that preceded this Court. Raw political partisanship that sees the Courtside with business interests is most apparent in environmental cases. The courts are in lockstep with the Right's attempts, outside the courts, to weaken the enforcement of environmental laws.

Minorities have run into a near impenetrable wall of "standing" law when they bring discrimination claims. The Rehnquist Court, building on the later years of the Burger Court, raised the toughest standing hurdles in cases in which minorities challenge racial or gender bias in zoning practices that keep minorities out of new or previously white areas. Poverty plaintiffs are barred from challenging the tax-exempt status of hospitals that deny them emergency services. In 1996, Thomas and Scalia, joined by Chief Justice Rehnquist, in *M.L.B. v. L.J.*,[72] indicated they would even permit states to prevent poor parents from appealing the termination of their parental rights by imposing high appeal and other fees, contrary to the majority's ruling. A portion of the dissent that not even Chief Justice Rehnquist would join showed that a Scalia-Thomas Court would overturn forty years of Supreme Court cases. One ruling they sought to overturn is the 1956 *Griffin v. Illinois*[73] case, in which the Court held for the "proposition that a State cannot arbitrarily cut off appeal rights for indigents while leaving open avenues of appeal for more affluent persons." If that case were overruled, high fees would even be allowed to prevent appeals by indigent criminal defendants facing the possibility of long prison sentences. However, standing requirements are relaxed when sustaining the unconstitutionality of federal subsidies for the nuclear power plant industry, for upholding offshore leasing policies, and for affirming tax credits to private schools.

In *Bragg v. Robertson*,[74] a 2001 case, homeowners joined an environmental group in West Virginia to sue state surface-mining officials for routinely issuing permits that allowed the environmentally devastating practice of mountain top–removal coal mining. Just as the name suggests, under this practice, the tops of mountains are literally blown up and removed and thousands of tons of rock and debris are dumped in adjacent valleys. These "valley fills" level forests, bury streams, and pollute the rivers fed by these streams. This causes flooding, dust, noise, and vibrations severe enough to crack the foundations of nearby houses. The federal appeals court, in its zeal to seal off traditional state responsibilities from federal law and injured plaintiffs, said that the state was immune from suit. The Supreme Court denied review.

It is hard to imagine how such a practice could be permitted under the federal Surface Mining Control and Reclamation Act (SMCRA), which is charged with protecting society from such adverse effects. Nonetheless, for years West Virginia surface-mining officials have routinely and expeditiously granted permits to do just that. The District of Columbia Circuit Court has also been striking a deaf ear. In the past few years, it has struck down or hindered a long list of critical environmental protections, ranging from wetland protections and Superfund site designations to guidelines on the treatment of petroleum wastewater.

Environmental controls are also on the way out. Alito and Roberts have consistently voted for the polluters. Chief Justice Roberts showed his hostility to environmental regulation when he narrowed the Commerce Clause to declare unconstitutional a provision of the Endangered Species Act.

In *Public Interest Research Group v. Magnesium Electron*,[75] a 1997 case, Judge Alito sided with the corporate polluter in a 2–1 ruling that wiped a $2.62 million fine off the books and restricted citizens' access to the courts. The plaintiffs proved that the defendant corporation had violated the Clean Water Act one hundred fifty times, discharging pollutants into a stream used by the plaintiffs for fishing and swimming. But Alito supported erecting new obstacles for environmental plaintiffs to have their day in court.

Three years later, in *Friends of the Earth v. Laidlaw*, 528 U.S. 167 (2000), the Supreme Court rejected the burden of proof Scalia raised for environmental plaintiffs, voting 7–2, with only Justices Scalia and Thomas dissenting.

Alito displayed a similar deference to corporate polluters in the *W.R. Grace & Co.* case in 2001.[76] Under the Safe Water Drinking Act, the Environmental Protection Agency (EPA) has emergency powers that allow it to protect a public water source from imminent threats to public health and safety, including terrorist attacks. In *W.R. Grace*, a polluter challenged an emergency order issued by the EPA to protect the public health from a large ammonia plume that threatened the drinking water of Lansing, Michigan. Alito joined a 2–1 opinion that overturned this emergency order and imposed a stiff burden on the EPA and other federal agencies in cases of environmental emergencies.

The first case Justice Alito heard on the Supreme Court, and the first environmental cases heard by Justice Roberts, attacked sections of the most important comprehensive environmental laws on the books, the 1972 Clean Water Act.

Rapanos v. United States[77] and *Carabell v. Army Corps of Engineers*[78] deal with the federal government's right, under the Commerce Clause, to regulate the wetlands and other waters because they theoretically affect interstate commerce. It's *Lopez, Morrison,* and *Garrett* redux.

Justice Kennedy and Chief Justice Roberts also pondered how to determine whether a large waterway clearly covered by the act had a "significant nexus" to a smaller tributary, which would place the smaller waterway under federal, not state, regulation.

Chief Justice Roberts asked whether a wetland that contributed "one drop a year" to a tributary of a navigable waterway should be subjected to regulation. The solicitor general said it would. Justice Scalia followed up, saying, "I don't know how a storm drain is a water of the United States."

The argument was disheartening. The moderates staked out positions while Alito and Roberts staked out radical positions. Souter asked why Congress would regulate navigable rivers without extending the same authority to the waterways and wetlands that free them.

Following this logic, Justice Souter said, "All you've got to do is dump the pollutant far enough up the water system to get away scot-free."

In arguing against the government, Justice Ginsburg asked if the wetland adjacent to the river counted as falling under the federal mandate. "Why not a stream that goes right into it? What sense does the distinction make?"

When the solicitor general, Paul D. Clement, rose to make his argument about the extent of federal jurisdiction, he was met with a volley of barbed questions, most from Justice Scalia. Scalia said that under the government's logic, "a storm drain, even when not filled with water, is a tributary." Minutes later, he added, "I suggest it's very absurd to call that 'waters of the United States.' It's a drainage ditch."

A few minutes later, Chief Justice Roberts told Clement, "You put a lot of weight on the tributary approach," and then added, "for those of us having trouble with the concept of 'tributary,' you don't give us much to fall back on." Clement replied by citing a major section of the law, saying it was "the clearest textual indication that Congress meant to regulate something" beyond the scope of navigable waters.

On June 19, 2006, in *Rapanos v. U.S.*, the four conservatives voted to severely limit the Clean Water Act's thirty-four-year-old protections. Stevens, Souter, Ginsburg, and Breyer voted to preserve the law that Congress had intended. Justice Kennedy, writing a narrow decision to form a majority, avoided the issue by sending it back to a lower court. The Court's 5–4 decision, reversing previous law, held that the Clean Water Act does not justify the regulation of all inland wetlands that connect to navigable waterways. As bad as the decision was, with one more conservative it would have been far worse.

The Scalia opinion, if it became a majority opinion, would gut an act passed under a Republican president. He said the law protected only "permanent, standing, or continuously flowing water bodies." This, the government says, would expose 60 percent of the country's waters to dredging, dumping, and developing.

The case arose when the Army Corps of Engineers refused permits to two Michigan real estate developers who filled in passageways, ditches, and drains where water flowed in "the waters of the United States." Two lower courts upheld the Army. Scalia, in writing the reversed decision, disagreed, pointing out that because of "the immense expansion of federal protection of the nation's waterways under the 1972 Clean Water Act," the amount of monies spent to protect our rivers was already too high, and if they did not reverse the Army, the costs would be even higher.

The Clean Water Act's objective "to restore the chemical, physical and biology of the nation's waters" and to give the government another tool to fight Katrina-like hurricanes and floods has now been so seriously cut back that it jeopardizes all our waterways.

Stevens' dissent pointed out that deference should be paid to Congress.

Justice Scalia, in a later case, made clear his rationale in the Clean Water Act case when dealing with acts of Congress. "The use of legislative history is illegitimate and ill advised in the interpretation of any statute."[79]

A week after the *Rapanos* decision, the Supreme Court agreed to decide whether the government can regulate "greenhouse" gases, especially carbon dioxide from cars. Spurred by states in a pollution battle with the Bush administration, the Court said it would decide if the Environmental Protection Agency is required under the federal clean air law to treat carbon dioxide as a pollutant harmful to health. The Bush administration said the EPA could not be forced to regulate the chemical. Their opponents said that *Massachusetts v. Environmental Protection Agency* "goes to the heart of the EPA's statutory responsibility to deal with the most pressing environmental protection of our time—global warming."

This will be the Court's first major statement on climate change. There is good reason to believe that the Supreme Court will give environmentalists a significant defeat.

The two sides of the issue each have their supporters. On one side are four former Environmental Protection Agency administrators (two Republicans and two Democrats), a star-studded assemblage of scientists, including Jared Dram and Edward O. Wilson, nine current and former members of Congress who drafted the Clean Water Act, and thirty-four states. The Bush administration reluctantly supported the law. On the other side are home building organizations, advocates for limited government, and farming and petroleum interests who want to be free to dump pollutants in smaller bodies of water that, they say, do not come under federal protection.

Early on in his career, Justice Rehnquist said the values jurists bring with them inform how they judge. In the economic area, the mindset of the majority justices helps them see economic issues through politically influenced personal lenses. They are not familiar with or sympathetic toward the group in society that most bears the brunt of a free market. None of them were elected to political offices—they have not had to listen to, see, work with, or apprehend disenfranchised members of our society. Whether Kennedy, acting in good faith, lets his constitutional interpretations lead to the same result as Rehnquist, Scalia, and Thomas, or whether he deludes himself into thinking that the malleable Constitution parallels his politics, ultimately matters very little to the people affected. The result—the defiling of our constitutional heritage—is the same.

America's never-ending political battles over the rights and duties of immigrants surfaced in a 2000 case that saw another substantial evisceration of civil rights law by the conservative majority. In the *Alexander v. Sandoval*[80] case, the Court upheld an Alabama law requiring an applicant for a driver's license to pass an English literacy test—a statute clearly aimed at keeping out non-English-speaking minorities. Spanish-speaking-only classes in our publicly financed school systems (for example, in California and New York), were made to appear as if they were coddling new immigrants and delaying their assimilation. *Alexander* is a powerful precedent that will help destroy bilingualism.

English-only laws have always been supported by Evangelicals and other groups of the Republican Right. It was a platform plank in Pat Buchanan's 1992 presidential campaign. Robert Dole in 1996 supported the English-only movement to protect "national unity." Newt Gingrich proclaimed that bilingualism threatened "the very fabric of American society." Language differences, he said, fostered "linguistic and cultural isolation" that could cause tension and unrest. The Washington Legal Foundation, one of the litigation arms of the New Federalists, argued in a case supporting Arizona's English-only law that the statute making English that state's official language was consistent with the hopes of those who wrote the Constitution and the Mayflower Compact. And after the 1997 census revealed that Hispanics were the majority minority, John

Tanton, the founder of a national advocacy group called U.S. English, warned of a "Latin onslaught." "Mongrelization" of America became one of his favorite images. In this atmosphere, a seemingly minor case like *Alexander* became a 5–4 decision to be used in severely limiting civil rights protection for the benefit of America's white majority.

More important than the English-only driver's license test upheld by the Court was the new test the Court imposed on those seeking to prove discrimination. Previously, an individual citizen could claim that a job requirement that appeared to be innocuous on its face was, in fact, a requirement meant to discriminate. For example, if all of California's and Alabama's rural street cleaners had to have high school diplomas, a requirement unrelated to the job, most minorities might be excluded. Similarly, a driving rule linked to literacy in California might prohibit licenses, and thus jobs, for non-English-speaking minorities, a substantial part of the population.

The federal appeals courts had allowed private plaintiffs to sue using the "results" standard of proof for three decades. But Scalia, as we saw, writing the majority opinion in *Alexander*, said suits could be brought only for intentional discrimination on the basis of race and national origin, not over policies that have a discriminatory impact. His ruling severely limited one of our most potent civil rights laws.

The *Alexander* decision restricted Title VI, a critical component of the Civil Rights Act, which was one of the most important pieces of 1960s legislation and acknowledged by Lyndon Johnson as his major achievement. Section 601 of that law provides that no person shall, on the grounds of race, color, or national origin, be excluded from participation in, be denied the benefits of, or be subjected to discrimination under any federally funded program. The law supports disparate discrimination claims, from discrimination in education and health care programs to bank red-lining of poor neighborhoods. Previously, both private individuals and the government could sue, but now a new standard prevails.

The *Alexander* decision is part of the Court's proposed blueprint. The Civil Rights Act was passed to stop blatant discrimination and to try to anticipate clandestine methods of discrimination, some that already existed and some that were sure to be created. The conservatives had failed in cases such as *Patterson*[81] to make sweeping changes, and they were aware, as Scalia said, that the public would stand for only so much change. They voted not to overrule the civil rights law but instead tried to nit-pick it to death.

In his dissenting opinion in *Alexander*, Justice Stevens said that "it makes no sense" to differentiate for the purposes of private lawsuits between intentional discrimination and discriminatory impact. "There is but one private action to enforce Title VI, and we already know that such an action exists." Stevens, speaking for himself, Souter, Ginsburg, and Breyer, said, "Today in a decision unfounded in our precedents and hostile to decades of settled expectations," the Court reverses twenty-seven years of law effectively "underlying the majority's dismissive treatment of our prior cases," in both a "flawed analysis" and "uncharitable understanding" of the intent of the Civil Rights Act. In *Alexander*, as in other cases, the majority refused to look at Congress' intent in passing the civil rights law, a practice uniformly observed prior to the Rehnquist Court. It was just another example—like *United States v. Lopez*, *Kimel v. Florida Board of Regents*, and *Morrison v. United States*—of disregarding Congress. As Justice Stevens put it, "The settled expectations of the Court undercut today's decisions not only from judicial decisions, but also from the consistent statements and actions of Congress."

Previous case law shows how radical the Supreme Court's *Alexander* ruling was. Of the twelve federal appeals courts, nine had addressed the issue and all nine had found that suits for discriminating impact could be filed under Title VI. But *Alexander* is a significant damper on other federal laws as well, for example, on those that prohibit sex discrimination in programs that receive federal money. Women who bring private lawsuits will be required to prove intentional discrimination. Scalia's *Alexander* decision affected the rights of many millions; far fewer claims are being filed, many of these are determined to be precluded from Court review, and of those that do go to trial, many more lose.

Scalia's majority decision, arguing that the case changes little, is misleading. All *Alexander* means, says Scalia, is that an individual discriminated against cannot sue unless he shows intentional discrimination directly aimed at him but that the government can sue on his or others' behalf. However, little federal money exists to fund such suits, and Republican administrations are not apt to rush to court to challenge laws such as these.

This problem becomes particularly acute, for example, when environmentalists want to attack a Department of Transportation regulation that they claim is discriminating, such as when companies that create pollutants are found in minority areas. According to Scalia, only the government can make the disparate impact claim, but there is no likelihood of a Republican Department of Justice bringing suit against a Republican Department of Transportation carrying out Republican policy.

Scalia's decision is strewn with language that can destroy other parts of the Civil Rights Act. Because few federally financed programs are overtly discriminatory, suits for intentional discrimination are rare, while lawsuits alleging discriminatory effects represent the biggest category of cases under Title VI. The law authorizes federal agencies to issue regulations that bring their own programs into compliance with Title VI, and many regulations go beyond intentional discrimination also to bar the use of federal money in programs with discriminatory effects. But, as we know, a private citizen can hardly win under those regulations.

Justice Stevens criticized the majority not only for its decision, but also for taking the case in the first place, as there was no conflict among the lower federal courts on the issue. While the newly conservative and right-wing circuit courts increasingly agree with one another, the Court, with more space on its docket, will continue to reach out, as it did in *Eastern, Patterson,* and *Alexander,* to change decisions and laws that it doesn't like, that are not before it, or that need not be before it. The conservative principle of judicial restraint—judges decide cases narrowly and do not decide cases that are not before them—is totally ignored by this Court. In *Bush v. Gore,* the Court majority, like in *Alexander* and *Patterson,* claimed they were obligated to decide the issues they felt were forced on them. This is nonsense; it's merely another example of an established outreach pattern. No other Court has done this in such a systematic way and been so disingenuous about its actions. The justice primarily responsible for this change in policy and demeanor was Chief Justice William Rehnquist.

Chapter Four

State Religion against the People

♦   ♦   ♦

Pat Robertson's resignation as head of the Christian Coalition in December 2001 "confirmed the ascendance of a new leader of the Religious Right in America." It was to be George W. Bush. Quoting the religious conservative Gary Bauer, Dana Milbank of the *Washington Post* reported, "Robertson stepped down because the position has already been filled." Christian publications shower George W. Bush with praise, preachers from the pulpit testify to his faith and point to his memoirs, describing his discovery of God with the help of Billy Graham. "Reverend Graham planted a mustard seed in my soul, a seed that grew over the next year. He led me to the path, and I began walking. It was the beginning of a change in my life." The Christian movement is no longer on the outside, or merely a player on the inside. The Religious Right is dominant in matters of church and state, and in parochial schools, morality, abortion, school prayer, and a host of other issues. John Ashcroft, who detests nonbelievers, considered running for president in 2000 as the candidate for the Religious Right. Most of the men and women being nominated for the bench share these views. This was exactly what the writers of the Constitution did not want.

Prior to the Constitutional Convention, the drafters had seen nearly a century of religious warfare in the colonies. The Puritans traveled three thousand miles to be free of the Church of England and the British government that enforced scriptural law as well as common law. They were determined to practice their religion freely, impose their morality on the communities they controlled, and brutalize those who flouted their orthodoxy. Execution, whippings, and floggings were common.

The Quakers, who could have safely stayed in Rhode Island, chose to confront the Puritans in Massachusetts to achieve martyrdom. The more the Puritans tried to keep them out, the more the Quakers came. The more the Puritans increased the punishments, the more the Quakers came. The persistence and courage of the Quakers and the relentlessness of the Puritans only confirm the length true believers will go to protect and practice their beliefs.

When the Constitution was first being conceived, there were no political parties. But the sects of the warring church groups formed political blocks to protect the free exercise of their religion while at the same denying that right to others in their state at the expense of other religions. That was their early vision of what government should be.

The history of religious persecution in Europe was repeated before the founding of the United States. For example, in Massachusetts, Quakers, Baptists, and other religious minorities were both brutalized and taxed by the established Congregational Church. In 1776, the Maryland "Declaration of Rights" stated that "only persons professing a Christian religion" were entitled to religious freedom, and not until 1826 were Jews permitted to hold public office. The South Carolina Constitution of 1778 stated that "the Christian protestant religion shall be deemed [the] established religion of this state." The reaction against the continuing persecutions reached its dramatic climax in Virginia in 1785–86, when Madison wrote his great Memorial and Remonstrance against renewal of "Virginia's tax levy for support of the established church" and the Virginia Assembly enacted the famous Virginia Bill for Religious Liberty originally written by Thomas Jefferson.

The Framers saw and heard all this in their daily lives, knew the history of religious massacres, and were determined not to let it happen in the new democracy they envisioned. After beating the British, they knew the greatest enemy of the new government could be warring church groups. Until very recently, the Establishment and Free Exercise Clause protected this country in the manner intended by the Constitution's writers.

The "establishment of religion" clause means at least this: Neither a state nor the federal government can set up a church; neither can pass laws that aid religion; neither can force nor influence a person to state a belief or a disbelief in a religion or force him either to go to church or not; no tax of any kind, in any amount, can be imported to support any religious institution; neither a state nor the federal government can participate in any religious institution, nor can a religious group participate in governmental decision making.

The Free Exercise Clause means that the government cannot punish anyone whose conduct is related to his religious belief. He cannot be punished for attending worship services, from abstaining from food or drink, proselytizing, abstaining from using certain modes of transportation, or not working on days that conflict with his beliefs.

Some of the delegates to the Constitutional Convention felt these clauses would stamp out religion. On the contrary, it has lead to a rich, pluralistic state, probably the most religious of any western state. That pluralistic free state is today under attack by coalitions of conservatives, Evangelicals, Fundamentalists, and the United States Supreme Court.

That coalition forms the core of the Republican Party. Priests on pulpits make clear the person and party to vote for. Religion and God are key issues in the political process. The Republicans are seen as the party of God, the party of personal morality, against abortion, for family values, against gay rights. The political parties can be identified by the religious groups that support them. Devout churchgoing Protestants and Catholics are generally Republican. The less committed Catholics and Protestants, Jews, Hispanics, and blacks are traditionally Democrats.

Jefferson sought liberty by privatizing religion and secularizing politics. Religion must be, he said, "a concern purely between God and our conscience." All religions should be free; the state should not establish any. Establishing one religion, Jefferson believed, would threaten all others. In 1802, after seeing the havoc caused by religion in the eighteenth century, he wrote, "Believing with you that religion is a matter which lies solely between a man and his God, that he owes account to none other for his faith or worship, that the legislative powers of government reach actions only, and not opinions, I contemplate . . . a wall of separation between Church and State." It was this model of religious liberty that the Supreme Court used in the landmark case *Everson v. Board of Education.*[82]

In the Court's first modern decision, *Everson v. Board of Education*, Justice Rutledge observed that "no provision of the Constitution is more closely tied to or given content by its generating history than the religious clause of the First Amendment." Justice Black "reflected in the minds of early Americans a vivid mental picture of conditions and practices which they fervently wished to stamp out in order to preserve liberty for themselves and for their posterity."

The First Amendment Establishment Clause "means at least this," Justice Black wrote for the *Everson* court: "Neither a state nor the Federal Government can set up a church. Neither can pass laws which aid one religion, aid all religions, or prefer one religion over another . . . no tax in any amount, large or small, can be levied to support any religious activities or institutions, whatever they may be called. Neither a state nor the Federal Government can, openly or secretly, participate in the affairs of any religious organizations or groups, or vice versa. In the words of Jefferson, the clause against establishment of religion by law was intended to erect 'a wall of separation between church and state.'"[83]

Professor Marci Hamilton of Cardozo Law School points out in her book *God vs. the Gavel*[84] religion was one of the most important motivating factors in the settlement of America. The Puritans and other settlers were refugees from religious wars that had ravaged England. Following John Locke's influence, the Founders created a separation of church and state, ensuring there would be protection for everyone to freely exercise nonorthodox as well as orthodox religions. The First Amendment clauses dealing with religion come out of our own early experiences.

In America during the eighteenth century, primarily prior to the

Revolution, religious organizations controlled politics. Churches were the first political parties. Professor Hamilton points out that many of those coming to America, who were oppressed by the British government's support of the Church of England, still set up their own churches and pushed hard to make them the official religion of the state. Congregationalists in New England and related Presbyterians in other regions—dissenters to the British crown—with traditions of hostility to the crown that reached back to the Puritan revolution, tried to keep the church out of government. The Quakers, powerful in Pennsylvania government and politics, were persecuted. James Madison and his colleagues at the first session of Congress put their religious concerns in the first of the Bill of Rights amendments.

The First Amendment contains two separate clauses dealing with religion: "Congress shall make no law respecting an establishment of religion, or prohibiting the free exercise thereof." These two clauses, elegantly and concisely written, exist in dynamic balance with each other. They and the interpretations given them, until very recently, have been remarkably effective in creating a balance that the Founders wanted.

The establishment clause of the First Amendment prohibits Congress from making any law "respecting an establishment of religion." This means not only that Congress cannot designate a national church but also that it cannot act to give any direct support to religion. We were trying to leave behind the English interlocking of church and state.

Freedom of religion is inevitably bound up with free speech, perhaps the better known guarantee of the First Amendment. The prime importance of the separation of church and state is manifested by the positioning of this freedom in the Constitution. Without the freedoms of speech and press, the expression and circulation of religious beliefs and doctrines would be impossible. Without the freedoms of assembly and association, the right to participate with others in public and private, religious worship would be curtailed.

The principle of separation of church and state had solid grounding. John Locke's famous *Letter Concerning Toleration* (1689), which had a great influence on several American founders, notably Thomas Jefferson, made an elegant plea for church and state to end their corrosive alliances and to end their corrupt abridgments of the liberty of conscience.[85] "[A]bove all things," Locke pleaded, it is "necessary to distinguish exactly the business of civil government from that of religion, and to settle the just bounds that lie between the one and the other."[86] The church, Locke wrote, must be "absolutely separate and distinct from the commonwealth."[87] The church is simply "a voluntary society of men, joining themselves together of their own accord in order to the public worshipping of God in such manner as they judge acceptable to Him, and effectual for the salvation of their souls."[88] Church members are free to enter and free to exit society. They are free to determine its order and organization and worship in a manner they consider most conducive to eternal life: "Nothing ought, nor can be transacted in this society, relating to the possession of civil and worldly goods. No force is to be made use of upon any occasion whatsoever. For force belongs wholly to the civil magistrate."[89]

The Court's move to the right comes at a time when it will soon be considering Bush's faith-based initiative. The Religious Right is determined to throw the massive weight of the federal government behind religious groups. "Problems like addiction and abandonment and gang violence, domestic violence, mental illness, and homelessness—we are called upon by conscience to respond," Bush said last year as he signed the executive order creating the new Office of Faith-Based and Community Initiatives. "As long as there are secular alternatives, faith-based charities should be able to compete for funding on an equal basis and in a manner that does not cause them to sacrifice their mission," he said.

As a policy initiative, this is a drastic policy change. For more than a century, the Supreme Court has said that church-run hospitals can receive government aid because these facilities are providing medical care, not promoting religion. But forcing taxpayers to subsidize church-based programs and bringing more of these programs into public institutions, such as prisons, hospitals, and schools, is qualitatively different. It is akin to forcing taxpayers to put money into the collection plates of churches, mosques, and synagogues.

Many states feel that they cannot contest the actions of church groups. Federal funds in parochial schools can lead to government monies being misused in extraordinary ways. State officials in Missouri were distressed in early 2001 when they received a complaint that a religious boarding school in the rural town of Bethel was punishing students by forcing them to muck out deep pits of manure. The state was unaware such a practice was going on. But there was no reason it should have known; in Missouri, residential schools and homes for troubled youth are exempt from virtually all state regulation if they are run by religious organizations. "They have no obligation to even make themselves known to us," said Denise Cross, director of the Missouri Division of Family Services. "There is no regulatory body for those facilities."

President Bush's proposal to increase federal financing for charitable works of religious organizations has allowed religions that receive federal money for charitable work to continue hiring solely within their faith. Many such organizations have refused to hire Jews, blacks, or Catholics. Under current law, religions are allowed to impose such a hiring restriction because they use private money. Had the Democratic-controlled Senate not made passage of the Bush bill conditional upon the removal of this employment provision, we would have seen federally financed discrimination in hiring. Even so, the newly passed initiative is an open invitation for mischief-making. Because the government always regulates what it finances, and regulation means control, the government can audit a church's books or prohibit a synagogue, mosque, or church from using funds in ways the government feels is wrong. The Bush faith-based federal handout, its critics point out, would also lead to competition between religions for funding, a result that would have appalled James Madison.

Justice Thomas is already on record in favor of abolishing the prohibition against supporting pervasively sectarian organizations with public funds; Justice Scalia, in a 1989 case, said he supported allowing tax exemptions for religious books and periodicals, even if nonreligious publications were denied the same benefit. The Texas law in question, he claimed, did not improperly favor religion. Everything we take for granted in church-state relationships is today being put into play.

The Supreme Court now permits tax dollars diverted to religious uses through school vouchers. The Bush administration, on July 6, 2001, asked the justices to review and then uphold an Ohio program that offers Cleveland parents tuition assistance to send their children to private schools, including religious schools. In a case like this, it is unusual for the solicitor general's office to file a Supreme Court brief until the justices either agree to hear the case or ask for the solicitor general's view on whether they should hear it. Filing a brief at this early stage is a way for the administration to put its position on record and to send a signal to the court about the high priority the administration attaches to the issue. Theodore Olson's brief said that the district court's ruling, based on a 1973 Supreme Court decision that struck down a tuition-reimbursement program in New York, was "at odds with" and "out of step with" the Supreme Court's more recent interpretations of the First Amendment's Establishment Clause. Policies that "benefit religion only indirectly as a result of the private choices of the program's beneficiaries" are constitutional, Olson wrote to a Court already predisposed to the solicitor's overall positions. Olson said that it was "in the nation's interest" for the court to take up the case, that policy makers needed to "know, without further delay, whether such programs are a constitutionally permissible option for expanding education opportunity for children enrolled in failing public schools across America, or whether other solutions must be sought for this critical national problem."

The Supreme Court agreed with Olson. This was the most important case of the new century. It was clear; it was unequivocal.

The voucher decision solidifies the many different themes of the Rehnquist Court. Vouchers come about because of the resistance of suburban schools to integration, their refusal to take inner-city students, and the failure of the courts to integrate urban schools, leaving, in many cities, bad schools that are really all black. Vouchers come about because many see public schools failing and want privatization and the end of a government monopoly on education. Vouchers pull together diverse conservative groups, free marketers, the Religious Right, and those who want to become free of a central government that intrudes too much into people's lives. The voucher case combines an unprecedented assault on the establishment of religion prohibition that could render the clause nearly meaningless with the views of the free marketers who want the privatization of the education system. The Ohio *Simmons-Harris v. Zelman*[90] case gives "preference to students from low-income families," defined as families with incomes that are less than 200 percent above the poverty line. "Scholarships may be awarded to students who are not from low-income families only if all students from low-income families have been given first consideration for placement." More than 60 percent of children receiving scholarships are from families with incomes at or below the poverty line.

But nearly all of the pupils receiving aid previously attended parochial schools, making it clear that the Ohio program was assisting people already out of the public school system. This makes suspect the claim that voucher programs are for the benefit of the poor. While there are other voucher programs in the country, the Ohio program is more beneficial to parochial schools than any other program presently operating. Although the amount of aid per child is small compared to private school cost, it is still relatively large and therefore more significant to the cheaper parochial schools.

Once the Supreme Court gives the green light to the Ohio program, other states will create programs and open the floodgates to state funding of parochial schools.

Fifty-six schools are currently registered to participate in the Ohio program; forty-six (82 percent) of those participating are church-affiliated. Under the voucher plan, the participating schools are permitted to use funds made available under the program for whatever purpose they deem appropriate, without restrictions. The Government was quite literally handing sectarian education a blank check, the Ohio district court decided, when it struck down the plan.

The alleged choice afforded both public and private school participants in this program is illusory, the District Court said. "We find that when, as here, the government has established a program which does not permit private citizens to direct government aid freely as is their private choice, but which restricts their choice to a panoply of religious institutions and spaces with only a few alternative possibilities, then the Establishment Clause is violated. We conclude that the Ohio scholarship program is designed in a manner calculated to attract religious institutions and chooses the beneficiaries of aid by non-neutral criteria."

Justice O'Connor began the voucher case by argumentatively asking Judith French, representing Ohio, whether the state's position would require the Supreme Court to overrule its leading church-state precedent on tuition assistance, a 1973 decision of the Burger Court, the *Committee for Public Education v. Nyquist* case.[91] In *Nyquist*, the Court, relying on the *Lemon* case,[92] struck down, in a decision with many different opinions, a New York program of tuition assistance to families with children in private schools, most of which were religious schools. *Nyquist* "certainly points the other way, doesn't it," Justice O'Connor commented, wanting to have that case distinguished.

French's argument and brief were successful direct appeals to O'Connor. French declared that the Ohio program met the objections the Court had to the New York program. The voucher program is not tailored only to private schools, she said. The Ohio program offers Cleveland parents the option of remaining in the public schools and receiving extra money for tutoring or transferring to other schools within the public system. O'Connor seemed satisfied.

Justice Souter interjected, trying to persuade O'Connor to join him in the vote against the program, and argued that "what bothers me and Justice O'Connor" was that despite those differences, the Ohio program appeared to have the same effect as the New York program.

"At the end of the day, a massive amount of money went to the religious schools in [the New York program], and a massive amount of money goes to the religious schools here," Justice Souter said, trying to persuade O'Connor that previous Supreme Court decisions concerning New York state required that the voucher program be held unconstitutional. "That's the sticking point."

"We don't agree," French said, directing her response to O'Connor's concerns that the money flowed not as "the result of government action" but because "that's what the parents have chosen." Ohio's is a "neutral program that offers a true private choice to parents," she said.

Scalia made clear in his questioning that, consistent with the Richard Epstein line, he believes public and private schools should compete in the marketplace—there should be no public monopoly, in large part because public education has failed in so many urban areas.

The Christian Coalition issued more than seventy-five million voter guides, many handed out and endorsed by the priest or minister from the pulpit.

Now is the time for the Religious Right to push their agenda. Christian Evangelicals, Fundamentalists, and Pentecostals are 40 percent of the party. The percentage of those from the Religious Right who vote is far higher than for more moderate Republicans.

Voucher cases that go before the Supreme Court will help parochial schools get enormous financial aid; they will go through an enormous expansion; public schools will shrink. The better the parochial schools get, the more the states will give them financial aid. O'Connor, who has paid more fealty to church-state separation than either Alito or Roberts, found that the law was constitutional because the parents, not the state, seemingly make a free choice even as they use state aid to enroll their child in a religious school. But it is as direct as aid could be to a religious institution, to a religion. The wall has totally broken down.

As more and more churchmen speak from the pulpit about political matters, as more and more Christian lobbying groups pass out supposedly apolitical "informative" material, telling readers which politician votes for or against positions taken by the Church, suggesting how the voter can satisfy Church doctrine by voting patterns, we recognize we have a powerful political party of God.

A lawsuit on February 24, 2004, in federal court charging the Salvation Army with religious discrimination against employees in its government-funded social services in New York City and on Long Island is one of the first cases, and the most significant, attacking Bush's faith-based initiative.

The lawsuit asks the federal court to order the 136-year-old charity to stop the practices and to rule that the government funding of The Salvation Army's faith-based discrimination against its social services employees working in foster care, adoption, HIV, juvenile detention, and other social services is illegal. Agencies for New York State, New York City, Nassau County, and Suffolk County are named also as codefendants. I am one of the attorneys representing the plaintiffs.

The Salvation Army provides social services for more than two thousand children each day who are placed with the charity by the government. The programs are funded almost exclusively by taxpayer money. The agency received $89 million in taxpayer funds for social services and employs about eight hundred people.

The Salvation Army can, as a religious entity, discriminate against blacks, gays, and Jews on their hiring and firing; they can hang crucifixes and religious posters and paintings throughout their buildings; they can require children and the homeless to pray.

The case, which will probably appear before the Supreme Court in 2007, is not about the right of the Salvation Army to practice or promote its religion. They have every right to do so, but not with government money. The Salvation Army cannot use taxpayer money, the suit argues, to practice religious discrimination against its social services employees or against the people they are paid to care for. New York State and New York City, which contributed a large portion of the money before the Salvation Army became much more religious, cannot now withhold funds or claim that how the Salvation Army gets these monies is unconstitutional.

Religious excess has become part of our culture. Eighty-three percent of Americans in a February 13, 2006, Zogby poll described themselves as Christians; 48 percent described themselves as born-again; 58 percent do not believe in evolution; of those who do, 34 percent believe God directed or had a hand in the evolutionary process. Nearly all of the Christian right believes there should be prayer in school and unlimited aid to religious institutions. Abortion is not the issue that brings the most mail and complaints to the Supreme Court; religion is. The single case that drew the most mail, *Lee v. Weissman*, prohibited prayer in school.

School boards throughout the country are putting intelligent design into the textbooks. Seventy-six percent of the voters in the Zogby poll said students should be taught intelligent design. School board fights have become acrimonious name-calling battles, ripping communities apart and injecting hostility against opponents that evoke days past.

Wisconsin, Pennsylvania, and Ohio have been recent battle-grounds. After Judge John E. Jones decided on December 20, 2005, that it was unconstitutional to teach creationism in a Pennsylvania high school, thirty thousand often vituperative, insulting emails were sent to members of an Ohio school board who opposed teaching creationism.

The Christian right's agenda goes beyond church-state issues. They dismiss global warming; reject, on religious ground, family planning, excoriating China's one-child policy and opposing UN aid to countries and entities that urge contraception; oppose stem cell research; disagree with geological studies showing fossil fuel depletion; and oppose not only gay rights but many women's rights as well. They have been effective. Stem cell research has all but ended in the United States, other countries are moving ahead in areas that are out-of-bounds to our aid-denied scientists. No other world power in recent memory has become such a captive of a scriptural commitment that dismisses modern science. The effect of the continual religious bombardment is the stuff of nightmares.

The Supreme Court's contribution to that movement has already been substantial. Now, with five Catholic judges, it will become enormous.

We could soon see a replay of the John Scopes trial of 1925, as cases from Pennsylvania and other jurisdictions may head toward a 2008 Supreme Court hearing.

Inherit the Wind, the famous 1960 movie, showed Spencer Tracy as Clarence Darrow, defending the twenty-five-year-old Scopes in a Tennessee courtroom against criminal charges for teaching Darwinian Theory. We thought the film recounted a part of history that was never to be repeated.

We were wrong.

The Scopes trial was one of the most famous cases in American history. But it resolved little. Scopes was convicted. He appealed, and the state supreme court, while reversing his conviction, did not set aside the statute that made it illegal to teach anything other than biblical creation. In 1987, Chief Justice Rehnquist and Scalia dissented from the Court's ruling that Louisiana violated the First Amendment when it passed a law that required any public school teacher who taught evolution to give equal time to teaching creationism. In a 7–2 decision, Justice William Brennan, writing for the majority, said that the law's purpose was to advance a religious viewpoint that "a supernatural created humankind."

Rehnquist and Scalia, arguing that the law should be upheld, said "political activism by the religiously motivated is a part of our heritage." Scalia said, "Today's religious activism may give us [this law], but yesterday's resulted in the abolition of slavery, and tomorrow's may bring relief for famine victims."

The Roberts Court's legitimization of any part of the intelligent design movement will increase the country's religious fervor. Alito, Roberts, Scalia, Thomas, and Kennedy, devout Catholics, combine their political, legal, and religious positions to justify increased aid to private schools, insensitivity toward minority religions, and more prayer in schools. Breyer, on church-state issues, often leans toward the conservatives. The result will be decades of proreligion antisecular decisions.

While we do not see today's Galileo punished for saying that the sun, not the earth, is the center of our universe, scientists opposing governmental policies are discharged or have their research monies cut.

Critics of the war that God authorized Bush to conduct in Iraq are facing unprecedented governmental invasion of their privacy because of their beliefs. Anti-Muslim sentiment has contributed to the Abu Ghraib and Guantanamo brutalities.

The Fundamentalists and Evangelicals lost some credibility after Jerry Falwell and Pat Robertson reacted to the September 11 terrorist attack by lashing out, claiming that the World Trade Center was destroyed because the country had embraced church-state separation, legalized abortion, allowed Internet pornography, and condoned materialism.

Robertson said: "God is lifting his protection from us. The Lord is getting ready to shake this nation. We have not felt His judgment on America. This thing that happened in New York is child's play compared to what is going to happen. It was a great tragedy when we saw that suffering but a wake-up call from God." Robertson later announced that he had received a congratulatory telegram from Ashcroft because of his statements.

Robertson and his Fundamentalist allies constantly repeated this refrain and stood up for Jerry Falwell's statement: "I really believe the pagans and the abortionists, the feminists, and the gays and lesbians that are trying to make that an alternative lifestyle, the ACLU people, People for the American Way, all of them who have tried to secularize America . . . [are to blame]," Robertson said. Two days later a group of Fundamentalist leaders said: "It is now easier in many schools to bring a weapon than a Bible. Commandments are out and condoms are in." After Falwell's and Robertson's failed attempts to refine their statements, they apologized.

Professor Marci Hamilton recently said, "The United States is in the midst of the greatest wealth transfer from government to religious entities in its history. The shift has been incremental and has occurred on a number of distinct fronts, and therefore has not been apparent to the casual observer."

Seventy-Five Years of Uncompassionate Conservatism

◆   ◆   ◆

The first year of the Roberts Court saw Kennedy help push a sharp right shift, not so much in the cases the Court decided but more so in the cases the Court decided to hear in the 2006–2007 term. Abortion and affirmative action cases were put on the calendar for Roberts' second year. Kennedy remains conservative on late term abortions, race, education, capital punishment, disability aid, women's rights, and national security. The cases decided not only saw the effect of Roberts and Alito, but they showed that far more often than not, Kennedy was to the right of O'Connor. Kennedy has joined the conservatives in 5–4 cases far more than O'Connor did or would have.

It is not surprising that Alito was far more conservative than O'Connor or that Alito and Roberts had the highest agreement rate of any two justices on the Court in nonunanimous decisions (88 percent). What was surprising was the defection of the Clinton appointees to the conservative bloc in several key cases. The two Republican appointed members of the moderate bloc, Stevens and Souter, were most consistently opposed to the conservative bloc, more so than Breyer or Ginsburg. Three cases, argued when O'Connor was on the bench, were reaffirmed after Alito came. Two were definitely changed by the switch of judges—the third perhaps as well.

What is sorely missing on the Court is a true liberal voice like Brennan, Marshall, Black, Douglas, or Warren. Rarely do today's moderates write with the passion of those liberal voices—they could not, for their lives and experiences have been different. Marshall's personal history of fighting poverty and racism, in Southern and Northern courts, as well as before the Supreme Court, was evident in his decisions. Warren's, Brennan's, Marshall's, Douglass' and Black's identification with the poor, the dissenters, and the oppressed is not found on this Court. That eloquence, if there today, could at least remind us of the significance of cases lost and barely seen. Even if it were only one justice, writing either sole dissents or writing for the dissenting minority or even writing the occasional majority opinion, it would give a substance and texture to the Court's public pronouncements in their opinions.

This Court's political composition is no surprise. Ginsburg, appointed in 1993, was the first Democratic appointee in twenty-five years, a quarter of a century. Seven of the nine justices on the Rehnquist Court were Republican appointees. The Rehnquist Court sat as a group for eleven years—the longest period of time in American history that the Court's composition did not change. Loosening and shifting the Court will take decades.

Scalia, Thomas, and Rehnquist—and Roberts and Alito in their circuit court decisions—use words and terms like *textualists, judicial restraint* and *stare decisis* when it suits them; when it does not, they assert the Court and the president's rights over the rights of Congress. The claim that Roberts favors judicial caution is inaccurate. Roberts favors judicial restraint when it comes to interfering with state court criminal convictions. He does not favor judicial restraint where Congress has passed laws he disagrees with—he does not favor judicial restraint when it comes to giving the president the broadest of powers. The Separation of Powers doctrine has been severly limited .

Many of today's Supreme Court justices and circuit court judges see the overriding principle of the law as the maximization of wealth, not social justice, as they aggressively champion corporate interests. Today, the Court is giving away rights desperately fought for over the past century so that in the future we will have to look to the "benevolent employer," not the state, for minimum wages and safety in the workplace. These and other hot-button issues that mobilize voters and make people and groups pay attention to the Court are the conservatives' issues. When conservative legislators, together with ideologues like Ralph Reed, Jerry Falwell, and Pat Robertson, blame feminists, abortionists, and liberals for creating an atmosphere that spawns terrorists, they articulate the feelings of a significant part of the country's voters. Issues of obscenity, limits on free speech and dissent, gun control, voting rights, and race infuriate committed right-wingers. Only in the abortion area is there a powerful committed group that fights the Right over Supreme Court issues. It is not surprising. The Democratic Party, heavily committed to labor, traditionally pays much of its attention to, and spends much of its political capital on, labor-related issues. Until very recently it was left primarily to private groups like the People for the American Way and Alliance for Justice in Washington, D.C., which are underfunded and underequipped, to fight the evangelists and Bible Belt conservatives on social issues. The judicial selection process for much of the past twenty years has been virtually ceded away. Churches today are the largest power bloc. Unless something drastic happens, this will continue. The knowledge the public gains by its brief focus on the Supreme Court nomination process does not last long.

Constitutional interpretation is often just politics under a different name. While it may be true that there are as many different interpretations of the Constitution as there are of *Hamlet*, there are, in fact, limits. Yet, its malleability and susceptibility to different interpretations are broad enough to allow justices to interpret the Constitution in whatever way suits their needs in any particular case. Furthermore, what Scalia and Rehnquist can clearly see in the Constitution, Stevens and Souter cannot. In truth, law is underdetermined by precedent. As Chief Justice Hughes said, 90 per-

cent of "judicial decisions are based on bias, prejudices and personal and political motivations, and the other 10 percent are based
on the law."

Judges do not live as our peers. Roberts and Alito, who worked
in the White House, first represented substantial corporate interests,
then they were circuit judges. Their backgrounds and the backgrounds of Justices Black, Marshall, Brennan, and Warren could
not have been more different. They occupied a different world than
most of us and even most of our public figures. Largely unknown
and unaccountable, tacking between applause-filled rooms at corporate meetings, Federalist meetings, universities, grand ball-
rooms, and the isolation of their chambers, they are in a cocoon.

Their black robes, unique among politicians, recall our glorious
history of two hundred years ago—with echoes of George Washington, Thomas Jefferson, and Abraham Lincoln, visions of noble
men drafting a Constitution in Philadelphia. The justices' secrecy,
their professional seclusion, only add to their aura; nine people
regarded with reverence and awe, thought to be far smarter and
more judicious than the rest of us, distinguished in a way that none
of us are, and engaged in a lofty legal dialogue, with politics and
self-interest rarely intruding. It is, of course, not true. But most of
the justices, particularly Justice Stephen Breyer, assure the public
that they are collegial, that they do their work dispassionately, with
no hard feelings. That statement, meant to assure, does the opposite. "The majesty of the law" too often permits the judges, like the
Wizard of Oz, to decide behind drawn curtains. We forget, and too
often the justices, too, forget, their humanity.

Increasingly, those like Roberts and Alito who come to the Court
have political activity and a track record working the political judicial ladder as their prime, or sole, credential. Politics has always
been a selection criteria, but it has moved to a new level. Both
Roberts and Alito saw the path early—they wanted to be Supreme
Court justices and they worked hard at it. It wasn't scholarship, or

greatness, or long years of excellence in judging that brought these justices to the court. Rehnquist, Kennedy, and O'Connor worked hard on the political campaigns of Barry Goldwater and Richard Nixon, while powerful mentors in the Senate advanced the judicial careers of Thomas, Souter, and Breyer. Roberts and Alito knew that aggressive partisanship is the necessary credential.

Politics has always been a prime element in the shaping of constitutional law. But no court in the past has seized power the way the Rehnquist Court did, and no court may leave as long a legacy. Bork's reasons for rejecting this assertion are set forth in his review of my book *Courting Disaster*:

> [Garbus] seems to have forgotten the Warren Court which, often without the slightest support in constitutional text, history, or precedent, produced one constitutional revolution after another and thoroughly politicized the interpretation of statutes dealing with such matters as antitrust, taxation, criminal law and procedure, patents, administrative law, and much more. The theme in its statutory interpretation as in its constitutional decisions was equality, regardless of what the law said.

Bork is in many ways correct—the Warren Court, like the Rehnquist Court, was political. And both were activist courts—but they sought very different ends. The Warren Court saw the Constitution emerging from a new nation seeking equality and the stated priorities of the Bill of Rights and the Fourteenth Amendment. The Rehnquist Court, however, never had equality as one of its goals.

The values of the Bill of Rights, conservatives say, should not apply to state citizens. They reject the concept that in order for there to be equality there must be judicial intervention. The Constitution rejects the elitism of Hamilton.

From 1937 until 1972, when Nixon appointee William Rehnquist came on the bench, the Supreme Court was basically an inclusive liberal body. I believe that a court interpreting our Constitution should deal with issues of race, class, poverty, religion, and power in such a way as to protect the majority of Americans, including the aged, the disabled, women, and minorities. Today, that has already been turned around, but the new Roberts Courts will be able to turn it further. It renders the disadvantaged more vulnerable, closes the courthouse door to lawsuits against states that violate constitutional rights, and puts state government assets into religious schools. More and more, the Roberts Court sees itself as the guardian of a free market by keeping business free from congressional regulation. By nullifying acts legitimately passed by the people's elected representatives, it forces the people out of power. The Rehnquist Court elevated the protection of property rights over personal rights to protect big business—the drug, tobacco, and oil companies—at the expense of the environment, the consumer, and the citizens. The Roberts Court will extend such corporatization to even greater excess.

The Supreme Court's decision in *Bush v. Gore* occurred against the backdrop of a legal revolution that is an unabashed conservative grab for power. By a vote of 5–4, the majority not only decided who would occupy the White House, but also secured the nominations of Roberts and Alito and probably at least one more justice. It gave the partisans of the political and religious Right the opportunity not only to make the Supreme Court theirs for the next twenty-five to thirty-five years but also to control nearly nine of the thirteen circuit courts.

The Court's composition may have a more lasting effect than a president's election. A president sits for four years; some Supreme Court justices sit for forty.

The Roberts Court will finish the wholesale assault made by the Rehnquist Court on the various and many benefits of the New Deal and Warren Courts, but they are creating a strong foundation for doing so through a steady accumulation of self-reinforcing and self-perpetuating precedents.

Imagine the effect on our lives if workplace standards for health and safety were severely cut back; if abortions were banned, no exceptions; if minimum-hour and wage laws were so reduced as to be meaningless; if child labor laws were abolished or weakened; if there were no gun control at all. Imagine what our world would look like if the law abolished equal rights, by use and misuse of dubious terminology like *color-blind* and *reverse discrimination*; if the state took money from public schools and gave it to parochial schools; if regulatory agencies like the Food and Drug Administration, the Securities and Exchange Commission, the Federal Trade Commission, or the Environmental Protection Agency were so gutted or handcuffed as to be completely ineffectual; if Congress' ability to pass needed social legislation ended. All this and more are the declared goals of the Radical Right who now dominate the Republican Party on matters related to the judiciary. The judicial revolution that began under Richard Nixon, which accelerated during Reagan's second term and peaked in the past five years, has become a runaway train. Since 1995, the Court has declared unconstitutional thirty acts of Congress. No other court in American history has done that. Today the law in America is what five justices say it is. Five people can put their thumbs up or down and determine some of the most important conditions of our lives. These unelected justices serving life terms have become an imperial judiciary.

We are witnessing a judicial revolution, potent and purposeful, that seeks to do no less than unravel long-settled law reaching back to the cases Justice John Marshall decided in the early 1800s, which gave structure to the new republic; to the legislative and judicial law created after the Civil War that extended equality to the newly freed; and to the new body of law created by the New Deal jurists to deal with the economic chaos of the Great Depression. The divisions in this country today are every bit as political as those that divided the justices in the 1840s (when the issues were property rights and slavery) or the 1930s (when the issue was the creation of the administrative states) or the 1950s (when the issue was race). But few other courts have moved on so many different fronts.

With no economic depression or world war to motivate it, as FDR's Court had, and no explosive domestic movements to inspire, guide, or legitimize its actions, as the Warren Court had, the Rehnquist Court felt free to assert its supremacy and to cut back on federal power at a time when it was particularly dangerous and inappropriate to do so. Justices Scalia, Thomas, and Rehnquist are ideologically motivated, much like the secessionists during the Civil War, who argued that the states were "independent and autonomous." The states' rights and the antifederal government movement they embrace are so deep-seated that even the September 11, 2001, tragedy—which has led both to the war against terrorism and to economic instability and which requires a powerful central government—will not stop the new Supreme Court from drastically reducing federal power.

Replacing O'Connor with Alito, an ultra-right ideologue, marks a 180-degree change in the Court's direction on many issues of fundamental rights and liberties. Thirty-five years have passed since Democratic president Lyndon Johnson appointed the last unabashed liberal justice to the Court, Thurgood Marshall.

Until Roberts joined the Court, the current situation was without historical precedent. Since 1937, an average of one vacancy has occurred every two years, but until Roberts, this Supreme Court had not had a vacancy since 1994. Only once before, in 1824, had we been so long without a vacancy. FDR made nine appointments in less than six years; Lincoln five in less than three years; Truman four in four years; Nixon four in thirty months; Clinton two in eight years. Given the age and health of the present members of the Court, George W. Bush, by appointing two younger justices, and possibly more, will leave the changes in the law as his greatest legacy.

It is not enough to say it's only natural that today's Supreme Court reflects right-wing voting patterns. An overarching strategy has dictated the appointments. The conservative Right's attention to preparation, commitment to youth, and purposeful takeover of the control of the Republican Party on Court appointments has led to this Court. The Roosevelt Court reflected New Deal politics. The fact that the Court is political does not mean we disregard it, or that we should not respect its authority. Politics can lead a court to choose many different values: political stability, moderate policy choices, social satisfaction, social justice, or economic efficiency. Oliver Wendell Holmes described previous courts as "nine scorpions in a bottle"; in order to live together, there will be, and always has been, horse-trading and compromise, essential elements of both politics and judging. But that horse-trading is no longer necessary. Justice Brennan's great skills as a compromiser are unnecessary on this Court.

The law generally moves incrementally. Today's decisions, built on foundations of the past twenty years, may not seem radical. But momentum is turning these seemingly incremental decisions into a landslide. Prior to the New Deal, and during the early years of the Great Depression, the courts refused to allow the federal government to try to end the brutal economic conditions most Americans experienced, striking down child labor and minimum-wage laws that in effect prohibited the New Deal from regulating business. Fought by conservative jurists, FDR openly acknowledged the political nature of the Court by threatening to pack it with his own appointees, ultimately crushing his legal and economic opponents.

The pro–free market Rehnquist-Roberts Court has found its own tactical weapons through its fresh and idiosyncratic reading of "newly" discovered parts of the Constitution to protect business and economic rights at the expense of individual rights. Rehnquist, Scalia, and Thomas want to reinstitute the free market to the extent they can. That America's biggest private financial disaster, Enron, was the fruit of a deregulated market will not stop the rush to deregulation.

The Evangelical right wing is succeeding in changing sixty years of law by taking down the constitutionally created wall of church and state, by giving direct funding to religious schools, by putting prayer back in the classroom, and by implementing faith-based initiatives. The Right wants to end affirmative action in education, at the workplace, and in the awarding of government contracts. They want to get the courts out of the school integration business and give back to the states the power they believe the Roosevelt and Warren Courts took away. And, through their black-robed allies, they do this in the way they read the Constitution. They can find it in the original intent of those who drafted the Constitution, or they find it in natural law, in a Constitution created under God. Senate Majority Leader William Frist was correct. "Alito is the Democrat's worst nightmare."

The five votes today, as often in the past, are based more on political power and less on legal reasoning. The Court's composition is determined by politicians, and in an increasingly polarized society there is little the appellate court and Supreme Court do that is entirely free of politics. But the change from O'Connor to Alito is in some ways smaller than we are lead to believe. Of the eight rulings on civil rights and job discrimination handed down in the 2000 term, all were decided 5–4 in favor of the conservative majority. One-third of cases in 2002 (26–79) ended in 5–4 rulings, the highest percentage of 5–4 rulings in a decade. Nearly all were conservative decisions, with the same 5–4 conservative majority. Alito and Roberts stand on the shoulders of Rehnquist and O'Connor.

Gerrymandering, giving minorities the right to vote but making the vote meaningless, is the future the Roberts Court has laid out in order to undercut the one man–one vote cases. Employers will find it much easier to fire employees; plaintiffs suing for on-the-job sexual harassment will lose under statutes that would require them to prove "hostile" or abusive work environments; victims of job-related injury will have to prove a much harder case. Students are not as protected against sexual violence by other students.

Segregated schools, caused by white flight to the suburbs, by the collapse of urban economies, or by changing housing patterns, are now becoming permanently placed beyond the reach of the legal system, while supporters of the NRA will have unprecedented access to it. Thomas's Second Amendment argument to give all citizens the right to bear arms, a view shared by Condoleeza Rice, George Bush, and the conservatives, can establish precedent to reject any restrictions on gun control. On May 7, 2002, the Department of Justice and the attorney general, reversing federal policy that stood for sixty years, told the Supreme Court that the Constitution "protects the rights of individuals to own firearms." They attacked a 1934 case, *United States v. Miller*,[93] which was the basis of the government's policy. Ashcroft and Olsen reversed the government's view of the Second Amendment, even though in 1999, the most recent year for which statistics are available, 28,874 Americans were killed by guns. The NRA, one of the administration's bigger financial supporters, immediately applauded this tragic change of position. In the summer of 2001, the NRA featured a picture of Ashcroft on the cover of its magazine, calling him "a breath of fresh air to freedom loving gun owners."

The Supreme Court is preparing to meet the legal issues that have been generated by this administration's supposed war on terrorism. During periods of war, it takes a very strong Court not to bow to the fears of the time. Benjamin Franklin's admonitions that "those willing to give up liberty for security are deserving of neither" will not become this Court's precept. This is not that Court.

As technology permits greater invasions of privacy, privacy rights will be drastically narrowed. September 11, the Patriot Act, and the surveillance laws fundamentally deny all of us the privacy rights we thought were forever ours. The Court makes moral value judgments that are often appalling. The trajectory of *Griswold* stands waiting to be cut back each time the Court is faced with a new privacy situation. Today four justices solidly support the criminalization of homosexuality based on the concept that gays are not "morally straight" and "clean."

Property rights triumph over personal rights. Congress is virtually unable to pass laws in the public interest once the Court decides they are noneconomic matters. This Court, and the Court to follow, will continue to conclude that Congress' fact-finding and conclusions are simply irrelevant. Instead of seeing the Constitution as an engine for promoting democracy, this Court sees the Constitution as giving disproportionate power to the people. This Court's special agenda is to change the structure of government.

Some kinds of discrimination cases have fared fairly well in the past six years. In a series of sexual harassment cases, the Rehnquist Court sided with plaintiffs in 5–4 decisions.

In May 2002, Theodore Olsen told the Supreme Court that the solicitor general's office would no longer necessarily defend all congressional legislation against constitutional attack. This had never happened before. Traditionally, the solicitor general's office, representing the government, defends congressional legislation and argues for constitutional interpretation that increases congressional flexibility. Today, that office picks and chooses which legislation to defend.

In the first two hundred years of the Constitution, one hundred twenty-eight acts of Congress were struck down, thirty of them since 1995. Not since before the New Deal has a bare majority been so intent on reining in Congress and resisting encroachment on state prerogatives. The acts it held unconstitutional not coincidentally denied claims involving individual's rights. The church-state balance eroded and *Brown v. Board of Education, Miranda v. Ari-*

zona,[94] and *Roe v. Wade* were eviscerated to the point where the "freedom" and "liberty" they stood for became nearly meaningless. The Court is now determined to impose its own political preferences over that of elected federal officials. The constitutional agreement that governed the Supreme Court for the past six decades, which gave Congress the primary role of protecting and balancing our personal and economic liberties, has been broken.

Over the next decades, the Scalia-Thomas dissents will become the law of the land in the same way the Rehnquist dissents from the 1970s and 1980s are the law of the land today. The case-by-case approach previously employed by O'Connor will no longer be possible. Instead of incremental, fact-specific decisions, the conservatives will write with bolder, broader strokes. The Court's mission definition will continue to come from the Right.

Let us take inventory. The 2000 *Stenberg* case reaffirmed *Roe v. Wade* in a 5–4 decision. The Court is ready to uphold a ban on parital birth abortions if there is a health exception. In *Planned Parenthood of Southeastern Pennsylvania v. Robert P. Casey*, the last important reproductive rights case preceding it, that majority was 6–3—with three of the six able to find no better reason to affirm than the authority of precedent and the need for this Court to retain its credibility and the public's respect. Today, the "undue burden" test and laws making it increasingly difficult for physicians to perform abortions can end abortion rights. The figures we have show that, from 1974 to 1997, there were three hundred ninety abortions for every one hundred thousand births; we do not know in how many of these abortions the mother's life was at stake. Further restricting *Roe* would cause untold damage to our country and especially to those who can least afford further harm.

Kennedy and O'Connor differed on affirmative action. Even the small area that O'Connor carved out to protect university admissions programs will fall by the wayside because of that difference. "A few years ago there was a feeling that an anti–affirmative action wave was sweeping the country," Columbia University president Lee Bollinger has remarked. "There's much more support for ethnic and racial diversity now." Indeed, said Bollinger, polls show rising support for affirmative action. "More people today (56 percent, up from 49 percent in 1995) say such programs are needed to counter bias against minorities and women." Yet Robert Bork calls me, together with other supporters of affirmative action, "the hardcore racists of reverse discrimination."

O'Connor was more likely to uphold affirmative action for women than for blacks and would accept it in the school context but in no other. She rejected it in the competition between minorities and the majority for government contracts. O'Connor makes distinctions that permit her inconsistent legal thinking in this area because it is all based on her values—how you select the facts you need for your decision. She distinguished between a "numerical goal"—a quota—and a plan that addresses blatant discrimination and societal discrimination. But these were only labels she applies to get the results she wants. A program that was enacted to remedy specific instances of past discrimination, with measurable goals and a precise timetable to achieve those goals, would pass muster with her but not in this court.

The final nail in *Brown*'s coffin comes next term. On June 5, 2006, the Roberts Court decided to review two school integration cases, nearly identical to those that, in the O'Connor years, the Court had refused to review.

The Supreme Court will review Federal Appeals Court decisions that upheld school plans in Louisville, Kentucky, and Seattle, Washington, that transferred students to maintain racial balance within individual schools.

The lower courts, seeing that the Supreme Court upheld Michigan's attempt to use affirmative action to achieve a degree of racial balance, said that the school districts were trying only to maintain a similar balance.

The cases will not only undermine *Brown*—they will also undermine affirmative action just three years after O'Connor's 5–4 *Gottinger* decision upholding a racially conscious admissions plan at Michigan Law School.

While O'Connor was in the Court, the Court refused to hear an appeal on a racially conscious student plan from Lynn, Massachusetts very similar to ones the Court has now decided to review. *Gottinger* dealt with colleges—the *Lynn* case dealt with elementary school. That plan, upheld by the Federal Court, was the law of the land until now. Nothing has changed since except the replacement of O'Connor by Alito.

The cases the Court has decided to review were filed in January 2006 and resulted in heated argument. The Seattle case was considered six times and the Louisville case seven times in six months before they were accepted in June 2006. Such an extended reconsideration of a decision very recently made, and the six-month debate that followed, is extraordinary. Justice Roberts' expressed desire for a harmonious court was about as true as his expressed commitment to precedent.

Predicting the outcome in the Kentucky and Washington cases is easy. Sharon L. Browne of the Pacific Legal Foundation, a conservative interest law firm, said, "I think the writing's on the wall."[95]

The reach of federal antidiscrimination laws and the Americans with Disabilities Act will again be challenged. O'Connor, after narrowing the law, was recently the fifth vote to spare those rights. Alito will reject Congress' decisions and go the other way. He has, in his circuit court decisions, repeatedly relied on the Supreme Court's *Morrison*, *Printz*, and *Lopez* decisions to cut back on Congress' power.

While O'Connor did not reject capital punishment outright, she found enough individual circumstances that narrowed the application of the law. Many of those decisions were 5–4, with Kennedy on the other side. The use of capital punishment will continually expand over the next twenty-five years.

Ideology (Radical Right), politics (*Bush v. Gore*), and current events (September 11) have combined to give this results-oriented Court an immense and frightening antidemocratic power. Today's Court has assumed the role of both legislature and court. It will continue to do so and expand the areas in which it acts. No Court has ever subjected Congress to such a strict judicially created evidentiary standard, nor has any Court so upset the traditional constitutional balance between the political and judicial branches. The legislature can no longer afford to cede its authority; the confirmation process is where they may begin to reclaim it.

We are heirs to a judiciary in pieces, and we must try to balance the judiciary, beginning with the nomination process. The conservatives have been clear and specific in wanting partisans, while moderates and liberals too often reach for what is at the present, and in the immediate future, unattainable. Where, they ask, are the Holmeses, the Brandeises? They are there, in ever decreasing numbers, but for now we shall not have them in the courts. There are now primarily two criteria, as the Republicans have shown us— youth and politics. The judiciary has become more like the civil service—jurists making their way up a professional ladder—outsiders not wanted. There is little commitment to merit appointments, just as this Court, and the one to follow, has little commitment to either justice or equality. Politics has replaced law, and politicians, who have not been important political figures, have, to a great extent, replaced jurists in the legal system. Their cases send a message to the circuits, especially the nine conservative ones, and to the state legislatures, that the Supreme Court will literally turn a winking blind eye on itself so these other institutions can make decisions even more conservative than the Supreme Court's.

With the Supreme Court taking fewer and fewer cases, the circuit courts' decisions increasingly become the law of the land. When the U.S. Court of Appeals for the Fourth Circuit upheld a South Carolina statute that effectively ended abortion in that state, we saw the

Supreme Court deny review, rendering that decision for all practical purposes not only the law of South Carolina, but also a guide to other states in the circuit (Virginia, North Carolina, Maryland), suggesting to them the kind of antiabortion legislation that will be upheld.

Political philosophy and ideology plays a large role in Court decisions. But there is a difference between political philosophy and a radical revision of the law fueled by ideology and partisan politics. The Roosevelt Court was, in fact, a cautious Court, deferential to Congress. The Court believed it was carrying out John Marshall's mandate in giving power to Congress. It certainly did not see itself, as the Rehnquist and Roberts Courts, as the pivot of government. The Courts in the 1940s and 50s were timid and only treading water. The Warren Court, seen as revolutionary, had its decisions expanding individuals' rights firmly rooted in the Constitution. Many of the most controversial expansions of individual rights did not come from the Warren Court. The Burger Court gave us both *Roe* and *Furman v. Georgia*,[96] the decision, which struck down the death penalty; *Bakke*,[97] upholding racial preferences; the aggressive expansion of *Brown*; and cases keeping high the wall between church and state.

The John Marshall Court, in its affirmation of nationalism, the New Deal Court, in its affirmation of Congress' control over commerce and protection of individual rights, and the Warren Court, in its affirmation of equality, all had political agendas and practiced judicial activism. The Roberts Court also has a political agenda. It will go further to limit Congress, make the states "kings," repudiate precedent, cut back Congress' role in dealing with the general welfare, seek a return to laissez-faire Darwinian economics, and try to put racial minorities back where they were fifty years ago.

A permanent counterforce to the Fundamentalists and the Federalists must be created. It must function in the political, public, and legal arenas. The conservatives have a twenty-year advantage. They used their time and their advantage very well. Several private organizations, working diligently in the past, going outside the Democratic Party, now hope to coordinate efforts to keep senators under constant pressure when the time comes to vote on judicial nominations. There is a long way to go.

De Tocqueville remained nervously optimistic about democracy. He knew that the kind of equality that had taken hold in America could lead to tyranny, but he also believed that it gave people a "taste for free institutions," which would lead them to resist. Equality "insinuates deep into the heart and mind of every man some vague notion and some instinctive inclination toward political freedom," he insisted, "thereby preparing the antidote for the ill which it has produced."

Justice Breyer has said that the Supreme Court should be and is transparent, that all Americans see how the Court functions and decides. That's not accurate. Even though the American legal system has expanded into the political arena and into our everyday lives, it has done so with limited public awareness and without debate. The future will see an ever-greater expansion. In the next twenty to thirty years, as technology and science continue to advance, as the permanent war against terrorists continues, the Court will play a larger role in this "democracy." New issues, increasingly, will not be bound by precedent—no Framer truly could contemplate genetic screening, brain fingerprinting, the use of DNA, the extent of globalization, or an "unending war." The questions this new Court deals with are far more overtly political than narrowly legal. With regard to the great political and human issues of our time—race, abortion, women's rights, voting rights, campaign finance, and even the presidential elections—the new Court is arrogant and pays little attention to any branch of government other than itself.

It is difficult, if not impossible, to rely on Democratic officials who keep tacking toward the center. The Democrats, hungry for more votes, do not get enough pressure from their liberal constituents. This was never clearer than during the Robert and Alito nomination process. Add to that the Democrats' inability to cross-examine the well-prepared witnesses. We know that although the witnesses were prepared for perhaps a hundred hours, we have never heard that any of the Democratic senators met with any skilled cross-examination experts, who could have written out the questions and taught them, in no more than a few hours, how to press for the answers the American public needed. Asking leading, unanswerable questions is not that difficult. What Senator Lindsey Graham did so easily with willing witnesses could as easily have been accomplished when they were unwilling witnesses responding to the Democrats' questions. Their ineptness brought to mind the very competent, persistent, brutalizing cross-examination of Anita Hill by Senator Arlen Specter, an experienced prosecutor.

While we do know that the Democrats relied on constitutional experts, it did not seem that anyone, other than Charles Schumer, had a sufficient enough grasp of the details to challenge experienced evasive jurists. There was no Joseph Welch, who could transmit the pain of the decisions these nominees had caused millions of Americans through their decisions.

Roberts, a die-hard conservative, and a fine actor, played many different parts. He was the well-scrubbed Boy Scout who helped older people cross the street, the perfect dinner guest whose modesty told you he knew it all. Polite, deferential to his supposed betters with a steely obsequiousness, he was a high-toned, aw shucks Jimmy Stewart, so honest and straightforward, his face so well calibrated to show each emotion, that it was impossible for his interlocutors to attack him head-on. His analogy that a justice is like an umpire brought us back to the good old days of summer baseball, with small stands in small American towns, where your friendly neighbor was the umpire. How long, I wondered, did it take the preparation team, or Roberts himself, to come up with that perfect picture of unbiased fairness?

I was surprised that three Democrats confirmed his goodness, seemed to believe him, voted for him. I was staggered when Russell Feingold was one of them. Hadn't they read the cases he had decided or participated in?

Alito was only himself. And with him the Democrats were more inept.

◆   ◆   ◆

Presidents and Congress alone do not get us into wars, create torture chambers and detention centers, and violate our privacy. President and Congress alone do not create a nation where poverty, crime, and school segregation increase. The courts must be complicit for all that to happen, and they are. The refusal and failure to see, to act, is complicity.

Many of us acknowledge the sad state of the union, the sad state of the presidency, and the sad state of the Congress. But we do not acknowledge the sad state of the judiciary, the least scrutinized and least understood branch of government in part because most of the public doesn't know or care about it. It's one of several pieces.

Protecting "public morality" is far more important to Scalia, Thomas, Roberts, and Alito than protecting the environment, the right to vote, the right to a religion-free education, or the rights of the poor. Conservatives, as Justice Scalia has pointed out, feel that dispensing justice is not the prime aim of our court system. Rather, it is the preservation of the old order.

Eleven percent of the population can name more than one Supreme Court Justice. Less than 3 percent can name more than three justices. But the majority of the country believes in the jury system and believes that some people, not all, will get a fair trial and that justice will most often be done. Most of America believes in the justice shown to them in *Law and Order*. The Supreme Court may be foreign, but they know Judge Judy and they think that lawyers may be the problem, not the justice system itself.

All of the race, class, and gender issues that pervade our politics pervade our judiciary. But the panoply of judges in black robes, and the clever deviousness of the Justices' nomination language, as well as their opinions written in legalese, keep us from seeing who our judges are, how they judge, and what our laws mean. The Democrats in Congress who voted for Roberts cannot claim, as some now do, that they were misled. Senator William Frist, the Republican Majority Leader, warned everybody. He was correct—Alito is the stuff nightmares are made of. So, too, is Roberts. They are twins. Recall that in Roberts' first term they voted together in 91 percent of all cases and 88 percent of nonunanimous cases—more than any other two judges that term.

Secrecy is power. Our legal system—celebrity trials and Court TV notwithstanding—is less penetrable by the public than the other two branches of government. News about the Court decisions that most affect our lives is hardly ever translated for mass consumption. As a result, we are often unaware of the lasting effect of decisions and the pain and suffering the Court can cause.

We elect senators every six years, presidents every four and members of the House every two. We can reject those of our elected representatives who do not perform, and reelect those who serve our interests. We cannot do that with the judiciary—the public is not directly involved and Supreme Court justices are appointed for life, while judges for the lower courts can sit until the age of seventy.

Presidents and congressmen must run in "open" political campaigns, so we learn over a period of months at least a little about our politicians. The nomination process for Supreme Court justices and federal judges, however, is so badly broken that it now rewards lying and evasiveness. It is tightly planned and meticulously orchestrated. There is no reason to believe it will get better and every reason to believe it will get worse.

The same political consciousness and actions that we brought to the civil rights struggle, and to ending war in Vietnam and, hopefully, Iraq, must be brought to our consideration of the legal system. The never-ending "war on terror" so terrorizes politicians of both parties that we can be sure further "sacrifices" will be asked of us—and that there are further deprivations the judiciary will force us to accept. Too many Americans have already lost their rights of liberty, equality, privacy, and freedom.

Some final thoughts. There should no longer be lifetime appointments for any member of any court. And lower court judges should not sit until seventy. The supposed benefit of lifetime appointments—that judges will not be unduly influenced by outside pressures—is not, today, a sufficient reason. Today's justices come in with carefully thought-out political agendas. Years ago, older, respected jurists were appointed; youth was never an important criterion. Twenty-year terms would be appropriate. But such a change would require a constitutional amendment.

In years past, justices resigned in protest when the Court became irresponsible. Benjamin Curtis, a distinguished justice who dissented in the *Dred Scott* case, resigned in protest of that opinion. In 1992, Judge Lee Sarokin of the New Jersey federal court did the same—he said the laws and court decision he was being forced to follow by the Rehnquist Court and by his federal circuit were unconstitutional and he would not be part of it. Both of these resignations, for a while, focused some attention on the courts. But dissenting justices and judges are rare.

When a new candidate for judgeship is proposed for the federal bench, there should be laws requiring the political party that proposes the judge to make information available on the Internet for a substantial period prior to the election or appointment and hold a number of public hearings on each appointment. At hearings, the public should be given ample opportunity to question the judges and to present their own witnesses. This would apply only to appointments at the highest level of the federal district trial court.

There has always been a debate over whether judges should be appointed or elected. The more important issue is giving the public access to their backgrounds and the laws they write. The truth may or may not make us free. But the transmission of information, newly powerful because of the Internet, may help. At present, anyone can go to www.scotus.com to read Supreme Court decisions or www.findlaw.com, whose contributors come from both sides of the political spectrum and write in language that makes the legalese understandable.

The government should maintain additional sites that give us all of the writings and opinions of any sitting judge or justice— including those briefs written while employed by the government and all other relevant briefs written while in private practice that do not raise confidentiality issues. There should be a separate site for the justices and judges, with all their opinions classified by subject.

The Democrats, both with Roberts and Alito, should have filibustered. It would have made it clearer to Americans how important these nominations were. They should not have collapsed because they could not win, or because they were afraid of being considered obstructants in a losing cause, or because they were picking their fights.

The wretched *Bush v. Gore* decision ending the 2000 election, effectively decided by five citizens whose votes counted more than the other three hundred million, showed us the naked partisanship of the Court. The legal spectacle briefly seemed to surprise and, for the first time, anger many Americans. Politics has always gone on in the judiciary, and the shock people expressed reminded me of Claude Raines' quip in *Casablanca* when he says, "I am shocked, shocked" when he sees gambling going on in Rick's backroom. But after the sensation died down, the public quickly lost interest in what the Court does and how it affects us. Part of that is because its deliberations are held in secret, part is because it takes place in legalese, and part is because there exists in America right now a sense of apathy and disinterest in part due to doubts about the integrity of past two presidential elections.

The most dramatic change will come from the ballot box—by electing a president and members of Congress who care about the people of the country and are prepared to fight as hard over judicial appointees as over other issues. Today's Democrats do not seem willing or able to do that—certainly the new conservative democratic senators will not.

More Americans know now than before that we are in a partisan battle and we must fight. How much of that will be remembered during the next nomination battle is impossible to predict. But it is still a small number. Whatever happens in politics, hardball or softball, should begin with the nomination process. Filibuster, stalling, trade-offs, and the force of interest groups are political tools that must be used in judicial fights. We ought not deny that the judiciary is political. We should embrace that fact and learn how to deal with it. We must have a say in how the Constitution is interpreted. What we are fighting over is too important for each of us not to look squarely at the Court's face. Only when the courts are again balanced can we consider judicial bipartisanship.

The people are at one end of the democratic process, the justices at the other. It can now be our turn. We can change the law that governs us by changing the governors. We must use the power of our vote, as well as the power of the expression of our opinions and ideas. But the range of options understood by the Framers to be available to the citizenry is not limited to the vote. Dissent, civil disobedience, and ultimately the right to overturn an undemocratic government are also included. We know that at least some of the justices are sensitive to shifts in the public mood. We also know which candidates reflect our principles, our sense of what democracy is. If we vote for that candidate and he is elected, it becomes our duty as voters to stay involved, to make the candidate honor his commitments.

As Senator Barack Obama made it clear to an Illinois audience after the Alito appointment, "If we don't win elections, you are not going to get the judges you want."

We have power. Balancing the Court will take many years. It is a continuing struggle, and we must now commit ourselves fully to reclaiming the great gifts of the Founding Fathers. There is no time to lose, for, as the great Judge Learned Hand said, "Liberty lies in the hearts of men and women. When it dies, no constitution, no law, no court can save it."

We need justice now.

Notes

◆　　◆　　◆

1. He was also durably correct when he said, "The most outstanding Americans are seldom summoned to public office."
2. *Brown, et al. v. Board of Education of Topeka, et al.*, 347 U.S. 483 (May 17, 1954).
3. *Roe, et al. v. Wade, District Attorney of Dallas County*, 410 U.S. 113 (Jan. 22, 1973).
4. *Griswold, et al. v. Connecticut*, 381 U.S. 479 (June 7, 1965).
5. *Rust, et al. v. Sullivan*, 500 U.S. 173 (May 23, 1991).
6. *Bray, et al. v. Alexandria Women's Health Clinic, et al.*, 506 U.S. 263 (Jan. 13, 1993).
7. *Lee, et al. v.Weisman*, 505 U.S. 577 (June 24, 1992).
8. *Baker, et al. v. Carr, et al.*, 369 U.S. 186 (March 26, 1962).
9. *United States v. Shawn D. Eichman, et al.*, 496 U.S. 310 (June 11, 1990).
10. *Texas v. Johnson*, 491 U.S. 397 (June 21, 1989).
11. *Plessy v. Ferguson*, 163 U.S. 537 (May 18, 1896).
12. *Bush v. Gore*, 531 U.S. 98 (December 12, 2000).
13. David Margolick, in his 2004 article in *Vanity Fair*, reported that a Supreme Court law clerk said, "We changed our minds every five minutes about whether the fix was in."
14. A liberal clerk said, "That infuriated us. It was typical Kennedy bullshit."
15. *Lochner v. New York*, 198 U.S. 45 (April 17, 1905).
16. *Youngstown Sheet & Tube Co., et al. v. Sawyer*, 343 U.S. 579 (June 2, 1952).
17. Bush both denies and admits his obligation to go to Congress. "If I wanted to break the law, why was I briefing Congress?" he asks. But it turns out his "briefing" of Congress was merely to insure that Congress could not take action against him.
18. *Shafiq Rasul, et al, v. George W. Bush, et al.*, 542 U.S. 466 (June 28, 2004).
19. David Cole, "Why the Court Said No," *New York Review of Books*, Vol. LIII, August 10, 2006, p. 41.
20. *Hamdi v. Rumsfeld*, 542 U.S. 507 (June 28, 2004).
21. For a while, the Bush administration tried to float that the legal justification for the wiretap program was a 34-year old conservative wunderkind, John Yoo, presently teaching at Stanford University. They claimed that Yoo, who has been called today's Robert Bork, determined Bush's policy.
22. Bruce Berkowitz and Kori Schake. 2005. "National Security: A Better Approach." *Hoover Digest* 4:58.
23. *Adamson v. California*, 332 U.S. 46 (June 23, 1947).
24. Newman and Gass, A New Birth of Freedom, Brennan Center, 2004.
25. *United States v. Cruikshank*, 92 U.S. 542 (March 27, 1876).
26. *Butchers' Benevolent Association of New Orleans v. Crescent City Live-Stock and Slaughter-House Company; Esteben, et al. v. State of Louisiana*, et al., 83 U.S. 36 (April 14, 1873).

27. There were five such cases decided under the heading Civil Rights Cases: *United States v. Stanley, United States v. Ryan, United States v. Nichols, United States v. Singleton, Robinson & Wife v. Memphis and Charleston Railroad Company*, 109 U.S. 3 (October 15, 1883).
28. China's figures are unknown.
29. *Riley v. Taylor*, 277 F. 3d 261 (2001).
30. *United States v. Alfonso Lopez, Jr.*, 514 U.S. 549 (April 26, 1995).
31. *Heart of Atlanta Motel, Inc. v. United States, et al.*, 379 U.S. 241 (Dec. 14, 1964).
32. *Wickard v. Filburn*, 317 U.S. 111 (November 9, 1942).
33. *United States v. Rybar*, 103 F. 3d 273 (U.S. Ct. Appeals, 3d Cir., 1996).
34. *Printz v. United States*, 521 U.S. 898 (June 27, 1997).
35. *Gibbons v. Ogden*, 22 U.S. 1 (March 2, 1824).
36. *United States v. Morrison*, 529 U.S. 598 (May 15, 2000).
37. *Garrett v. Univ. of Ala.; Ash v. Alabama Dept. of Youth Services*, 344 F. 3d 1288 (2003).
38. *Kimel v. Florida Board of Regents*, 528 U.S. 62 (January 11, 2000).
39. *Dred Scott v. John F.A. Sanford*, 60 U.S. 393 (March 5, 1857).
40. *Federal Maritime Commission v. South Carolina State Ports Authority*, 535 U.S. 743 (May 28, 2002).
41. *Missouri v. Jenkins*, 515 U.S. 70 (June 12, 1995).
42. *Baker, et al. v. Carr, et al.*, 369 U.S. 186 (March 26, 1962).
43. *Shaw v. Hunt*, 517 U.S. 899 (June 13, 1996).
44. *Easley v. Cromartie*, 532 U.S. 234 (April 18, 2001). See also *Hunt v. Cromartie*, 526 U.S. 541 (May 17, 1999).
45. *Gonzales v. Raich*, 125 S. Ct. 2195 (June 6, 2005).
46. *Goodridge v. Dep't of Pub. Health*, 440 Mass. 307, 798 N.E. 2d 941 (November 18, 2003).
47. *Planned Parenthood v. Casey*, 505 U.S. 833 (June 29, 1992).
48. *Stenberg v. Carhart*, 530 U.S. 914 (June 28, 2000).
49. *Greenville Women's Clinic v. Bryant*, 66 F. Supp. 691 (1999).
50. *Hope Clinic v. Ryan*, 530 U.S. 1271 (June 29, 2000).
51. *Hammer v. Dagenhart*, 247 U.S. 251 (June 3, 1918).
52. *United States v. Darby*, 312 U.S. 100 (Feb. 3, 1941).
53. *United States v. Carolene Products Co.*, 304 U.S. 144 (April 25, 1938).
54. *National League of Cities v. Usery*, 426 U.S. 833 (June 24, 1976).
55. *Garcia v. San Antonio Metro. Transit Auth.*, 471 U.S. 1049 (April 15, 1985).
56. *Goldberg v. Kelly*, 397 U.S. 254 (March 23, 1970).
57. *King v. Smith*, 392 U.S. 309 (June 17, 1968).
58. *Pennsylvania Coal Co. v. Mahon*, 260 U.S. 393 (December 11, 1922).
59. *Miller v. Schoene*, 276 U.S. 272 (February 20, 1928).
60. *First Evangelical Lutheran Church v. County of Los Angeles*, 482 U.S. 304 (June 9, 1987).
61. *Pennell v. San Jose*, 485 U.S. 1 (February 24, 1988).
62. *Lucas v. S.C. Coastal Council*, 505 U.S. 1003 (June 29, 1992).
63. *Pennsylvania Coal Co. v. Mahon*, 260 U.S. 393 (December 11, 1922).
64. *Dolan v. City of Tigard*, 512 U.S. 374 (June 24, 1994).
65. *E. Enters. v. Apfel*, 524 U.S. 498 (June 25, 1998).

66. *Kelo v. City of New London*, 125 S. Ct. 2655 (June 23, 2005).
67. *Chittister v. Dept. of Community & Economic Dev.*, 226 F.3d 223 (3d Cir. 2000).
68. *Nev. Dep't of Human Res. v. Hibbs*, 538 U.S. 721 (May 27, 2003).
69. *RNS Servs. v. Secretary of Labor, MSHA*, 115 F. 3d 182 (1997).
70. *Flast v. Cohen*, 392 U.S. 83 (June 10, 1968).
71. *Friends of the Earth, Inc. v. Laidlaw Envtl. Servc (TOC), Inc.*, 528 U.S. 167 (January 12, 2000).
72. *U.S. v. Miller*, 307 U.S. 174 (1939).
73. *Griffin v. Illinois*, 351 U.S. 12 (April 23, 1956).
74. *Bragg v. Robertson*, 2001 WL 410382 (4th Cir. 2001).
75. *Public Interest Research Group v. Magnesium Elektron*, 123 F. 3d 111 (1997).
76. *W.R. Grace & Co. v. United States EPA*, 216 F. 3d 330 (2001).
77. *Rapanos v. United States*, 533 U.S. 913 (June 18, 2001).
78. *Carabell v. United States Army Corps of Eng'rs*, 126 S. Ct. 415 (October 11, 2005); 391 F. 3d 704 (2004).
79. *Zedner v. United States*, No. 05-5992 (June 5, 2006).
80. *Alexander v. Sandoval*, 532 U.S. 275 (April 24, 2001).
81. *Patterson v. McLean Credit Union*, 491 U.S. 164 (June 15, 1989).
82. *Everson v. Board of Education*, 330 U.S. 1 (February 10, 1947).
83. *Everson*, 330 U.S. at 15–16.
84. Hamilton, Mari A. *God vs. the Gavel*. Cambridge University Press, 2005.
85. John Locke, *Letter Concerning Toleration* (1689), in *The Works of John Locke*, 12th ed., 9 vols. (1824), 5:1–158. Locke wrote two subsequent such letters and had a fragment of a fourth letter underway on his death in 1704. It was the first letter of 1689 that was best known in America.
86. Ibid, 9.
87. Ibid, 21.
88. Ibid, 13.
89. Ibid, 16.
90. *Zelman v. Simmons-Harris*, 536 U.S. 639 (June 27, 2002).
91. *Comm. for Public Educ. & Religious Liberty v. Nyquist*, 413 U.S. 756 (June 25, 1973).
92. *Lemon v. Kurtzman*, 411 U.S. 192 (April 2, 1973).
93. *U.S. v Miller*, 307 U.S. 174.
94. *Miranda v. Arizona*, 384 U.S. 436 (June 13, 1966).
95. Linda Greenhouse, "Court to Weigh Race as a Factor in School Roles," *New York Times*, June 6, 2006, p. 15.
96. Furman v. Georgia, 408 U.S. 238 (June 29, 1972).
97. Regents of Univ. of Cal. v. Bakke, 438 U.S. 265 (June 28, 1978).

Index

•   •   •

ABOUT THE AUTHOR

Named by *Newsweek* magazine as "legendary . . . one of the best trial lawyers in the country," MARTIN GARBUS, who has taught at both Yale and Columbia University, has appeared before the United States Supreme Court and the highest courts throughout the nation. *The National Law Journal* and others cite Garbus as one of the U.S.'s "ten top trial lawyers" and "one of America's most prominent First Amendment lawyers." He has taught at Yale and Columbia and lectured at law schools throughout the country as well as in France and Germany. He has represented dissidents throughout the world, including Nelson Mandela in South Africa, Vaclav Havel in Czechoslovakia, and Andrei Sakharov in Russia, and participated in the writing of constitutions and media laws in Russia, Rwanda, China, and Czechoslovakia. The author of five widely-acclaimed books, Garbus has written for *The New York Times, Los Angeles Times, Chicago Tribune, Washington Post,* and other periodicals and appeared regularly as a television commentator on the major networks. His next book, coming out in 2008, describes China's extraordinary attempt to create a twenty-first-century legal system. A partner at Davis & Gilbert, he practices throughout the country.

ABOUT SEVEN STORIES PRESS

Seven Stories Press is an independent book publisher based in New York City, with distribution throughout the United States, Canada, England, and Australia. We publish works of the imagination by such writers as Nelson Algren, Octavia E. Butler, Assia Djebar, Ariel Dorfman, Lee Stringer, and Kurt Vonnegut, to name a few, together with political titles by voices of conscience, including the Boston Women's Health Book Collective, Noam Chomsky, Ralph Nader, Gary Null, Project Censored, Barbara Seaman, Gary Webb, and Howard Zinn, among many others. Our books appear in hardcover, paperback, pamphlet, and e-book formats, in English and in Spanish. We believe publishers have a special responsibility to defend free speech and human rights wherever we can.

For more information , visit our Web site at www.sevenstories.com or write for a free catalogue to Seven Stories Press, 140 Watts Street, New York, NY 10013.